The Field Is White

The Field Is White

Harvest in the Three Counties of England

Carol Wilkinson *and*
Cynthia Doxey Green

Published by the Religious Studies Center, Brigham Young University, Provo, Utah, in cooperation with Deseret Book Company, Salt Lake City. Visit us at rsc.byu.edu.

© 2017 by Brigham Young University. All rights reserved.

Printed in the United States of America by Sheridan Books, Inc.

DESERET BOOK is a registered trademark of Deseret Book Company. Visit us at DeseretBook.com.

Any uses of this material beyond those allowed by the exemptions in US copyright law, such as section 107, "Fair Use," and section 108, "Library Copying," require the written permission of the publisher, Religious Studies Center, 185 HGB, Brigham Young University, Provo, Utah 84602. The views expressed herein are the responsibility of the authors and do not necessarily represent the position of Brigham Young University or the Religious Studies Center.

Cover design and interior layout by Carmen Cole.

Library of Congress Cataloging-in-Publication Data

Names: Wilkinson, Carol, 1954- author.
Title: The field is white : harvest in the three counties of England / Carol
   Wilkinson and Cynthia Doxey Green.
Description: Provo : BYU Religious Studies Center, 2017. | Includes index.
Identifiers: LCCN 2016057400 | ISBN 9781944394158
Subjects: LCSH: Church of Jesus Christ of Latter-day
   Saints--Missions--England--History--19th century. | Mormon
   Church--Missions--England--History--19th century.
Classification: LCC BX8661 .W525 2017 | DDC 289.3/320942--dc23 LC record available at https://lccn.loc.gov/2016057400

In memory of Paul Peterson,
kind, wise colleague and friend.
We miss you.

Contents

Preface ix
1: The Church in Britain before 1840 1
2: A People Prepared 23
3: Wilford Woodruff's Mission to the Three Counties 41
4: The Missionaries and Their Labors 57
5: The Harvest of Converts 91
6: Emigrating or Remaining in England 137
7: From Then Until Now 173
Appendix 201
Bibliography 225
About the Authors 233
Index 235

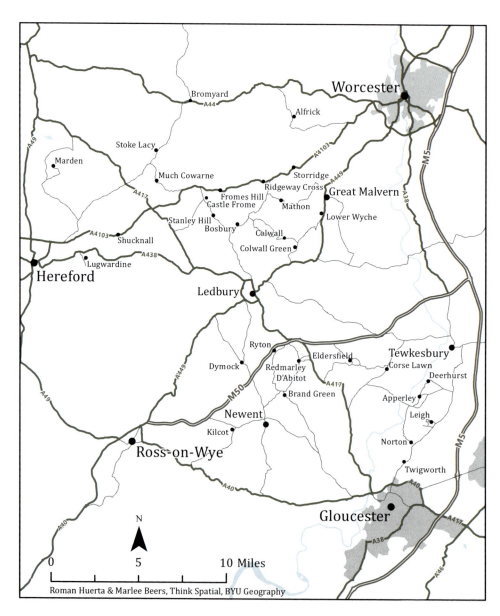

Map of the triborder area of the Three Counties.

Preface

THE GENESIS OF THIS BOOK occurred in 2005 when a member of the stake presidency from the Cheltenham Stake of The Church of Jesus Christ of Latter-day Saints in Gloucester, England, contacted administrators at Brigham Young University, Provo, Utah, asking if it was possible for scholars from the university to write a history of the early days of the Church in the counties of Herefordshire, Gloucestershire, and Worcestershire (commonly referred to as the Three Counties). The stake presidency was specifically interested in finding out more about the missionary work of Wilford Woodruff in the early 1840s, to provide clarification of the number of baptisms that took place during this time period. Although there was a general understanding that a large group of people joined the Church as a result of Wilford Woodruff's preaching, some people have questioned the actual number of baptisms.

The university administrators directed the member of the Cheltenham stake presidency to talk to Paul Peterson, the chair of the Department of Church History and Doctrine. After discussing the proposal, Paul agreed to take on the project and invited us to join him in the endeavor. Paul, Carol Wilkinson, and Cynthia Doxey Green began researching the history of the Church in the Three Counties using records that were available in Utah. Through generous grants from Brigham Young University's International Vice President's Office, Religious Education, and the Church History and Doctrine Department, all three of us were able to spend time researching on-site in Herefordshire, Worcestershire, and Gloucestershire at different times over the next couple of years. Sadly, in 2007, Paul succumbed to the cancer he had been battling for years, leaving the project for us to finish. The story of Wilford Woodruff's great success in the Three Counties area of England has previously been documented to some degree but, based on the charge given to us, we felt it necessary to explore these missionary experiences in more detail.

In this book, before commenting on Wilford Woodruff's activities in the Three Counties, we explore the background of what had occurred in England prior to Elder Woodruff's arrival there in 1840. To accomplish this, chapter 1 focuses on the experiences of the first missionaries who arrived in England in 1837 and the early efforts to give the Church a base there. In chapter 2 we look at the background of the Three Counties area and the people who initially joined the Church to see how the political, social, economic, and religious milieu of the time influenced their lives and prepared them for the message of the restored gospel initially brought to them by Wilford Woodruff. Chapter 3 moves on to describe Wilford Woodruff's missionary experiences in this part of England. One of the strengths of this research is that we accessed a number of journals and life stories of other missionaries, including British missionaries, who labored in this area. Chapter 4 describes many of these stories, providing a more complete picture of the growth of the Church.

Because this research was initiated to determine the number of baptisms during the time of Wilford Woodruff's mission to the Three Counties, we discuss the research process we used and our findings from a variety of records to augment the reports from Wilford Woodruff's own words. Chapters 5 and 6 briefly describe how we created two databases of converts from the Three Counties: one coming from names listed in missionary and member journals, and the other coming from names found in the Church membership records of the time. In addition to compiling the names and any identifying information about these converts from those original records, we searched for information about their lives in public records such as Family Tree (from FamilySearch.org), census records, and emigration records. For the interested reader desiring to know more details about the research processes, the appendix explains the sources we used, along with the way we found many of the records and homes of many of the early converts from the Three Counties.

Chapter 5 looks at how many converts joined the Church during Wilford Woodruff's mission, also describing the demographic information about the converts: gender, age, occupations, and social status. Chapter 6 answers many questions about what the converts did after their initial acceptance of the gospel: How many converts emigrated to America to join the body of the Saints? How many went west with the Saints from Nauvoo to Utah? Why did many of the converts remain in England? Interspersed in the analyses of our databases, we include stories of many of the English converts who left journals or reminiscences of their lives, describing their joys and struggles as they embraced their newfound faith. This is not a comprehensive history of all the converts from the Three Counties. We know there are many converts whose stories we have not told. We focused on the primary sources that we could locate, knowing that there are other stories that the converts' descendants could tell.

Finally, in chapter 7, we conclude with a look at the current situation of the Church in the Three Counties area at the beginning of the twenty-first century to see how the Church has changed, and how current members of the Church have forged links with the legacy left to them from this amazing time of harvest in the mid-1800s. We also share information about places of historical interest as found in the Three Counties today.

Acknowledgments

We would like to express appreciation to Brigham Young University's International Vice President's Office, Religious Education, and the Church History and Doctrine Department for their generous support of this project in providing funds for our research both in England and for student research assistants at Brigham Young University. We appreciate the invaluable help of Wayne Gardner and Simon Gibson, with whom we visited in the Three Counties of England, in helping us understand current efforts of

Church members to connect with the legacy left to them from the time of harvest in the 1800s. We also appreciate the help of William W. Slaughter, Emily Utt, Jay Burrup, and many others at the Church History Library of The Church of Jesus Christ of Latter-day Saints who provided insight and access to several of the journals and photographs used in this research. We want to thank Sharon Black for her wonderful editorial help with the manuscript. We express gratitude to Thomas A. Wayment, Joany O. Pinegar, Brent R. Nordgren, Devan Jensen, Leah Emal, Allyson Jones, and Carmen Cole of the Religious Studies Center. Finally, we appreciate the numerous student assistants who helped us conduct the family history research for the hundreds of people who joined the Church in the Three Counties in the mid-nineteenth century. There are too many students to mention, but we want them to know their work was important to the success of this project.

The Church in Britain before 1840

WE NEED BACKGROUND PERTAINING TO the history of The Church of Jesus Christ of Latter-day Saints in the British Isles to understand the growth and development of the Church in the Three Counties area in England (Herefordshire, Worcestershire, and Gloucestershire). On 6 April 1830, Joseph Smith formally organized the Church with a small group of attendees in Fayette, New York. The following year the body of the Church moved to Kirtland, Ohio, where they organized a settlement and built a temple.

A subsequent revelation specified Independence, Missouri, as the place where Zion would be built, so Church members began to move west to that area. The group experienced great opposition from their neighbors, and many were driven out of their homes. The following year, Joseph Smith gathered a group of members in Kirtland and formed a band of volunteers totaling around two hundred, referred to as Zion's Camp, to travel to Missouri to regain the lost properties. When they were not successful, some of the volunteers became disgruntled and angry. As Joseph disbanded the camp, he voiced a promise from the Lord for those who had been faithful: "I have heard their prayers, and will accept their offering; and it is expedient in me that they should be brought thus far for a trial of their faith" (D&C 105:19).

In February 1835, Joseph Smith ordained the Quorum of the Twelve Apostles, nine of whom had been participants of Zion's Camp.[1] They had proven themselves through this difficult trial.

This pattern would be repeated many times in the future with additional trials, just as it is repeated today: good news (the restoration of the gospel and the designation of the geographical location of Zion), followed by trials (loss of property in Missouri and inability to regain it), followed by increased faith that ultimately leads to blessings (becoming members of the Quorum of the Twelve Apostles).

The pattern occurred again in 1836 when the dedication of the Kirtland Temple brought an outpouring of spiritual manifestations which many of the Saints were able to witness and record. However, by May 1837, trials had engulfed the fledging Church. Many Church members engaged in financial speculation (prevalent through the nation); Joseph Smith described this spirit of speculation:

> As the fruits of this spirit, evil surmisings, fault finding, disunion, dissension, and apostasy followed in quick succession, and it seemed as though all the powers of earth and hell were combining their influence in an especial manner to overthrow the church at once, and make a final end. Other banking institutions refused the "Kirtland Safety Society's Notes; The enemy abroad, and apostates in our midsts united in their schemes; flour and provisions were turned towards other markets; and many became disaffected toward me as though I were the sole cause of those very evils I was most strenuously striving against; and which were actually brought upon us, by the brethren not giving heed to my council.
>
> No quorum in the church was entirely exempt from the influence of those false spirits, who were striving against me, for the Mastery; even some of the Twelve were so far lost to their high and responsible calling, as to begin to take sides, secretly with the enemy.[2]

During this difficult time of financial speculation, God revealed to Joseph that "something new must be done for the salvation of his church."[3] On 4 June 1837, Joseph spoke to Heber C. Kimball in the Kirtland Temple. Heber's grandson Orson F. Whitney recorded the occasion as Joseph said to Heber, "Brother Heber, the Spirit of the Lord has whispered to me: 'Let my ser-

Heber C. Kimball. (Church History Library.)

Orson Hyde. (Church History Library.)

vant Heber go to England and proclaim my Gospel, and open the door of salvation to that nation.'"[4] Heber was feeling overwhelmed and unfit for the work, so he asked if Brigham Young could accompany him. However, Joseph had other plans for Brigham. Although Heber felt a tremendous burden, his journal entry indicates his great faith:

> The idea of being appointed to such an important office and mission, was almost more than I could bear up under. . . . However, all these considerations did not deter me from the path of duty . . . but the moment I understood the will of my heavenly Father; I felt a determination to go at all hazards, believing that he would support me by His almighty power; and endow me with every qualification that I needed. And although my family were dear to me, and I should have to leave them almost destitute; yet I felt that the cause of truth, the gospel of Christ, outweighed every other consideration.[5]

Orson Hyde was present when Heber was ordained to the mission; Orson asked forgiveness of his faults and offered to accompany Heber.[6] Willard Richards, a good friend of Heber, was also anxious to join the group and obtained permission to do so.[7] The previous year on a mission to Canada, Parley P. Pratt had

Willard Richards. (Church History Library.)

Parley P. Pratt. (Church History Library.)

introduced John Taylor to the message of the restored gospel of Jesus Christ. John had joined the Church along with Joseph Fielding; both had family in England. Joseph Fielding was in Kirtland at the time of Heber's mission call and was ready to accompany him to England. Three other Canadian converts—John Goodson, Isaac Russell, and John Snyder—prepared to meet the group in New York. All seven missionaries sailed on the *Garrick* on 1 July and reached Liverpool in eighteen days. They were assisted by good weather and a wager from a rival ship, the *South America*, which never managed to pass the *Garrick* during the voyage.[8] Instead of joining the other passengers in boarding a steamer to reach shore, Elders Kimball, Hyde, Richards, and Goodson jumped in a small rowing boat and leaped onto the dock ahead of the steamer. Liverpool was England's main port, and the port through which many emigrants left their homeland. After three days, the missionaries felt led by the Spirit to travel north by coach to the industrial city of Preston, where Joseph Fielding's brother was a Methodist minister.[9]

John Taylor. (Church History Library.)

Joseph Fielding. (Church History Library.)

Church Beginnings in Lancashire

The group of missionaries arrived in Preston on 22 July during a parliamentary election. As the missionaries alighted from the coach, they noticed a gilded banner with the motto "Truth will Prevail." Involuntarily, they exclaimed, "Amen. So let it be."[10] While the rest of the missionaries found lodging, Joseph Fielding located his minister brother, James, who welcomed Joseph Fielding.

After James preached the following Sunday morning, 23 July, he offered to let the missionaries preach from his pulpit that afternoon. News of their arrival had spread among the community, so when the community heard that one of the elders would preach later in the day, a large number of people gathered at the Vauxhall chapel to hear them. Many people were interested in the message, so Reverend Fielding opened his chapel again to the elders the following Wednesday. Following the preaching of Elder Hyde that day, many rejoiced and wished to be baptized. At the mention of baptism and the possibility of losing his flock, James Fielding shut his doors to the missionaries. Speaking later

Obelisk in Market Square, Preston. (Photo by Cynthia Doxey Green.)

of those first sermons, Reverend Fielding said, "Kimball bored the holes, Goodson drove the nails, and Hyde clinched them."[11]

Nine people committed to baptism on Sunday, 30 July, but despite all the good news, the missionaries would face a test of their faith. That morning around daybreak, the missionaries had an encounter with satanic forces at their lodging in St. Wilfrid Street. Isaac Russell awoke Elders Kimball and Hyde, telling

Vauxhall chapel, Preston. (Church History Library.)

Interior of Vauxhall chapel, Preston. (Church History Library.)

them that he was afflicted by evil spirits and asked them to pray for him to receive relief. Elder Kimball described what transpired during that blessing:

> While thus engaged I was struck with great force by some invisible power and fell senseless on the floor, as if I had been shot; and the first thing I recollected was, that I was supported

The missionaries' lodgings on St. Wilfrid Street, Preston. (Photo by Carol Wilkinson.)

by Brothers Hyde and Russel, who were beseeching a throne of grace on my behalf. They then laid me on the bed, but my agony was so great that I could not endure, and I was obliged to get out, and fell on my knees and began to pray, I then sat on the bed and could distinctly see the evil spirits who foamed and gnashed their teeth upon us. We gazed upon them about an hour and a half, and I shall never forget the horror and malignity depicted on the countenances of these foul spirits, and any attempt to paint the scene which then presented itself; or portray the malice and enmity depicted in their countenances would be vain. I perspired exceedingly, and my clothes were as wet as if I had been taken out of the river. . . . I felt exquisite pain, and was in the greatest distress for some time. . . . Yet, by it I learned the power of the adversary, his enmity against the servants of God, and got some understanding of the invisible world.[12]

With great faith, the missionaries overcame the effects of this terrifying experience and performed the first baptisms in England in the River Ribble. Two of the nine converts were so

River Ribble, ca. 1845. (Church History Library.)

eager to be baptized that they raced each other to see who would be the first to reach the river. The missionaries continued to preach in Preston, experiencing both success and rejection. They decided to spread further afield, and on 1 August, Russell and Snyder went north to Alston and Goodson, and Richards went south to Bedford.[13]

Joseph Fielding continued to live at his brother's house in Preston, but James's feelings towards the message of the restored gospel became so bitter that the atmosphere in the home was intolerable, and Joseph left.[14] His sister Ann, who was married to the Reverend Timothy Matthews of Bedford, also rejected the gospel message along with her husband when Brothers Goodson and Richards taught it to them. Joseph wrote, "I am now as a Stranger in my Native land, and almost to my Father's house. There is not one that I can look to with any Confidence. I am

River Ribble, Preston. (Photo by Cynthia Doxey Green.)

something like Joseph when sold by his Brethren. The Devil would suggest perhaps I am wrong, but it cannot be. I have too much Evidence of the Truth to give way to such a thought. May the Lord help me to stand fast in the Liberty of the Gospel and my Calling."[15]

Although the Matthews family rejected the message in Bedford, many members of Reverend Matthews's congregation chose to be baptized.[16] So two ministers in the Fielding family had initially opened their doors to the missionaries, and although they were not interested in the gospel message, they became instrumental in helping many to enter the waters of baptism.

The work in Preston continued into August, and a young woman by the name of Jenetta Richards from Walkerfold, a village further up the River Ribble, was baptized and confirmed. Her father, John Richards, was a minister in Walkerfold, whose home was situated next to the chapel. He opened his doors for Elder Kimball to preach three times during the following week. But when Reverend Richards saw that members of his flock were leaving, he told Elder Kimball in a kindly way that he must close the doors of his chapel to further preaching. Other individuals opened their homes for preaching, and the elders were able to baptize several converts. The preaching continued in private homes, and Walkerfold was the first of many villages in the surrounding area to accept the message of the restored gospel.[17]

By the middle of September, some ninety people had joined the Church in the Preston area, and members began to meet in the centrally located "Cock Pit," previously a site for cock fights, but at that time a meeting place for preaching and temperance groups.[18] By Christmas Day of 1837, over three hundred Saints attended the first general conference of the Church in England.[19] Elders Kimball and Hyde planned to return to America in the spring, so they began to strengthen existing congregations in addition to continuing with missionary work.

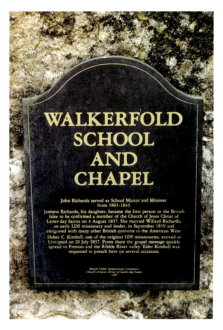

Plaque outside Walkerfold school and chapel. (Photo by Carol Wilkinson.)

Reverend Richards's school and chapel. (Photo by Carol Wilkinson.)

Reverend Richards's home in Walkerfold. (Photo by Carol Wilkinson.)

Chatburn village. (Photo by Carol Wilkinson.)

Stream location in Chatburn where early LDS baptisms were performed. (Photo by Alan Wilkinson.[21])

The missionary success in the villages of Downham and Chatburn on the upper River Ribble in Lancashire are noteworthy. When Elder Kimball had first mentioned his interest in going to these villages to share the gospel, local people told him that the area was wicked and the villagers were hardened against the gospel.[20] Undeterred, Heber took Joseph Fielding with him to preach in these two villages; many of the inhabitants accepted the gospel and requested baptism.

A bond of friendship developed, uniting the missionaries and their converts in Downham and Chatburn. Prior to departing for America in April 1838, Elders Kimball and Fielding experienced an emotional farewell with their new English friends. Elder Kimball described the occasion:

> The next morning [the villagers] were all in tears, thinking they should see my face no more. When I left them my feelings were such as I cannot describe, as I walked down the street followed by numbers, the doors were crowded by the inmates of the houses to bid us a last farewell, who could only give vent to

Homes in Downham. (Photo by Cynthia Doxey Green.)

View of Downham from the parish church. (Photo by Cynthia Doxey Green.)

Plaque designating the site of the Cock Pit. (Photo by Carol Wilkinson.)

their grief in sobs and broken accents. While contemplating this scene we were induced to take off our hats, for we felt as if the place was holy ground—the Spirit of the Lord rested down upon us, and I was constrained to bless that whole region of country, we were followed by a great number, a considerable distance from the villages who could hardly then separate themselves from us. My heart was like unto theirs, and I thought my head was a fountain of tears, for I wept for several miles after I bid them adieu.[22]

In recounting this particular experience in Elder Kimball's life, Orson F. Whitney described how the Prophet Joseph was able to explain the holy feeling that Heber perceived: "The Prophet Joseph told him [Heber] in after years that the reason he felt as he did in the streets of Chatburn was because the place was indeed 'holy ground,' that some of the ancient prophets had traveled in that region and dedicated the land, and that he, Heber, had reaped the benefit of their blessing."[23]

On Sunday, 8 April 1838, over six hundred Saints from Preston and the surrounding area met at the Cock Pit for a mission conference. Joseph Fielding was chosen to be the mission president, with Willard Richards and William Clayton (an English convert) as his counselors.[24] The English Saints raised the money to pay for the Apostles' trip back to America, and Elders Kimball and Hyde sailed on the *Garrick* on 20 April, landing in New York City on 12 May 1838. Elders Kimball and Hyde left approximately a thousand members in England.[25]

Difficult Times for the Church in America

During the time the missionaries had been in England, dissension had occurred within the Church, and persecution had continued from outside the Church. As a result, the Ohio Saints had left to join the Saints in Missouri. Heber arrived in Far West, Missouri, on 25 July 1838, but a couple of weeks earlier the prophet had received a revelation that would send Elder Kimball back to England accompanied by other apostles. The revelation directed the reorganization of the Quorum of the Twelve Apostles, calling men to take the places of those who had fallen and specifying the time that they should leave for the next mission. "And next spring let them depart to go over the great waters, and there promulgate my gospel . . . and bear record of my name. Let them take leave of my saints in the city of Far West, on the twenty-sixth day of April next, on the building-spot of my house, saith the Lord" (D&C 118:4–5).

These were trying times, as apostasy continued to be a problem in the Church. The Apostles were not immune: four of them had left the Church after the difficult times in Kirtland. By the end of 1838, Thomas B. Marsh turned against the Church and Apostle David W. Patten was killed. That same year, Governor Lilburn Boggs of Missouri issued an order that the Saints should be "exterminated," the Hawn's Mill Massacre occurred, Joseph Smith and several Church leaders were imprisoned in Liberty Jail, and the Saints in Missouri had to move to Illinois. Yet, during these trying times, the revelation came to send the Apostles abroad. The mission would prove to be a strengthening experience for the Apostles and would have positive ramifications for the future of the Church.

As the senior member of the Twelve Apostles, Brigham Young helped direct the move to Illinois. Despite the dangers of returning to Missouri, the brethren were determined to fulfill the direction received in Doctrine and Covenants section 118 for meeting at Far West. During the early morning of 26 April 1839, Brigham Young, Heber C., Kimball, Orson Pratt, John Taylor, George A. Smith, John E. Page, Wilford Woodruff, and eighteen other Church members met at the designated spot at Far West. After ordaining Wilford Woodruff and George A. Smith as Apostles, they held a short service and placed a symbolic cornerstone for the temple.[26] The men then quickly made their way back to Commerce, Illinois, to join the rest of the Saints. Several months would pass before any of the Apostles left for England, because they had to settle their families in Illinois.

Disease was common in the swampy area in which the Saints had settled, and they were already weak from their trials and deprivations. Yet miraculous healings rewarded the faith of many. During the summer of 1839, Joseph Smith met often with the Apostles to give them instruction on spiritual matters and leadership to help prepare them for their mission.[27]

Departure of Apostles for England

Even though they were battling sickness, Wilford Woodruff and John Taylor were the first to leave for the mission field on 8 August 1839; both were unwell for several weeks on their journey east. Brigham Young and Heber C. Kimball were the next Apostles to leave. Both were extremely ill as they prepared to depart, and their families were in a similarly dire condition. In these difficult circumstances, Brigham left Montrose, Iowa, crossed the Mississippi River, and arrived at Heber's home in Commerce, Illinois, the same day, 16 September. His wife followed to help nurse him. The following day as Brigham and Heber left Commerce in a wagon, Heber described his feelings as he left his wife Vilate and two of their three children sick in bed: "It seemed to me as though my very inmost parts would melt within me at the thought

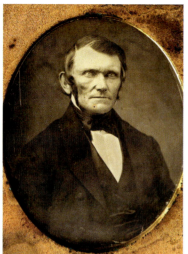

Above left: Wilford Woodruff. Above right: Brigham Young. (Church History Library.)

of leaving my family in such a condition." The two men decided to give a cheer to their families. They stood up in the wagon, and waving their hats they cried, "Hurrah, hurrah, hurrah for Israel!" Vilate got out of bed and joined Mary Ann Young in bravely calling back to their husbands, "Good bye; God bless you." The men returned the prayer and left for their mission.[28]

Three other members of the Quorum of the Twelve Apostles also made their way to the East as they turned their faces toward England to begin their missions: George A. Smith, followed by Parley P. Pratt and his brother Orson Pratt. Of the seven Apostles who went to the British Isles at that time, Wilford Woodruff and John Taylor were the first to arrive in England on 11 January 1840. The remaining five Apostles arrived in Liverpool on 6 April 1840. Two days later, in company with John Taylor, they traveled to Preston to hold a conference. At the conference on 14 April, they ordained Willard Richards, who had remained in England since the 1837 mission, as an Apostle.[29]

By the time the Apostles arrived from America in 1840, Church membership in Britain had increased to 1,850, and missionary work had started in Scotland.[30] With their experience, enthusiasm, and priesthood direction, the Apostles and other missionar-

Above left: George Albert Smith. Above right: Orson Pratt. (Church History Library.)

ies under their direction were able to effect further growth in the Church in England. One of the areas where the Church saw exponential growth and development was in the Three Counties area of Herefordshire, Worcestershire, and Gloucestershire, hereafter referred to as the Three Counties. The remainder of this book will focus on the Three Counties area, including the preparation of the people for the preaching of the gospel, the missionary work that proceeded there, and the contribution of the Saints who lived in that area.

Notes

1. Record of the Twelve, 14 February–28 August 1835, *The Joseph Smith Papers*, http://josephsmithpapers.org/paperSummary/record-of-the-twelve-14-february-28-august-1835.
2. History, 1838–1856, volume B-1 [1 September 1834–2 November 1838], http://josephsmithpapers.org/paperSummary/history-1838-1856-volume-b-1-1-september-1834-2-november-1838?p=215.
3. Joseph Smith, *History of the Church of Jesus Christ of Latter-day Ssaints*, ed. B. H. Roberts, 2nd ed. rev. (Salt Lake City: Deseret Book, 1974), 215.

4. Orson F. Whitney, *Life of Heber C. Kimball* (Salt Lake City: Bookcraft, 1967), 104.
5. Heber C. Kimball, *Journal of Heber C. Kimball* (Nauvoo, IL: Robinson & Smith, 1840), 10.
6. History, 1838–1856, volume B-1 [1 September 1834–2 November 1838], http://josephsmithpapers.org/paperSummary/history-1838-1856-volume-b-1-1-september-1834-2-november-1838?p=215.
7. History, 1838–1856, volume B-1 [1 September 1834–2 November 1838], http://josephsmithpapers.org/paperSummary/history-1838-1856-volume-b-1-1-september-1834-2-november-1838&p=216.
8. History, 1838–1856, volume B-1 [1 September 1834–2 November 1838], http://josephsmithpapers.org/paperSummary/history-1838-1856-volume-b-1-1-september-1834-2-november-1838&p=219.
9. Kimball, *Journal*, 15–16.
10. Kimball, *Journal*, 16.
11. Kimball, *Journal*, 16–18.
12. Kimball, *Journal*, 19.
13. Kimball, *Journal*, 19–20.
14. Joseph Fielding, "Diary of Joseph Fielding," 8, BX 8670.1 .F46, L. Tom Perry Special Collections, Harold B. Lee Library, Brigham Young University, Provo, UT.
15. Fielding, "Diary," 10.
16. Kimball, *Journal*, 24–25.
17. Kimball, *Journal*, 21–23.
18. Kimball, *Journal*, 25–26.
19. *On the Potter's Wheel: The Diaries of Heber C. Kimball*, ed. Stanley B. Kimball (Salt Lake City: Signature Books, 1987), Christmas 1837.
20. Kimball, *Journal*, 33.
21. Carol Wilkinson, "Mormon Baptismal Site in Chatburn, England," *Mormon Historical Studies* 7, nos. 1 & 2 (Spring/Fall 2006): 83–88.
22. Kimball, *Journal*, 34.
23. Whitney, *Life of Heber C. Kimball*, 188.
24. Kimball, *Journal*, 37–38; Fielding, "Diary," 19.
25. Fielding, "Diary," 19.
26. Smith, *History of the Church*, 3:336–39.
27. Smith, *History of the Church*, 3:383–92.
28. Kimball, *Journal*, 84–85.

29. James B. Allen, Ronald K. Esplin, and David J. Whittaker, *Men with a Mission, 1837–1841: The Quorum of the Twelve Apostles in the British Isles* (Salt Lake City: Deseret Book, 1992), 134.
30. Stanley B. Kimball, *Heber C. Kimball: Mormon Patriarch and Pioneer* (Urbana: University of Illinois Press, 1981), 70.

A People Prepared

IN 1830, PARLEY P. PRATT, OLIVER COWDERY, Ziba Peterson, and Peter Whitmer accepted a call to serve a mission for the Church to the Lamanites in a wilderness area of the midwestern United States. Parley had recently embraced the gospel while serving a mission in western New York for the Baptist Church. He received a copy of the Book of Mormon, read it overnight, became convinced that it was true, and was baptized in September of 1830. En route to teach the Lamanites, he and his three missionary companions passed through the Kirtland area of Ohio, where they shared the gospel message with Parley's Baptist friend Sidney Rigdon and members of Rigdon's congregations; Rigdon and many of his followers embraced the message.

A Kirtland Comparison

The people of Kirtland were prepared to receive the gospel. Sidney was a former Baptist preacher who had become one of the founders of the Campbellite movement (named after Alexander Campbell), which focused on a return to Christian Primitivism—what they perceived as the original gospel from the time of Christ. By 1824, Rigdon could no longer agree with Campbellite doctrines. His belief in baptismal regeneration (baptism for the remission of sins) put him at odds with the Campbellites. They excommunicated him, and most of his congregation left with him (though the Baptist account does not mention this). Rigdon spoke

Sidney Rigdon. (Church History Library.)

of restoring the "ancient order of things," which included laying all of one's possessions down for the use of the members, which he referred to as his "common stock system."[1] After he had joined the Latter-day Saints, a personal revelation instructed Sidney: "I have heard thy prayers, and prepared thee for a greater work. Thou art blessed, for thou shalt do great things. Behold thou wast sent forth, even as John, to prepare the way before me, and before Elijah which should come, and thou knewest it not" (D&C 35:3–4).

Like Parley P. Pratt, Wilford Woodruff experienced amazing missionary success among a people prepared for the message of the restored gospel. His success was not in Kirtland in the 1830s, but in the Three Counties area of England in 1840. This chapter considers the conditions that prevailed in England in the latter part of the eighteenth century and early decades of the nineteenth, prior to the arrival of Wilford Woodruff and his colleagues.

Social, Political, and Economic Conditions in Britain

During this period, the changing social, political, and economic conditions culminated in a fertile ground for a ripening crop in Herefordshire, Gloucestershire, and Worcestershire prior to the arrival of the Latter-day Saint missionaries. The population in England and Wales increased substantially from 6.5 million in 1750, to nearly 9 million in 1801.[2] Landlords wanted to try new farming methods to meet the increased demand for food for the expanding population. During the Middle Ages, cultivation had been in an open field system, with land partitioned into strips with a common area. Gradual changes had occurred over the centuries, but after 1760, the practice of enclosure greatly accelerated new practices. The landlords introduced updated farming methods to meet the increased demand for food, focusing on large-scale farming by which estates absorbed small holdings. The modern English landscape of small hedge-lined fields dates from the enclosures that existed during the eighteenth and early nineteenth centuries. Within the villages, these changes in farming practices produced social displacement and distress for many of the inhabitants.[3]

With the onset of industrialization in the latter half of the 1700s continuing into the 1800s, many workers moved from rural areas to work in city factories. The conditions often meant working long hours and dealing with the high expense of urban living; for many families, women and children had to work to help keep households solvent. Some children had to work fourteen-hour days and occasionally nineteen-hour days. Child beatings at work were commonplace.[4] Through the 1833 Factory Act, parliament sought to limit child labor, but harsh conditions remained.

A state of unrest prevailed in England during this period due to several conditions and events: social and economic pressures associated with industrialization, the French Revolution in 1789, England's wars with France during the Napoleonic period (until 1815), and pressures for political reform in England. As a result, in 1832 the Reform Bill was enacted by parliament to enfranchise a larger portion of the male population. In towns, the privilege to vote was given to £10 householders, and in the counties, the vote was extended to include £50 tenants. The result increased the total electorate by about a half, although the vote in England was still restricted to one man in five. This legislation first took effect in the 1837 election.[5]

With the spread of the enclosures after 1760, and the increase in food prices during the French wars, the number of poor people needing help rapidly increased.[6] The New Poor Law of 1834 sought to do away with the old system of poor relief, which many felt was encouraging indolence. Under the new law, workers who had previously received government or parish aid had to labor in workhouses, where conditions were worse than the lowest paying job.[7] Economic depression during the 1830s and 1840s further exacerbated financial despair.

Religious Conditions in Britain

The years immediately following the French Revolution of 1789 brought a political component to the religious environment in Britain. The Church of England rallied in support of the establishment to preserve order and control. Sermons condoned the monarchy and condemned democracy, and the upper and upper-middle classes viewed established religion with renewed interest. Conservatives saw the parish organization of the Church of England as a way to preserve a paternalistic, hierarchical society.[8] People of lower social status were not to mingle with "their betters" on the social scale. The wife of a local parson in Warwickshire would sit in state in her pew, and the poor women had to walk up the church aisle and curtsey to her before taking their assigned seats. The squire and other individuals of status did not wish to look at agricultural laborers in the congregation, nor did they wish the laborers to gaze at them while they worshipped; so they had curtains erected to hide them from the vulgar gaze of the workers.[9]

This conservative approach to maintaining order in the country discredited the Church of England for those who wanted political reform and further alienated the working classes. The 1790s saw a great acceleration in the growth of Noncomformist religions, which continued for several decades.[10] Table 2.1 shows the number of Dissenters' places of worship for this time period. These groups included the Protestant dissenters, Congregationalists, Baptists, Presbyterians, and Quakers.[11] Table 2.1 demonstrates the burgeoning growth of dissenting religions throughout the country during these years of social and political upheaval. The largest occupational group of Nonconformists was artisans rather than the poorest people.[12]

Methodism began with John Wesley's attempts to seek reform within the Church of England by focusing on a return to the gospel message, itinerant preaching, and "religious societies,"

Table 2.1 Dissenters' Places of Worship

Decennial periods	Places of worship
1771–1780	158
1781–1790	251
1791–1800	832
1801–1810	1,470
1811–1820	2,645
1821–1830	2,880

which were voluntary associations of clerics and laymen meeting regularly in search of spiritual fellowship unavailable in the ordinary services of the Church of England. Wesley did not wish to leave the Church of England, but the Church would not accept his ideas.[13] Methodism became a separate denomination after Wesley's death in 1791. Methodists are not represented in table 2.1, probably because many Methodists did not register their places of worship as "Dissenters."[14] The Methodist Church grew rapidly from the birth of the movement until 1840, when the second group of Latter-day Saint missionaries arrived in England; growth slowed from this time.[15]

Primitive Methodist Church. By the early years of the nineteenth century, some felt that the original mission of Wesley had been repressed by the Methodist Church. For example, Lorenzo Dow, an American Methodist who visited England between 1804 and 1807, displayed his flamboyant preaching in open-air gatherings referred to as camp meetings, which were large gatherings that focused on lay preaching and praying. Camp meetings were condemned by the English Methodist Church because such meetings condoned improper behavior.[16] English Methodists Hugh Bourne and William Clowes continued to hold camp meetings because they liked the down-to-earth manner of preaching and recognized that lay preaching in the open air had been espoused by John Wesley himself. The Methodist Church disagreed and shortly expelled Hugh Bourne and William Clowes,[17] who in 1812 formed the Primitive Methodist Church. The same year, the New

John Wesley's chapel, London, England. (Photo by Carol Wilkinson.)

Toleration Act extended the freedom accorded to Nonconformist congregations by the Toleration Act of 1689.

Wesley's methods and organization, his teachings, and most important, his original evangelical aims, were the inspiration of the Primitive Methodist founders and leaders.[18] They believed that everyone sinned, but all could be saved if they repented of their sins. Preaching was of supreme importance to them. They considered the Bible to be the word of God, an infallible guide in life.[19] The "Ranters," as they were called, believed God speaks directly to men through dreams and visions, so when the Bible offered no direct answer to questions, they turned to direct inspiration. Both male and female preachers were involved.

This new religion appealed to the working classes. Its teachings built their self-esteem in a society that constantly told them they were rough and uncultured.[20] Becoming a Primitive Methodist meant affirming that one's soul was important, not only in an eternal sense but to other Primitive Methodists. Working-class people were linked together in a community in which each member had responsibilities and chances to serve.[21] According to Werner, "For the inner dynamic of revivalism to function well, four prerequisites had to be met: there had to be a corps of effective revival preachers, a desire for an out-pouring of the spirit, a willingness to let decorum fall by the wayside, and some means of communicating revival experiences from one place to another. The Ranters measured the worth of a preacher according to the number of souls won. Women, local preachers, and self-appointed missionaries were all welcome to participate so long as they furthered the 'converting work.'"[22]

Letting decorum fall by the wayside was just one of the religion's interesting behaviors. The Primitive Methodists believed in witches, "physical manifestations of the Devil, miraculous healings and special providences," that were common in England at this time. To them, the world was a battlefield where God and the devil fought for the souls of men and women.[23] However, Primitive Methodism transformed the frustrations many Methodists felt with contemporary Wesleyanism into positive action.[24] The following describes the process of involvement in the Primitive Methodist Church:

> A convert who became a Primitive Methodist did more than add his name to a membership roll. The society was less an organization than an extended family in which shared values were substituted for blood ties. To join was to be adopted into that

family. Instead of traveling the way of holiness alone, the spiritual pilgrim gained the support and counsel of fellow members and was expected to reciprocate. A newcomer who asked to join, if "accounted eligible," was given a probationary ticket and a copy of the rules. If he could read, he was to study the rules; if he was illiterate, the preacher was supposed to read and explain the regulations to him. After a quarter spent in attending meetings and endeavoring to live according to Primitive Methodist precepts, the probationary member was given a "complete" ticket and took his full place in society.[25]

A Primitive Methodist minister described the down-to-earth lay preaching methods of Primitive Methodism in the 1840s on the Yorkshire Wolds as a focus on the three Ss—shortness, sense, and salt. Many whose lives were dull and monotonous found, in the various aspects of Primitive Methodist meetings, "a life, a freedom, and a joy to which they had been strangers."[26]

The United Brethren. Thomas Kington was a preacher for the Primitive Methodists who had labored in Herefordshire until May of 1832.[27] His favorite text was, "Except ye repent, ye shall all likewise perish."[28] Sometime after leaving Herefordshire, Kington left the Primitive Methodists and founded a group known as the United Brethren. John Wesley, the founder of Methodism, had had dealings with and was influenced by the Moravians,[29] a Protestant group wishing to return the practices of the Roman Catholic Church to the purer practices of Christianity. The 1835 *Primitive Methodist Magazine* included the following explanation: "In the year 1453, the Hussites having done with wars, being in a suffering state, a number of them repaired to Lititz, on the borders of Moravia and Silesia, and formed themselves into a church, under the title of "THE UNITED BRETHREN." . . . In the year 1467, the United Brethren, having received assistance from the Waldenses, desired a closer connexion with the Waldenses in Austria, but it did not take effect. It may be proper to observe, that the Moravians in England are of these United Brethren."[30]

Thomas Kington may have been aware of this history when he decided to use the name United Brethren for his own offshoot group. A description from 1833 to 1840 of the Cwm Circuit of the

Primitive Methodist Church, where Kington had labored, indicated some possible disturbances among the membership, which may have been referring to the departure of Kington and others to form the United Brethren:

> While Pilawell Circuit was extending its borders in Herefordshire and Monmouthshire, Cwm Circuit was also laudably employed in missionary efforts in the same counties. In the town of Bromyard, in the east of Herefordshire, and at many villages and hamlets around, the missionaries belonging to this circuit labored with zeal and diligence, in the midst of much opposition and despite many hardships and privations. They, however, met with a measure of success. A room was taken on rent in Bromyard and opened for worship on 4 August 1833, and a new chapel was opened there about two years afterwards. But the societies in this part of the country did not flourish like those in the upper part, several untoward circumstances having occurred which retarded their progress.[31]

Thomas Kington, superintendent of the United Brethren. (Church History Library.)

Thomas Kington became the superintendent of this group of the United Brethren, which also included a standing committee. By 1840, there were forty-seven male and female preachers (with eight on trial) who attended to the spiritual needs of people in forty-two places of worship.[32] The chief preachers met once every three months to arrange the dates and places for preaching on a preachers' plan for the next quarter. As with the Primitive Methodists, lay preaching was the main practice of the United Brethren. Some preached several times on Sunday and on most

"United Brethren Preachers' Plan of the Frooms Hill Circuit, 1840." (Church History Library.)

evenings of the week, whereas others with more labor commitments preached only on Sunday.[33] They used much of the organization of the Primitive Methodists, including a preachers' plan that was almost identical.

By 1840, the United Brethren group numbered around six hundred people; they had a chapel at Gadfield Elm, along with many houses and barns licensed for preaching in the Three Counties.[34] They had formed into two circuits (or conferences), called Froom's Hill and Gatfield Elm.[35] We found several of their homes by looking for the names of the United Brethren on the licenses for preaching. We then located these names and their properties on the tithe survey maps in the appropriate county record office. Once we had found the places on the 1¼-inch to 1-mile scale Ordnance Survey maps, we drove to the homes and barns and took photographs. More details of this process are

Gadfield Elm chapel ruin. (Photo by Alec Mitchell.)

noted in the appendix. The locations of the homes are accurate and some of the dwellings are the original homes of members of the United Brethren. A sample of some of those homes follows. Other photographs appear to illustrate stories in later chapters.

Little is known of the doctrine and practices of the United Brethren, but preaching was interspersed with individual praying, which so affected the congregation that several might be heard praying simultaneously. The group encouraged families and individuals to pray vocally. Sometimes, as people listened to

Joseph Trehern of Whiteleaved Oak. (Photo by Cynthia Doxey Green.)

5

1. James Shin of Whiteleaved Oak, Herefordshire. (Photo by Cynthia Doxey Green.)

2. James Hadley of Ridgeway Cross, Herefordshire. (Photo by Cynthia Doxey Green.)

3. Benjamin Warr of Ryton, Gloucestershire. (Photo by Cynthia Doxey Green.)

4. Joseph Simmonds of Wynds Point, Herefordshire. (Photo by Cynthia Doxey Green.)

5. James Holden of Brooms Green, Gloucestershire. (Photo by Cynthia Doxey Green.)

6. William Rowley of Suckley, Worcestershire. (Photo by Cynthia Doxey Green.)

7. Sarah Davis of Bosbury, Herefordshire. (Photo by Cynthia Doxey Green.)

Joseph Sheen of Whiteleaved Oak, Herefordshire. (Photo by Cynthia Doxey Green.)

the preachers, members of the congregation—frequently young females—"would fall down on the floor in a fit of noisy desperation concerning their supposed awful condition of sins committed and unforgiven."[36] After the preacher had exhorted the individual to believe and the person had agreed to do so, "the young person would spring up and dance around in a noisy fit of ecstasy."[37] Regarding the beliefs of the United Brethren, Job Smith, who attended their meetings, observed, "There was, beyond all controversy, a deeply devout feeling, devoid of all ostentation, intense opposition to all forms of pride, profanity and every form of immorality."[38]

These were the social, political, economic, and religious conditions that existed in Britain when Wilford Woodruff and his fellow missionaries arrived in 1840. Just as Sidney Ridgon and his group had their minds in readiness to receive the message of the restored gospel when Parley P. Pratt and his companions arrived in the Kirtland area of the United States, the people were prepared for the same message when Wilford Woodruff and other Latter-day Saint missionaries arrived in the Three Counties area of England.

William Peart of Kilcot, Gloucestershire. (Photo by Cynthia Doxey Green.)

William Phillips of Lime Street, Worcestershire. (Photo by Cynthia Doxey Green.)

Itinerant and outdoor preaching, shared personal testimonies, a lay ministry and lay member participation, and acceptance of dreams and visions as manifestations of divine intervention were all part of their religious experience. Hence, they would not have been shocked when the missionaries used these methods as they preached the message of the restored gospel.

Notes

1. Richard S. Van Wagoner, *Sidney Rigdon: A Portrait of Religious Excess* (Salt Lake City: Signature Books, 1994), 29, 31.
2. J. F. C. Harrison, ed., *Society and Politics in England, 1780–1960: A Selection of Readings and Comments* (New York: Harper and Row, 1965), 4.
3. Harrison, *Society and Politics*, 22–23.
4. Samuel Coulson, "Child Labor in the Factories," in *Society and Politics in England, 1780–1960: A Selection of Readings and Comments*, ed. J. F. C. Harrison (New York: Harper and Row, 1965), 150–52.
5. Harrison, *Society and Politics*, 124.
6. *The Reading Mercury*, 11 May 1795, "The Speenhamland System," in *Society and Politics in England*, 43.
7. His Majesty's Commissioners, "The 1834 Poor Law Report," in *Society and Politics in England*, 148.
8. Hugh McCleod, *Religion and the Working Class in Nineteenth-Century Britain* (London: Macmillan, 1984), 18.
9. Joseph Arch, "Rich and Poor in the Parish Church," in *Society and Politics in England*, 175.
10. McCleod, *Religion and the Working Class*, 18.
11. Alan D. Gilbert, *Religion and Society in Industrial England: Church, Chapel and Social Change, 1740–1914* (New York: Longman, 1976), 34.
12. Gilbert, *Religion and Society*, 66.
13. Gilbert, *Religion and Society*, 19–21.
14. Gilbert, *Religion and Society*, 33, 35.
15. Gilbert, *Religion and Society*, 30–31.
16. Geoffrey Milburn, *Primitive Methodism* (Peterborough: Epworth Press, 2002), 3, 5.
17. Milburn, *Primitive Methodism*, 3, 5, 11.
18. Milburn, *Primitive Methodism*, 7.

19. McCleod, *Religion and the Working Class*, 26.
20. McCleod, *Religion and the Working Class*, 29.
21. Julia Stewart Werner, *The Primitive Methodist Connexion: Its Background and Early History* (Madison: The University of Wisconsin Press, 1984), 175–76.
22. Werner, *The Primitive Methodist Connexion*, 174.
23. McCleod, *Religion and the Working Class*, 27.
24. Werner, *The Primitive Methodist Connexion*, 185.
25. Werner, *The Primitive Methodist Connexion*, 158.
26. Henry Woodcock, "Piety among the Peasantry," in *Society and Politics in England*, 187–88.
27. "Memoir of Sarah Harding (Of Frooms Hill, Herefordshire, Cwm Circuit)," *Primitive Methodist Magazine* 3 (1833): 64–65.
28. Job Smith, "The United Brethren," *Improvement Era*, May 1910, 821.
29. Milburn, *Primitive Methodism*, 28.
30. "An Ecclesiastical History, chapter 80, The Fifteenth Century, p. 172–74," *Primitive Methodist Magazine* 5 (May 1835): 174.
31. John Petty, *The History of the Primitive Methodist Connexion from Its Origin to the Conference of 1859* (London: Danks, 1860), 298.
32. "United Brethren Preachers' Plan of the Frooms Hill Circuit, 1840," 248.6 U58p 1840, Church History Library, Salt Lake City.
33. Job Smith, "The United Brethren," *Improvement Era*, July 1910, 820.
34. Wilford Woodruff, *Leaves from My Journal* (Salt Lake City: Juvenile Instructor Office, 1881; republished by LDS Archive Publishers, Grantsville, UT, 1997), 126–27.
35. Smith, "The United Brethren," 819.
36. Smith, "The United Brethren," 820–21.
37. Smith, "The United Brethren," 821.
38. Smith, "The United Brethren," 821.

Wilford Woodruff's Mission to the Three Counties

AS CHAPTER 1 RECOUNTS, THE FIRST GROUP of Latter-day Saint missionaries to go to England arrived in Liverpool in July of 1837. They began their work in the Preston, Lancashire, area, later expanding north and south. At the time of the apostolic mission to Great Britain in 1840, when eight of the Twelve were in the British Isles at same time, the missionaries were able to travel to various parts of the country, creating more branches and strengthening those already organized. Wilford Woodruff and John Taylor were the first of the Quorum of the Twelve to arrive in Liverpool, landing on 11 January 1840.[1]

These Apostles began their efforts by splitting into groups with other missionaries and going to a variety of places. Elder Woodruff and his companion, Theodore Turley, headed south to Staffordshire, to the area known as the Potteries because it was a center of ceramic production. Preaching by other American missionaries and British members had opened the work in that area, and Elder Woodruff was able to preach and to baptize several members. He soon sent Elder Turley to the Birmingham area, remaining in the Potteries with Elder Alfred Cordon.[2]

Despite the opposition of local clergy, Elder Woodruff had reasonable success in the area of Hanley, Staffordshire. On his birthday, 1 March 1840, while preaching to a large congregation, he announced that he would be leaving the area, much to the group's surprise. Later in his life, he described his subsequent actions thus: "In the morning, I went in secret before the Lord, and asked Him what His will was concerning me. The answer I got was that I should go to the south; for the Lord had a great work for me to perform there, as many souls were waiting for the word of the Lord."³ Elder Woodruff discussed his plans with his friends William and Ann Benbow, recent converts who lived in Hanley. William suggested that Elder Woodruff should visit his brother John in Herefordshire. William offered to pay his way and accompany him there.⁴

Wilford Woodruff's Meeting with the United Brethren

The Lord had directed Elder Woodruff to go south. Through the instrumentality of William Benbow, Woodruff found the exact area where he needed to go. John Benbow was a member of Thomas Kington's United Brethren group who were seeking truth and enlightenment. Accordingly, on 3 March 1840, Wilford Woodruff and William Benbow, along with Benbow's young son William, rode an omnibus for twenty-six miles to Wolverhampton. The next day they took a coach for thirty-four miles to Worcester, then walked another sixteen miles to John Benbow's farm in Castle Frome, Herefordshire. In his journal, Elder Woodruff described John Benbow as a farmer who cultivated about three hundred acres of land.⁵

John Benbow and his associates in the United Brethren were "in a preparation to hear the word" like the poor of the Zoramites who accepted Alma's preaching (Alma 32:6). When Woodruff arrived at John Benbow's farm in early March 1840, he found approximately six hundred members of the United Brethren who had been preaching the gospel of faith, repentance, baptism, and the remission of sins through the Atonement of Jesus Christ, with the desire to be born again through the Holy Ghost.⁶ In his recollections of the United Brethren, Job Smith related a story told to him by Thomas Steed. As Susan Brooks and another preacher were conversing on the Sunday prior to Woodruff's coming, one asked the other, "What are you going to preach today?" The reply was "I don't know. I have preached all I know. What are you going to preach?" The other said, "I, also, have preached all I know. I hope the Lord will send us light."⁷ The United Brethren were

Wilford Woodruff. (Church History Library.)

John Benbow. (Church History Library.)

prepared and eager to listen to the words of a missionary from America who claimed to have the fullness of the gospel.

Woodruff described the United Brethren in a letter to the editor of the *Millennial Star*, dated 9 July 1840: "This people almost universally appeared willing to give heed to the exhortation of Solomon, to hear a matter before they judged or condemned [it]. They opened their doors for me to preach, and searched the Scriptures daily to see if the things which I taught were true; and on finding that the word and spirit agreed and bore record of the truth of the fullness of the everlasting gospel, they embraced it with all their hearts."[8]

Intense Missionary Activities

When Woodruff arrived at the Benbow home, he first taught the gospel to his hosts, who accepted his words. John and Jane Benbow then invited Woodruff to preach the gospel at their home for others to hear. Their friends and neighbors came to learn from this American missionary who was an Apostle of Jesus Christ. After Woodruff preached the gospel on Thursday, 5 March 1840, he prophetically recorded in his journal, "I spent the day at Mr

Hill Farm, Herefordshire. (Photo by Cynthia Doxey Green.)

Benbows & preached at his house & had the testimony that there was many present that would be Saints."[9] The following day, Elder Woodruff baptized the Benbows and four of their friends. He recalled that he spent the rest of the next day (Saturday) clearing out the pond near the Benbows' home, where he would perform more baptisms on Sunday.[10]

By Sunday, word of an American preacher in the area had spread swiftly, and Elder Woodruff preached three sermons in three different locations for a combined total of almost one thousand people. The local Anglican parish church reported only fifteen attendees for that day. Upset by this disparity in attendance, the local rector in the Castle Frome parish sent a constable to arrest Wilford Woodruff as he preached his last sermon of the day at the Benbows' home. When the constable came forward with his warrant at the beginning of the meeting, Elder Woodruff pointed out that he had a license to preach, just like the rector, but would be willing to speak to the constable after the meeting.[11] Elder Woodruff recalled, "The power of God rested upon me, the spirit filled the house, and the people were convinced."

Castle Frome Parish Church. (Photo by Cynthia Doxey Green.)

At the end of the meeting, seven people presented themselves for baptism, including the constable who had planned to arrest Elder Woodruff.[12]

Not giving up on his designs, the parish rector sent two of his church clerks to listen to the next sermon, hoping that they could find something he could use against Elder Woodruff. After listening to the sermon, these clerks also believed the message and desired to be baptized. The rector did not send anyone else to listen to Elder Woodruff. Several other ministers in the area also complained about the Mormon missionaries, asking the archbishop of Canterbury to petition Parliament to stop Elder Woodruff from preaching and "cause [his] religion to cease out of the land."[13] The Archbishop of Canterbury refused the request, stating that "if [these ministers] had the worth of souls at heart as much as they valued the ground where hares, foxes, and hounds ran, they would not lose so many of their flock."[14]

The community of United Brethren was a fertile ground in which Wilford Woodruff could plant the seed of the restored gospel, from which fruit matured in hours or days for many individuals.

Pond at Hill Farm, the location of many baptisms by Wilford Woodruff. (Photo by Cynthia Doxey Green.)

In that group, he found many homes and chapels already licensed for preaching, along with many welcoming individuals who desired to hear his words and receive baptism.[15] Within a short time, John Benbow invited Thomas Kington to hear this new gospel message as preached by Elder Woodruff. This was a crucial development in Elder Woodruff's missionary labors. Thomas Kington, the superintendent and leader of the United Brethren, was willing to listen. Kington's acceptance of the gospel message was a great blessing to the work. If he had refused to hear Wilford Woodruff and consider the gospel he preached, Kington might have counseled others of the United Brethren to avoid it as well. Elder Woodruff later described their meeting: "Mr. Kington received my testimony and sayings with candor, and carried the case before the Lord, made it a subject of prayer, and asked the Father in the name of Jesus Christ, if these things were true, and the Lord Manifested the truth of it unto him, and he went forth and was baptized, he and all his household. I ordained him an elder, and he went forth and began to preach the fulness of the gospel."[16]

Thomas Kington's baptism and his inherent zeal for preaching and teaching helped move the work forward rapidly. Kington gave Wilford Woodruff the "United Brethren Preachers' Plan," which provided a systematic method for preaching at their places of worship.[17] Elder Woodruff had already baptized many of the original preachers from the United Brethren; these individuals followed the established preachers' plan, but preached the restored gospel to their friends and neighbors in place of their previous teachings. Drawing upon the network of family and friends who had been a part of the United Brethren, Wilford Woodruff saw the progress of the work move quickly. By the time of the first conferences in Castle Frome and Gadfield Elm Chapel in June 1840, many preachers from the United Brethren—then ordained to the priesthood as teachers, priests, and some elders— were able to preach and baptize in the surrounding communities.[18]

Inspired Preaching

During this time period, the Book of Mormon had not yet been printed in Great Britain. The only copies available were those carried by the missionaries as they traveled. Elder Woodruff said he "preached unto them the first principles of the gospel, viz., faith in Christ, repentance and baptism for the remission of sins, and the gift of the Holy Ghost by the laying on of hands."[19] He affirmed, "The Spirit of God accompanied the preaching of the word to the hearts of men. Whole households, on hearing the word, have received it into good and honest hearts, and gone forth and received the ordinances of the gospel."[20] Elder Woodruff taught by the Spirit, and the Spirit testified of the truthfulness of the restored gospel to the people who heard him.

Job Smith, who was only eleven years old when he first met Wilford Woodruff, recollected:

> President Woodruff and Elder Kington arrived at father Bundy's house in the afternoon of April 8th, 1840. The usual weekly meeting of the United Brethren was on every Wednesday evening at one of the member's houses a short distance down the

Home of William Simmons in Hawcross, Redmarley D'Abitot, Worcestershire. (Photo by Cynthia Doxey Green.)

street. The member's name was William Simmons, and the name of the street or hamlet was called Haw Cross, in the parish of Redmarley, County of Worcester. At the usual hour the gentlemen above named with my uncle and aunt Bundy, and myself repaired to the meeting place. Reports had arrived previously of some new and strange things happening at Froom's Hill [Fromes Hill] and other places in Herefordshire, and the advanced report succeeded in filling the large kitchen to over flowing, many being unable to gain admission.

An anxious audience then listened with open ears and anxious hearts for two hours while the apostle explained the first principles of the gospel together with the manner in which it had been revealed through the ministering of angels to one Joseph Smith, through whom a church had been organized with Apostles, elders, priests and teachers, with all the gifts, healings, and manifestations enjoyed by the ancient church of Jesus Christ in Jerusalem, and other places in the days of the apostles whom Christ himself had ordained.[21]

A pond in Hawcross. (Photo by Cynthia Doxey Green.)

Job Smith recorded that after the meeting, many people offered themselves for baptism. The group went to a nearby pond for the baptisms, but because of a mob that had gathered, they had to postpone the ordinances until midnight, hoping the mob would disperse. The rowdy crowd did not leave. Wilford Woodruff's journal recorded the event: "I went down into the water & Baptized 5 persons in the midst of a shower of stones flung at me by the mob, & while they were pelting my Body with stones one of which hit me in the top of my head which nearly knocked me down into the water with the man that I was Baptizing but the Lord saved me from falling & I continued untill I had closed my Baptizing & my mind was stayed on God."[22]

Job Smith wrote that after this experience, he spoke with Elder Woodruff. "I also asked him if I was old enough to be baptized, which he answered in the affirmative, and when shaking hands with him I asked him if there were any of the apostles now in England, to which he replied, 'You have hold of one of their hands.' Subsequently the remainder of the members of the [United Brethren] were baptized."[23] Although Job Smith stated

Gadfield Elm chapel, restored. (Photo by Cynthia Doxey Green.)

that all of the United Brethren were baptized, Wilford Woodruff corrected this to "except one person."²⁴ One of the original United Brethren preachers, Edward Phillips, mentioned the one preacher who was not baptized as being Philip Holdt.²⁵

These statements might create an impression that baptizing the remaining members of the United Brethren was a routine matter, as if they all became model Church members the moment they heard Wilford Woodruff's preaching. However, the process of converting the group may not have been as simple as it sounds. In a statement to Willard Richards, Elder Woodruff mentioned that he had to contend with some unusual behaviors in the new converts. He employed one of his oft-used fishing analogies to describe his approach:

> You see, by this time, Brother Richards, I am not idle, but have much to do, and need much wisdom from God to do it well; for it

Brigham Young. (Church History Library.)

Willard Richards. (Church History Library.)

is the strongest fishing that I have ever done. I expect that while gathering the salmon, I will get from among them some eels and snakes, for some already, after being baptized, went pitching and bending like a porpoise and jumped and rolled like a hen with their head cut off, manifesting every kind of spirit, except that of order; and if ever an Elder had any trimming to do, I expect to have my share of it by and by, for in doing such a rapid work as this, I have to become all things to all men; I cannot get time to do much trimming as yet; in fact, some have, before I was aware of it, bounded into the water to me stark naked, excepting a loose cloth round their legs, but I put a stop to all disorder as fast as possible, and again I am having a mighty struggle against this Methodist power of falling down like a dead man, stiff as a stake, which is in some of the preachers as well as the people. I have to handle all these things in wisdom.[26]

In short, although the United Brethren were prepared to hear and accept the preaching of Wilford Woodruff, they perhaps were not equally ready to give up some of the behaviors and traditions of worship they had learned during their time as Primitive Methodists.

View from Herefordshire Beacon. (Photo by Cynthia Doxey Green.)

Arrival of Brigham Young and Willard Richards

Wilford Woodruff left the Herefordshire area for a few days while he traveled to Preston for a Church conference on 15 April 1840, where he was able to reunite with his fellow Apostles. During the conference, he shared his experiences with the United Brethren and described the great success he was having in that part of the country. He reported that within one month and five days of preaching in that area, he had baptized Thomas Kington, the superintendent of the United Brethren, along with 48 of their preachers and 112 of their members. Because this group of Saints had previously licensed their homes as places of worship, along with the chapel at Gadfield Elm, all of these established meeting places were now available to Wilford Woodruff and other missionaries. He petitioned help from some of his brethren to return with him to that part of the vineyard where so many people were interested and ready to be baptized. After a few days, Brigham

Young accompanied Wilford Woodruff to Herefordshire, and Willard Richards followed a short time later.[27]

Under the leadership of Wilford Woodruff, Willard Richards, and Brigham Young, supported by the local priests and elders, the work moved forward rapidly. The three brethren of the Twelve met together on two significant occasions while in the Three Counties. The first was on 18 May at a feast day in Dymock, at the home of Thomas Kington. Elder Woodruff wrote that the feast day "had been a custom among the United Brethren. But as they now were all receiving the fulness of the gospel they had become Saints."[28] Although there is no record of exactly where Thomas Kington lived in Dymock, either the home or the surrounding property must have been large enough to accommodate one hundred people.

After the meal, Brigham Young spoke to the assembled gathering. Three individuals were confirmed, and the first miraculous healing in the Three Counties region took place. Mary Pitt, Thomas Kington's sister-in-law, "had not walked except on crutches for 11 years" and had been "confined 6 years to her bed" because of problems with her spine.[29] Wilford Woodruff related that she was healed by the laying on of hands and that when he saw her a couple of weeks later on 3 June, "her ancle [sic] bones received strength & she now walks without the aid of crutch or staff."[30]

The second important meeting of Brigham Young, Wilford Woodruff, and Willard Richards occurred on 20 May 1840. The three walked up to the top of Herefordshire Beacon, one of the major hills in the Malvern range. After a prayer, they counseled together and felt inspired that Brigham Young should leave immediately for Manchester to publish three thousand copies of the Book of Mormon, along with a collection of hymns. They had collected money from the local Saints for these publications.[31] The biggest donations came from John Benbow, who contributed £200, and Thomas Kington, who provided £100.[32] Brigham Young left to go north after the meeting atop Herefordshire Beacon, but Willard Richards continued to preach in the Three Counties area until he and Wilford Woodruff went north for a general conference in Manchester, held on 6 July.[33]

Continued Growth

Demonstrating the rapid growth of the Church in the Three Counties area, the first Church conferences were held on 14 June 1840, at the Gadfield Elm Chapel in Eldersfield, Worcestershire, and on 21 June, at Stanley Hill near Castle Frome, Herefordshire. At these conferences, the branches were organized into two conferences: the Bran Green and Gadfield Elm Conference, consisting of twelve branches, and the Frome's Hill Conference, which consisted of nineteen branches.[34] In his journal, Wilford Woodruff praised the Lord for his goodness. The Church, at this time, consisted of "more than 500 souls whare a little less than four months since ther was not one to be found or the fulness of the Gospel herd [sic]."[35] The growth of the Church in this area was truly remarkable and significant, due in part to the preparation of the United Brethren and to the tireless efforts of Wilford Woodruff and his companions in preaching the word to the Brethren's families and friends.

Elder Woodruff traveled through the Three Counties a few more times during the rest of his mission in England in 1840 and 1841. He also labored in London, in the Potteries, and in other places, but the experiences he had in and around the Three Counties made a lasting impression upon him. He was beloved by the people there, many of whom eventually emigrated to Nauvoo and later to Utah. Many years later, as Elder Woodruff looked back on his work among the United Brethren, he recalled, "They, as a people, were prepared for the word of the Lord, and I wanted to catch them in the gospel net."[36] His mission to the Three Counties demonstrates how the Lord can guide and direct his servants to the people who have been prepared to hear the message of the gospel. His service in the Three Counties provides an example of the faithfulness of a servant of God who preached the gospel with all the energy of his heart, fulfilling the calling of an Apostle to testify of the divinity of Jesus Christ.

Notes

1. James B. Allen, Ronald K. Esplin, and David J. Whittaker, *Men with a Mission, 1837–1841: The Quorum of the Twelve Apostles in the British Isles* (Salt Lake City: Deseret Book, 1992), 80.
2. Allen, Esplin, and Whittaker, *Men with a Mission*, 118–19.
3. Woodruff, *Leaves from My Journal*, 124.
4. Allen, Esplin, and Whittaker, *Men with a Mission*, 121.
5. *Wilford Woodruff's Journal*, 1:423 (3–4 March 1840).
6. James Palmer, "James Palmer Reminiscences, ca. 1884–98," 5, MS 1752, Church History Library, Salt Lake City.
7. Job Smith, "The United Brethren," *Improvement Era*, July 1910, 823.
8. Wilford Woodruff, "Correspondence," *Millennial Star* 1, no. 3 (July 1840): 72.
9. *Wilford Woodruff's Journal*, 1:423–24 (5 March 1840).
10. *Wilford Woodruff's Journal*, 1:424 (7–8 March 1840).
11. Woodruff, *Leaves from My Journal*, 128–29.
12. Woodruff, *Leaves from My Journal*, 129.
13. *Wilford Woodruff's Journal*, 1:430 (29 March 1840).
14. Woodruff, *Leaves from My Journal*, 130.
15. Woodruff, *Leaves from My Journal*, 126–27.
16. Wilford Woodruff, "Correspondence," *Millennial Star* 1, no. 3 (July 1840): 72.
17. "United Brethren Preachers' Plan of the Frooms Hill Circuit, 1840," 248.6 U58p 1840, Church History Library, Salt Lake City.
18. *Wilford Woodruff's Journal*, 1:457–60 (14 June 1840), 463–67 (21 June 1840). In the Conference Minutes recorded by Wilford Woodruff, we find the names of presidents of branches, along with others who were sustained to be ordained as priests and elders. Many of them are also found as preachers on the United Brethren preachers' plan.
19. Wilford Woodruff, "Correspondence," *Millennial Star* 1, no. 3 (July 1840): 72.
20. Woodruff, "Correspondence," *Millennial Star* 1, no. 4 (August 1840): 82.
21. Job Taylor Smith, "Job Smith Autobiography, circa 1902," 1–2, MS 4809, Church History Library, Salt Lake City.

22. *Wilford Woodruff's Journal*, 1:433 (9 April 1840). Woodruff records this event as happening on 9 April 1940, but Job Smith records it as 8 April 1840. Woodruff mentions that he spoke "to a vast mass of human beings & not a quarter of the people could not get in to the house."
23. Smith, "Autobiography," 2.
24. Woodruff, *Leaves from My Journal*, 131.
25. Edward Phillips, "Biographical Sketches of Edward and Hannah Simmonds Phillips, 1889, 1926, 1949," 1, MS 11215, Church History Library, Salt Lake City.
26. *British Manuscript History, Part 1, 1837–40*, Wednesday, 25 March 1840, 1–2, LR 1140, Series 2, Reel 7, Church History Library, Salt Lake City.
27. *Wilford Woodruff's Journal*, 1:439–40 (15–16 April 1840).
28. *Wilford Woodruff's Journal*, 1:450 (18 May 1840).
29. *Wilford Woodruff's Journal*, 1:450 (18 May 1840) and 1:455 (3 June 1840).
30. *Wilford Woodruff's Journal*, 1:455 (3 June 1840).
31. *Wilford Woodruff's Journal*, 1:451 (20 May 1840).
32. *Wilford Woodruff' Journal*, 1:449 (14 May 1840), 451 (19 May 1840).
33. Woodruff, "Correspondence," *Millennial Star* 1, no. 4 (August 1840): 83.
34. *Wilford Woodruff's Journal*, 1:457–60 (14 June 1840), 463–67 (21 June 1840). These branches closely parallel the locations where the United Brethren had established licensed places of worship, as found in their preachers' plan.
35. *Wilford Woodruff's Journal*, 1:462–63 (20 June 1840).
36. Wilford Woodruff, in *Journal of Discourses* (London: Latter-day Saints' Book Depot, 1854–86), 18:124.

The Missionaries and Their Labors

WILFORD WOODRUFF'S MISSION to the Three Counties was essential in establishing and building the Church in that area. But with the preparation of the United Brethren and their desire to learn the truth, more people were interested in the gospel than he had time or energy to teach and baptize. Brigham Young and Willard Richards were the first to join him in the Three Counties. Soon, additional missionaries from America and other parts of England arrived.

As they joined the Church, several of the preachers and other members from the United Brethren were ordained to the priesthood and called to go and preach the restored gospel to their friends and neighbors—traveling, preaching, and baptizing throughout the Three Counties and across the border of Wales into Monmouthshire. Some of the leaders of the United Brethren who participated in sharing the gospel in those first few months included Thomas Kington, Daniel Browett, John Cheese, John Gailey, James Barnes, and John Spiers. Wilford Woodruff's journal contained a baptismal record of 1840 that shows that these men baptized some of the converts on the list.[1] Elder Woodruff wrote to the *Millennial Star* that although many people wanted to hear the gospel, there were not enough laborers, "notwithstanding there were about fifty ordained elders and priests in this part of the vineyard."[2]

Fortunately, several of the early missionaries to the Three Counties area wrote journals or reminiscences about their missionary service, some including the names and baptismal dates

"United Brethren Preachers' Plan of the Frooms Hill Circuit, 1840." (Church History Library.)

of the people they taught. As companion texts to Elder Woodruff's journal, these other missionary writings provide the modern reader with a sense of what it was like to be a missionary at that time, how their message was received, and who was listening and responding. Some of these missionaries described their experiences in great detail, providing important insights into the process of missionary work in the mid-nineteenth century.

Because of the preparation of the United Brethren, missionary work in this area was successful. Along with many licensed places to preach, the group had a well-planned system for preaching at all the locations. The Church History Library holds a copy of the "United Brethren Preachers' Plan." The plan lists the names of forty-seven preachers along with eight others who were on trial, as well as forty-two places of worship with the dates and times of the meetings.[3] Many of the converted and baptized male preachers who had been ordained as teachers or priests may have continued to preach according to the preachers' plan. Those ordained as priests and elders often traveled with the teachers to perform the ordinances of baptism and confirmation.

Understanding the "United Brethren Preachers' Plan" can be somewhat difficult at first glance. Two general "branches" or groups are organized within the Three Counties region: the Froom's Hill [sic] Branch and the Brangreen [sic] and Gadfield Elm Branch, names used later for the Church conferences created by Wilford Woodruff and Thomas Kington. The preachers' plan listed the names of the villages or hamlets where the preaching would take place (presumably at someone's home or barn), along with a three-month schedule for preaching. Apparently, meetings took place on Sundays at all the venues and on a weekday at a few places. The numbers listed next to each village name designated the assigned preacher, as listed on the right side of the page, so that each preacher would travel to different places to preach on Sundays and weekdays. For example, Edward Ockey lived at Moorend Farm, where meetings were scheduled for 6 p.m. on Sundays and every other Friday. The preachers scheduled to teach there on Sundays during April 1840 were J. Pullin, M. Possons, and T. Jenkins. As the members and preachers of the United Brethren accepted the gospel preached by Wilford Woodruff,

Barn at Moorend Farm, the home of Edward Ockey. (Photo by Cynthia Doxey Green.)

this elaborate schedule could still be followed but with the preachers who were members of The Church of Jesus Christ of Latter-day Saints teaching the truths of the restored gospel.

Although the names on the preachers' plan include only first initials and surnames, the majority of those names are found in Wilford Woodruff's baptismal record. The plan includes at least twelve women among the preachers, some who were married to other preachers (e.g., Ann and Thomas Oakey) and some who seem to have been either single or married women whose husbands were not involved in preaching. Although these women were not ordained to priesthood duties when they were baptized, they probably continued to teach their neighbors and friends about their newfound faith. They would also have been involved in the activities of the missionaries and in building up the branches of the Church.

Members assisted with the missionary effort in numerous ways. Many shared their homes and food with missionaries. Sarah Davis Carter remembered, "My father kept an open house for the elders. Many, many times my father and mother gave their bed

Sister Jones lived in this home, called "The Stoney," Garway Hill. (Photo by Carol Wilkinson.)

to the elders, while they would take a quilt and sleep on the floor in another room, never letting the elders know they had given up their bed for them. They always made the elders feel welcome and fed them the best they had."[4] Several missionaries' accounts also mention how the Latter-day Saint members cared for them by providing food and shelter. For example, James Palmer noted that both Sister Morgan and Sister Jones cared for the missionaries' temporal needs when they were in Garway.[5]

Similarly, John Spiers said that when he was very ill in September 1841 in Worcester, Sister Wright took "the greatest care of me possible to be taken, scarcely leaving me night or day" and that while praying for him, she heard a voice assuring her that Brother Spiers would not die.[6] These faithful members helped the missionaries fulfill their callings to preach the word of God throughout the area.

Turkey Hall, Eldersfield, Worcestershire. (Photo by Cynthia Doxey Green.)

Groups of Missionaries

Three basic groups of missionaries preached the gospel in this area during the 1840s. The first group included the members of the Quorum of the Twelve Apostles, as well as a few other American missionaries who arrived soon after Wilford Woodruff's first encounter with the United Brethren. The second group included recent converts from other parts of Britain who were assigned to labor in the Three Counties area. The third group was comprised of local members, many of whom had been preachers with the United Brethren.

American Missionaries. The American missionaries, including Wilford Woodruff, Brigham Young, George A. Smith, Willard Richards, and Levi Richards, have some prominence in Church history. Some of their stories have been told because they produced journals and writings about their experiences in England.[7] The American missionaries were obviously well-versed in the teachings of the restored gospel, having had extensive experience with the Prophet Joseph Smith and a relatively long period as members of the Church. Their missionary efforts are important because they were the first to preach the gospel in the Three Counties. Their enthusiasm blessed the people they taught and baptized. As British missionaries began to preach during these early years, the American Church leaders trained them for the work, helping them to gain greater doctrinal understanding and providing the authority for priesthood ordinations.[8]

Although Brigham Young and Willard Richards did not spend a great deal of time in the Three Counties area, their service was significant. In his journal, Brigham Young described his travels in the area, stating that he traveled and stayed with members in villages such as Fromes Hill (at the home of John Benbow), Eldersfield (Turkey Hall, home of Benjamin Hill), and Dymock (at the home of Thomas Kington). In his travels, Brigham Young preached at various places—baptizing, confirming, holding sacrament meetings, and ordaining priesthood holders. Sometimes he traveled with Wilford Woodruff or Willard Richards from place to place, and sometimes he traveled on his own, perhaps meeting up with one of the other brethren when he arrived at his destination.[9] Although the American missionaries often met each other during their travels, their journals do not indicate whether they planned their travels together or just happened to find one another at certain meetings and stayed together for a day or two before going off to other villages.

Willard Richards wrote a letter from Ledbury, Herefordshire, dated 15 May 1840, sharing some insight into his travels and describing the way he, Wilford Woodruff, and Brigham Young were able to spread out to share the gospel with the help of some of the local members. He reported that in the previous two weeks, the three had parted, going to various places in Herefordshire, Worcestershire, and Gloucestershire, "preaching daily, talking night and day, and administering the ordinances of the gospel as directed by the Spirit." When they met again on the day the letter was written, they compared their experiences and found that "there has been in these two weeks about 112 baptized; 200 confirmed; 2 elders, about 20 priests, and 1 teacher ordained—and the Church in these regions now numbers about 320." He concluded by saying that there were far too many people interested in hearing the word for the leaders to meet with all of them, and

Street in Ledbury, Herefordshire. (Photo by Cynthia Doxey Green.)

that the Saints should pray for more laborers in the field to help them accomplish their work.[10]

As described more fully in chapter 3, these three brethren of the Twelve met together on at least two important occasions toward the end of Brigham Young's stay in the area. The first occasion was the feast day in Dymock with the converts from the United Brethren, and the second was the council they held together on top of Herefordshire Beacon where they decided to publish the Book of Mormon in England. After Brigham Young left the area, Willard Richards and Wilford Woodruff continued preaching the gospel. The two of them conducted two local Church conferences, one held on 14 June in Gadfield Elm Chapel and another on 21 June at Stanley Hill. At these meetings, the

Three Counties were organized into two main conferences. The southern area was called the Bran Green and Gadfield Elm Conference, with twelve branches, and the northern region was called the Fromes Hill Conference, with twenty branches.[11] Establishing these branches was essential to the growth of the Church because on 23 June 1840, both Wilford Woodruff and Willard Richards went north for a conference to be held in Manchester, and Elder Woodruff did not return until nearly a month later.[12] By the time they left, a number of other missionaries and leaders were available for carrying on the teaching and organization of the Church. Elder Woodruff's "Baptismal Record" ended after he left on 23 June, and he no longer listed the names of the people who were baptized in the region.[13]

George A. Smith, another member of the Quorum of the Twelve, accompanied Wilford Woodruff back to the Three Counties at the end of July and stayed in the region for nearly a month. He preached often in Ledbury, one of the larger market towns near Fromes Hill. Wilford Woodruff first preached there on 30 March 1840 when he said that "many flocked around to see me."[14] He said that the Baptist Minister allowed him to preach in his chapel, and afterwards "bid [Woodruff] God speed."[15] Apparently, Ledbury was a center for Elder George A. Smith; Wilford Woodruff mentioned several times that Elder Smith had preached in Ledbury.

In Dymock, Elder Woodruff and Elder Smith met another member of their quorum, Heber C. Kimball, on 12 August 1840, and for a few days they joined together in preaching and meeting with the Saints in the area of Deerhurst and the Leigh, Gloucestershire. On 18 August 1840, they left the Three Counties to travel to London.[16] Elder Woodruff returned several times over the next few months before he left England entirely in April 1841. Brigham Young returned to the area in December. He attended conferences in Gadfield Elm and Stanley Hill while he was there and reported that the Church in those two conferences, along with the newly-formed Garway Conference, had 1,261 members, with a growth of 254 new members since the previous general conference in October in Manchester.[17] This growth occurred largely due to the work of the British members and missionaries, as none of the Quorum of the Twelve had been in the Three Counties

Wilford Woodruff preached at the Ledbury Baptist Church. (Photo by Cynthia Doxey Green.)

since September 1840. Certainly the service of the American missionaries, including the members of the Quorum of the Twelve Apostles, was vital as the missionary work began in the Three Counties, but other British missionaries continued moving the work forward when Wilford Woodruff and his brethren were not present.

In response to Willard Richards's plea for more laborers in the field, additional missionaries came into the area. The minutes of the July general conference in Manchester include assignments for many local and American missionaries. For example, Elder Thomas Kington, along with William Kay and T. Richardson (both from other parts of England) joined the missionaries in Herefordshire. Brother D. Wilding went to serve in Garway, working with James Morgan, who was from that neighborhood. Brother Price was asked to give up his business and "labour under the advice of Elder Kington, as the way opens."[18] These brethren who preached in the Three Counties represent the two types of British missionaries of this era: those who came from other counties and those who served in their local area.

British Missionaries. Among the British men from other parts of the country who were preaching the gospel in the Three Counties at the time of the October 1840 general conference were William Snailam, Joseph Knowles, John Needham, and Thomas Richardson.[19] Some of the missionary journals mentioned other British missionaries serving in the area such as Henry Glover, William Kay, and Elder Martin Littlewood. Many more may have been serving there from other parts of England, but no comprehensive list is available.

John Needham was a British missionary who left a detailed journal of traveling, preaching, and baptizing in the Three Counties.[20] Having grown up in Warrington, near Manchester, Needham learned of the Church when he was working in Preston as a draper. He joined the Church in 1838 and was ordained a priest soon afterward. In April 1840, he left his work and began traveling and preaching in Lancashire and Staffordshire. He did not write of how he received his assignment to go to the Three Counties, but he did describe arriving in Worcestershire sometime in November 1840 in company with some other brethren he did not name. His journal, which ends the following November, gives details of his journeys and missionary experiences in and around the Three Counties, over the border into Wales, and his travels north to attend Church conferences and to visit his family. This journal provides a wealth of information about missionary work in the British Isles in general, along with stories about experiences he had preaching, people he met, and hardships he passed through.

John Needham. (Church History Library.)

British Missionaries from the Three Counties. The final group of missionaries serving in the Three Counties during this period were local brethren who had joined the Church and were assigned to preach in congregations and neighborhoods in the area. Diaries or journals are available for several of these local missionaries, including James Palmer, John Spiers, James Barnes, and John Gailey.[21] Their journals, along with writings and reports from the other missionaries, indicate that many of the local brethren started teaching and baptizing others soon after their own baptism. Wilford Woodruff's "Record of Baptisms, 1840" records the names of others besides himself who were teaching and baptizing. For example, John Cheese, one of the first to be baptized on 6 March 1840, was ordained a priest a few days later on 15 March. Elder Woodruff was gone for ten days in April to attend the general conference in Preston, and upon his return he wrote that "Priest John Cheese [had baptized] 20."[22] The Church in this area had no lack of priesthood leadership because many of the branch leaders and missionaries serving in the region had previously been lay preachers for the United Brethren, with experience teaching and preaching.

One of the most prominent of these missionaries is Thomas Kington, the superintendent of the United Brethren when Wilford Woodruff first came into the area in March 1840. While he did not leave a journal or diary, several individuals described his involvement in the Church. On 17 March 1840, he first met Wilford Woodruff, who baptized him on 21 March and ordained him an elder on the following day.[23] Kington soon became a key figure in moving the Church forward in the Three Counties area. Elder Kington's leadership is evident in reports of his activities, which included representing the Herefordshire Saints in the Church conferences in Lancashire, as well as providing direction to the work of the local Saints and missionaries.[24] At the first local conference in the Gadfield Elm Chapel, held on 14 June 1840, Elder Kington participated quite notably. He proposed that the branches be formed into the Bran Green[25] and Gadfield Elm Conference of the Church. Along with Wilford Woodruff, Thomas Kington also proposed and participated in priesthood ordinations. Together they made assignments for leadership in various branches in the conference. Elder Kington participated similarly in the meeting held on 21 June 1840 for the area of the Fromes Hill Conference. At each conference, Elder Kington was asked to be the presiding elder over all the churches in the area.²⁶ He appears to have been fully involved as a leader of both the missionaries and the members, in spite of having been a baptized member for less than three months. By the July general conference held in Manchester, Wilford Woodruff reported that the combined conferences in the Three Counties had 1,007 Church members. At that time, Thomas Kington accepted the assignment to oversee the three conferences in the area: Fromes Hill, Bran Green and Gadfield Elm, and Garway.²⁷

John Spiers was another of the United Brethren preachers who became a local missionary soon after his own conversion. Wilford Woodruff baptized him on 6 April 1840, Willard Richards ordained him a priest on 4 May, and he began preaching and baptizing as often as his circumstances would allow.²⁸ At the 14 June 1840 conference at Gadfield Elm chapel, John Spiers was called to preside over the local branch in the Leigh, Gloucestershire, where he was living with Daniel Browett's family.²⁹ He fulfilled that assignment until November of the same year, while still preaching in the surrounding villages, "sometimes walking on Sundays more than twenty miles and preaching to people."³⁰ His journal reported that on 25 September 1840, Thomas Kington called on him, as well as Brother Daniel Browett and Brother Jenkins, "to give up our business and devote all our time to the spread of the work." He admitted that "this was a severe task for me, and I would gladly have done anything else, but as I had been councelled [sic] I arranged my business as fast as I could and prepared to go out."³¹

John Spiers. (Church History Library.)

Preparation to Preach

Missionaries for The Church of Jesus Christ of Latter-day Saints in the twenty-first century usually have at least one year of experience in the Church before their mission call. They also receive training as missionaries, first at a missionary training center and later from mission presidents, leaders, and companions. Thus, they are generally well prepared to share the gospel. In contrast, most of the missionaries of the early Church were recent converts who had minimal training and experience. Latter-day Saints of the twenty-first century may question how these early missionaries learned the gospel doctrines and practices well enough to go out to preach so soon after baptism.

Many of the early missionaries from the Three Counties had been baptized only days or weeks before they went out to preach the gospel. Many were experienced preachers for the United Brethren, but they were still young in their understanding of the restored gospel. Some training came from Wilford Woodruff and the other Apostles who taught gospel doctrines while they were in the area. Some of the local leaders and missionaries also attended the Church conferences in Manchester, where they learned more about the gospel principles. Additionally, although the members of the Quorum of the Twelve did not remain in the Three Counties, they periodically returned to meet with the Saints and to give counsel. For example, in December 1840, Brigham Young came to the Three Counties for conferences at Gadfield Elm, Garway, and Stanley Hill, where John Spiers stated that he "received much instruction."[32]

Most of the local Saints and missionaries had not even read the Book of Mormon before going out to preach. One of the early converts, Job Smith, recollected the day when he first read from the Book of Mormon. Job was a young boy living with his uncle, George Bundy, when Willard Richards first visited their home. Job wrote, "I was reading a history of a noted Methodist preacher who had suffered some severe persecution. Brother Richards after looking at the book, asked me to put it aside for a book which he would lend me. I did so, and he lent me his Book of Mormon, turning to the Book of Ether to where the story of the voyage of Jared and his brother is written."[33] The experience of reading from the Book of Mormon was probably rare for the new Church members and missionaries until after the first copies printed in England became available in February 1841.[34] Without the scriptures, the local British missionaries had to learn the gospel doctrines through the teachings of others, primarily from the members of the Quorum of the Twelve or more experienced missionaries from America or other parts of Britain.

One of the important methods of disseminating information to the Saints throughout Britain was the *Latter-day Saints' Millennial Star*, a periodical that was first published in May 1840. This monthly publication was intended to "prepare all who will hearken for the Second Advent of Messiah, which is now near at hand."[35] It included letters or reports from Church leaders and missionaries, conference reports, editorials from Parley P. Pratt and others, instruction from Church leaders, and extracts from scriptural writings and revelations. In addition, as a "harbinger of the millennium," the *Millennial Star* published interesting world news that might be signs of the approach of the Savior's Second Coming.[36]

By reading this publication, missionaries and other Latter-day Saints could learn of Church doctrines and practices, as well as other information that could increase their understanding of the gospel. When the *Millennial Star* began publication, Job Smith was responsible for delivering copies on foot to members, and he read it with great interest.[37] This publication communicated the Church's beliefs to members scattered throughout the country, similar to the function of Church magazines today.

Levi Richards. (Church History Library.)

The journals of the early missionaries described the council meetings and gatherings where they learned from other missionaries and from more experienced leaders. For example, after Levi Richards came into the area in December of 1840, he began

The Kitchen, home of Thomas Arthur, Garway, Herefordshire. Many missionaries stayed there. The Garway Conference met here on 8 March 1841. (Photo by Carol Wilkinson.)

to oversee the churches and missionaries in the area.[38] James Palmer, one of the local missionaries, described Elder Richards as "an excellent man in concil [sic] sound in judgement, and endowed with a noble and generous disposition."[39] Several times over the next few months, Levi Richards was noted in the journals as being the presiding elder for the region, presiding at conferences or meeting with the Saints and the missionaries, teaching doctrine, and providing counsel.[40]

Missionary Methods

While missionaries did not appear to have set companions, their journals mention that two of them would work together for a few days and then separate and meet other missionaries in other villages or towns. For example, as James Barnes recounted his travels from one village to another during a month in 1840, from time to time he met Elder John Cheese, Elder Clark, Elder James Hill, Elder Wilford Woodruff, and Elder John Gailey. Except for the few times when Church councils were convened, Barnes's account does not mention whether there had been plans to meet with the other brethren; thus, many of these meetings may have happened by chance. Barnes described going to Church meetings in different villages, visiting a member's home, or just finding the other brethren while he was walking from place to place.[41]

The missionary accounts tell very little about how the missionaries decided where to travel. Mention of a set schedule was usually because of a particular meeting they had previously arranged or because of a council meeting or conference. For example, soon after John Needham arrived in the Three Counties in November 1840, he wrote about traveling from place to place in the Garway area, usually staying with Church members like the Arthur family in Garway or the Morgan family in Little Garway.[42] The Arthur home was referred to as "the Kitchen" in most of the missionaries' journals, and many missionaries mentioned staying there as they traveled through Garway. The meetings of the Garway Conference were held at the Kitchen in December 1840 and again in March 1841, with Brigham Young and Levi Richards in attendance at the first and Wilford Woodruff at the latter meeting.[43]

After the December Garway conference, John Needham went to a conference at Gadfield Elm, with Brigham Young and Elder Levi Richards, who "had lately come from America," in attendance.[44] Although there was another conference at Stanley Hill, John returned to Garway and its environs rather than following the group to Stanley Hill.[45] He focused his missionary efforts for some time on Garway and Monmouthshire, although he did not specify whether he chose to go to that area himself or if Church leaders had assigned him to go there.

In one rather unusual example, John Spiers mentioned why he decided to go to preach in the northwestern area of Herefordshire, including Leominster and other villages. He had been teaching in the villages of Deerhurst and the Leigh, as well as the

Little Garway Farm, the home of the Morgan Family. Wilford Woodruff stayed here and held Church meetings. (Photo by Carol Wilkinson.)

town of Cheltenham in Gloucestershire, much of the time working with Elder Henry Glover. On 29 January 1841 he recorded in his journal, "I met Br. Samuel Warren who was about starting on a mission in to the upper part of Herefordshire and he wished me to go with him. I told him I would go providing Elder Glover was willing, he therefore met Elder Glover and it was agreed to."[46] After taking leave of the Saints in Gloucestershire, John Spiers walked with Brother Warren to Fromes Hill, attending meetings with the members there. Then they made their way north, stopping to visit with Church members such as William Jay's family in Marden, Herefordshire.

Although it had been less than a year since Wilford Woodruff had arrived in the area, the connections of the close-knit United Brethren had spread the gospel to many villages, establishing branches and preparing missionary contacts. The members opened their homes for the traveling missionaries to hold meetings, also providing food and shelter for them. Many of these early members also invited their families and friends to hear the missionaries' message. However, not all of the members' fami-

Fireplace at Little Garway Farm, where Wilford Woodruff warmed himself after walking many miles in inclement weather. (Photo by Carol Wilkinson.)

Home of William Jay, Marden, Herefordshire. (Photo by Cynthia Doxey Green.)

lies were interested or willing to hear. For example, John Spiers stated that his mother and brother did not join the Church, and they were not pleased when he accepted baptism and set out to preach.[47]

With the initial foundation for Church membership established in the areas prepared by the congregations of the United Brethren, the missionaries began to travel a little further from the three main focal points of Gadfield Elm, Fromes Hill (or Stanley Hill), and Garway. Brigham Young noted that when he came to the area for conferences in December, he stopped in Cheltenham, where Elder Glover was doing good work in preaching and baptizing.[48] Although Cheltenham did not have a congregation of the United Brethren, it became a focal point of missionary work during the fall of 1840 because of its size and importance as a town. Early in 1842 the Bran Green and Gadfield Elm Conference changed its name to the Cheltenham Conference. In the general conference held in Manchester on 15 May 1842, the Cheltenham Conference had 540 members with 17 branches.[49] The Cheltenham Conference membership records show that over 700 people were baptized from 1840 to 1863.[50] Today, Cheltenham is the central place of the stake in the Three Counties.

John Spiers provided insight into a missionary's lifestyle in those early days. He described his service as he moved from Gloucestershire into northwest Herefordshire, where he opened up a new area of preaching:

> This was now getting beyond the branches of the Church. During my mission in Gloucestershire I had become much discouraged at having no more success and especially so as very many people seemed to despise my testimony because of my youth and because I lacked a beard. I now felt determined to find a people who were willing to obey the truth. I therefore went before the Lord and asked Him to let me see the fruits of my labours, and also covenanted with the Lord that I would find a people willing to obey the gospel or I would die trying.[51]

In spite of Spiers's discouragement and challenges, his covenant with the Lord to try his best to find individuals willing to obey the gospel is inspiring. He carried on teaching throughout the area for many more months, baptizing over eighty people during his mission, even while suffering with illness and persecution. For example, one evening he fainted in the middle of his speech in front of a large congregation. His companion, Brother Warren, carried on preaching until Spiers woke up again and could stand up and finish his discourse.[52] This example of determined discipleship shows these young local missionaries' full conversion and dedication to the gospel they had embraced.

Missionaries today, often with the help of their families and ward members, bear a majority of the responsibility for their temporal needs while they are serving. In contrast, the missionaries of the 1840s traveled without purse or scrip (see D&C 24:18), meaning that they depended on local individuals (Church members and others) to provide shelter and food. When the missionaries ventured further from the established congregations of the United Brethren, they had to find people willing to invite them into their homes. At times they had little to eat and no place to sleep. John Spiers and Brother Warren traveled to the village of Kingsland, where they did not know anyone. They found only a hay loft where they could sleep, "but the calves kept up such a bleating as to keep us awake [a] great part of the night."[53]

Sometimes after a meeting in a new village, one of the attendees would invite the missionaries to his or her home. Often, the individuals who invited missionaries into their homes were later baptized. For example, James Barnes related that on a Wednesday he walked eleven miles to Abinghall, where he entered the home "of Elijah Clifford tarried there and lodged there and [bore] testimony." After staying with them several days and preaching in their home and neighborhood, on Sunday, 5 September 1840, Barnes baptized Elijah and his wife, Margaret.[54] Other missionaries had similar experiences as they ventured beyond the established branches of the Church. John Spiers recorded that as he entered the town of Leominster, "some people named Wright" fed him and then introduced him to Mrs. Tunks, who provided shelter for the night, "and from this time we had a home with these people who treated us with the greatest of kindness."[55] Mrs. Tunks and many of her family members joined the Church over the next few months.[56]

Although Wilford Woodruff's missionary service in the Three Counties provided the foundation, perhaps some of the real strength of the Church in this area came from those who

Herefordshire countryside. (Photo by Cynthia Doxey Green.)

followed him and continued to teach the gospel, helping Church membership grow. The missionaries and members were spread all over the Three Counties, not centered only in one or two locations. Branches with strong membership developed in areas such as Garway, Eywas Harold, and Orcop in southwestern Herefordshire. Other branches in Herefordshire included Leominster, Fromes Hill, Lugwardine, Stanley Hill, and Colwall. Worcestershire had branches around Gadfield Elm and Berrow, as well as the Malvern Hill areas of Alfrick and Suckley. Strong branches in Gloucestershire included Dymock, Deerhurst, Apperley, Cheltenham, and the Forest of Dean, to name just a few. Some of the missionaries also ventured into Monmouthshire, going over the mountains from Garway into Abergavenny and Llantony Abbey. Perhaps because the early Church members had friends and relatives scattered throughout the region, the gospel spread farther afield more quickly than if the missionaries had gone randomly from place to place.

These early missionaries' diaries show that they rarely stayed long in the same area. They may have stayed a day or two with the same family, teaching and baptizing in a particular village, but then they would move on to another town where they had made appointments to preach. They often crisscrossed each other's paths, as one would mention going to Garway and Orcop while another would be leaving from Garway and going to Dymock or Lugwardine. They may have had certain places they would return to visit regularly, but very rarely would they stay for more than a few days. For example, James Palmer mentioned that when he passed through Orcop he stayed at the Pigeon House Estate with Mr. Daniel Price, his widowed niece who served as his housekeeper, Mrs. Elizabeth Knight, and her younger sister, Miss Mary Ann Price.[57] Later in his reminiscences, Palmer recalled that on the day he baptized Mary Ann Price, the Spirit revealed to him that "I had baptized the person that was designed by providence to become my wife."[58] This young woman may have provided a motive for James's many visits to the Pigeon House. He stated that Mr. Price received him very kindly but never joined the Church and that Mrs. Knight was baptized but eventually turned against the Church.[59] James Palmer married Mary Ann Price in March 1842 in Liverpool, before they embarked on the ship to travel to Nauvoo.[60]

The missionaries preached in open-air meetings or in the streets, but they also focused on finding homes, meeting places, or churches in which to deliver their message.[61] The homes and barns of the United Brethren, already licensed for preaching by the local governments, became the central meeting places for the newly formed branches and for local conferences and leadership meetings. As the missionaries moved into places with no established branches, they would seek out meeting places and arrange to preach wherever they could. For example, John Needham had planned to meet at the home of Mr. Jones in Longtown, Herefordshire, but arrived when Mr. Jones was not at home. He then found a Mrs. Davis who was willing to have the missionaries preach in her home, and a large and attentive congregation gathered.

Mr. Davis gave permission for them to preach at his home another time.[62]

In contrast, John Spiers told how after he had been preaching and baptizing in Leominster, many in the town turned against the Church, and he could not obtain a house in which to preach. So he found it necessary "to resort to some stratagem to obtain one; accordingly we sent one of the members to take a house as though for private use," and they were able to hold their meetings.[63] Two months later, John Spiers applied for and received a license for a place to preach in Leominster at a building hired by Isaac Tunks in the Corn Market Square; thus they were eventually able to establish a better meeting place.[64]

Content of the Preaching

The early missionaries had no set lesson plans or discussions to share with investigators. The journals provide a few examples of the missionaries' methods of teaching the doctrines of the gospel. James Palmer described Elder Woodruff's preaching. When Palmer first heard Wilford Woodruff preach, this "noble man of God" shared "gods divine law," using the scriptures, "giving chapter and verse line, upon line here a little and there a little until we were all satisfied and our hearts ware filled with Joy [sic]."[65] Palmer testified that the Holy Ghost enlightened Wilford Woodruff as the prophets of old were inspired by the Holy Ghost to write the commandments of God. This knowledge led him and others to desire baptism.[66] Although they did not have printed materials readily available, the missionaries focused their preaching on the first principles of the gospel, the plan of salvation, the organization of the primitive church in Christ's day, and the Second Coming of Christ.[67]

The journal of William Williams, a very dedicated preacher for the United Brethren, gives an interesting perspective about what the missionaries preached. Williams's first experience with the Mormons came with hearing the preaching of John Cheese, a former United Brethren preacher who was a newly ordained priest in The Church of Jesus Christ of Latter-day Saints. Williams's description of the things he heard and the change that had come over John Cheese since his baptism shows an effective contrast between the styles of preaching of the United Brethren and the missionaries for the Church. His entry is as follows:

> After Singing & Prayer [John Cheese] Began Preaching in a Plain Simple Stile Concerning the doctrines of the Church of Jesus Christ Called Latterday Saints he said God had Spoke from heaven that it was our duty to repent of our Sins be baptized for the Remission of them get the gift of the Holy Ghost by the Laying on of hands Believeing in doctrine of the Resurection & eternal Judgment for God was a going to do a great work & to cut it Short in righteousness to gather the meek & Honest in Heart to Zion while Judgments Rolled thro the Nations of the earth Such in Part was the Principels upon which he discoursed he did not seem to want for any thing but Seemed to Proceed with perfect ease from first to last No excitement but a Perfect calm No Thunderings of Hell & damnation to Scar[e] us but each Part as he Proceeded he Proved from our own Bible what a change in him he seemed to teach as one having authority and we felt it and felt abashed.[68]

William Williams recognized the change that Church membership had made in John Cheese, noticing a contrast in his new preaching style as he taught about repentance, baptism, and the gift of the Holy Ghost. Even without printed materials to read, people were converted to the gospel because of the message of truth and the testimony received through the Holy Ghost. The changes apparent in John Cheese's preaching style and the reactions of William Williams are evidence that people were convinced of truth, not merely because the preacher was exciting, but because the Holy Ghost communicated the truthfulness of the words of the preacher, who had authority from God.

Persecution

According to the pattern explained in chapter 1, experiencing joy after accepting the gospel and going out to preach in the Three Counties was followed by times of testing and trial. Although these missionaries had many successful interactions with the people as they taught and baptized in the Three Counties area, they also had their share of opposition and persecution. Sometimes the persecution was instigated by the clergy from other local churches who feared losing their parishioners. For example, in Dymock, Wilford Woodruff attributed some of the mob action to the local parish rector, saying that this religious leader stirred up the townspeople against the Saints. Elder Woodruff recorded that during one meeting in September 1840, at Thomas Kington's house in Dymock, the local populace paraded up and down the street outside the house, beating drums, pots, and pails, trying to disrupt the meeting. They also threw stones, bricks, and rotten eggs at the home. Although the windows were shuttered, some windows and roof tiles were broken. Wilford Woodruff reports that the local brethren did not allow him to go outside for fear he would be injured by the mob, but they went out to record the names of the mob leaders so they could report them to the law. After the mob broke up, the Saints had to clear away the debris, and then they "had a good nights rest [sic]."[69]

Other missionary journals mention ministers and preachers interrupting meetings, defying doctrine, and trying to convince the listeners that the Latter-day Saints were preaching falsehoods. Despite their relative youth and inexperience in the Church, the missionaries were able to overcome those disturbances by the help and guidance of the Spirit. James Palmer wrote of a Methodist minister who got up to disturb a meeting, but after listening a little longer to the missionaries, he gave them two pence to help sustain them.[70] Not long after this incident, however, Palmer related that another minister rose up in opposition to the missionaries and demanded a sign. The missionaries replied that this heckler was part of a wicked and adulterous generation seeking for signs; afterward, the congregation left, disgusted at the way the missionaries had been treated by the minister. Palmer said the missionaries rejoiced because their sufferings for Christ's sake would be recompensed at the last day.[71] John Spiers related a time when a minister became so combative that the congregation got into an uproar, and they called in the local constable to bring order back to the meeting.[72]

Dymock Village. (Photo by Carol Wilkinson.)

Even a local newspaper noticed that the Latter-day Saints were being treated differently than other religious groups. An article from the *Hereford Times* on 14 November 1840 reads as follows: "Proceedings at Dymock: 'The Dymock Lads' (as the male part of the population of that parish are generally called) and lasses too, have been amusing themselves very much of late by shooting, hanging, and burning effigies, which they dressed to represent some of the leaders of the 'latter day saints' of that neighbourhood."[73]

Apparently, burning effigies was not a one-time or one-place occurrence for the Saints. John Spiers related that in Dilwyn, Herefordshire, the local "good Christians" influenced the rebels in the village to disturb the Latter-day Saint meeting, threatening to throw Spiers into the well and to burn the house down. Instead, they burnt him in effigy, and the next day he was accompanied out of the village by the sound of a "gang of kettles."[74]

Some individuals followed the missionaries, taunting them or trying to frighten or injure them. John Gailey wrote that after he tried to raise a voice of warning in Ross-on-Wye, one of the villagers hit him on the shoulder with an egg, and a multitude escorted him to the edge of town, crying out against him.[75] James Palmer told of ruffians who attended a meeting and afterward followed the missionaries, throwing stones and snowballs at them, finally demanding money to let them go in peace. The missionaries gave the crowd all they had: "the enormous sum of one shilling and sixpence half penny."[76] James Palmer noted, somewhat sarcastically, that the amount of money, which would be worth about ten dollars in the twenty-first century, was not quite the enormous sum the ruffians would have liked.

Persecution of missionaries and Church members has been seen throughout the history of the Church. These stories from the Three Counties provide representative examples of how the missionaries and members were able to overcome the challenges placed before them.

Importance of the Early Missionary Journals

Most published accounts of the early success of the Church in the Three Counties have focused on the work of Wilford Woodruff and many of the American Church leaders and missionaries in the area. However, other missionaries' journals show that many faithful British Saints and missionaries also were important to the growth of the Church in this area. While it is impossible to know how many British missionaries served in the area in the 1840s and 1850s, due to incomplete Church records, the service they rendered in leaving their homes and going out to preach made it possible for many branches of the Church to be established.

The missionary journals provide insight into how these local individuals shared the gospel effectively, even without the resources of the present day. Most had few printed materials, but they preached the basic doctrines of the gospel with the power of the Spirit. The Book of Mormon was not easily available in Britain until after February 1841, but the *Millennial Star* was an important resource for teaching the doctrines of the gospel. The missionary journals relate that the early missionaries in the Three Counties often found their best converts among the friends and relatives of the members of the Church, an important reminder that Church members are the best sources for referrals to the missionaries.

These journals also demonstrate that although the missionaries in mid-nineteenth-century England had many challenges, they had great faith and perseverance to carry on preaching the gospel in the face of adversity.

Notes

1. "Wilford Woodruff's Baptismal Record, 1840," in *Wilford Woodruff's Journal*, 1:377–95. The list contains 479 names of baptized individuals. Sometimes he wrote that others actually performed some of the baptisms.
2. Woodruff, "Correspondence," *Millennial Star* 1, no. 4 (August 1840): 82–83.
3. "United Brethren Preachers' Plan of the Frooms Hill Circuit, 1840," 248.6 U58p 1840, Church History Library, Salt Lake City. Although the preachers' plan and the journals or reminiscences of others often spell the place "Frooms Hill," the name as seen on 1851 jurisdiction maps on maps.familysearch.org and on current maps all spell the name "Fromes Hill." Unless quoting directly from a source, we will use the correct spelling of the place.
4. Sarah Davis Carter, "She Came in 1853," in *Our Pioneer Heritage*, comp. Kate B. Carter (Salt Lake City: Daughters of Utah Pioneers, 1969), 12:227.
5. James Palmer, "James Palmer Reminiscences, ca. 1884–98," 19 (January 1841), MS 1752, Church History Library, Salt Lake City.
6. John Spiers, "John Spiers Reminiscences and Journal, 1840–77," 29 (13–14 September 1841), MS 1725, Church History Library, Salt Lake City.
7. At the Church History Library, journals or reminiscences can be found for Wilford Woodruff, Willard Richards, Brigham Young, and Levi Richards discussing their missionary activities in this area.
8. Spiers, "Reminiscences," 33 (12 November 1841). Spiers states that Levi Richards helped him organize the Leominster Branch; he ordained men to the priesthood and "gave us much useful instruction."
9. Brigham Young, *Manuscript History of Brigham Young, 1801–1844*, comp. Elden J. Watson (Salt Lake City: Smith Secretarial Service, 1968), 73–76.

10. Willard Richards, "To the Editor of the Mil. Star, Ledbury, Herefordshire, May 15 1840," *Millennial Star* 1, no. 1 (May 1840): 23.
11. Woodruff, "Correspondence," 83. "Minutes of the Conference Held at Gadfield Elm chapel, in Worcestershire, England, June 14th, 1840," *Millennial Star* 1, no. 4 (August 1840): 84; "Minutes of the Conference Held at Stanley Hill, Castle Frome, Herefordshire, June 21st, 1840," *Millennial Star* 1, no. 4 (August 1840): 86.
12. *Wilford Woodruff's Journal*, 1:470 (23 June 1840), 1:487 (22 July 1840).
13. In his journal after this date, Wilford Woodruff sometimes mentioned baptisms, but the little notebook of baptisms has no names listed after the time he left the region on 23 June 1840.
14. *Wilford Woodruff's Journal*, 1:430 (30 March 1840).
15. *Wilford Woodruff's Journal*, 1:430 (30 March 1840).
16. *Wilford Woodruff's Journal*, 1:491–93 (12–18 August 1840).
17. Brigham Young, "News from the Elders," *Millennial Star* 1, no. 9 (January 1841): 239. The letter was written 30 December 1840.
18. "Minutes of the General Conference," *Millennial Star* 1, no. 3 (July 1840): 70–71.
19. "Minutes of the General Conference," *Millennial Star* 1, no. 6 (October 1840): 168. Thomas Richardson may have been the same T. Richardson who was sent to Herefordshire in July.
20. John Needham, "John Needham Autobiography and Journal, 1840 August–1842 December," Transcript, MS 4221, Church History Library, Salt Lake City.
21. Palmer, "Reminiscences;" Spiers, "Reminiscences;" James Barnes, "James Barnes Diary, 1840 August–1841 June," MS 1870, Church History Library, Salt Lake City; John Gailey, "John Gailey, Reminiscence and Diary, ca. 1840–41," MS 1089, Church History Library, Salt Lake City.
22. *Wilford Woodruff's Journal*, 1:425 (15 March 1840) lists John Cheese's ordination; The quote about Cheese baptizing others is on 1:440 (16 April 1840). John Cheese's baptism is listed on 6 March 1840 in "Wilford Woodruff's Baptismal Record, 1840," 379.
23. *Wilford Woodruff's Journal*, 1:425–427 (17, 21, 22 March 1840).
24. "Minutes of the General Conference," *Millennial Star* 1, no. 3 (July 1840): 68–69. Page 68 shows Elder Kington submitting the minutes from the conferences held in Herefordshire, and on page 69 we see a proposal for Thomas Kington to be ordained a high priest. Wilford

Woodruff, "Correspondence," 82. In his letter to the editor, Wilford Woodruff mentions that Elder Kington had "given himself wholly to the work of the ministry."

25. Bran Green is spelled a variety of ways in the records, including Brangreen, Brandgreen, and Brand Green. Unless the record to which we are referring spells it differently, we will consistently spell it "Bran Green." On a map today it is spelled Brand Green.
26. "Minutes of the Conference Held at Gadfield Elm chapel, in Worcestershire, England, June 14th, 1840," 85; "Minutes of the Conference Held at Stanley Hill, Castle Frome, Herefordshire, June 21st, 1840," 87.
27. "Minutes of the General Conference," *Millennial Star* 1, no. 6 (October 1840): 165–68. The conference was held 6 July 1840 in Manchester. Wilford Woodruff reported 1,007 members from "Herefordshire, Gloucestershire, etc.," 166. On page 168, Elder Thomas Kington received the assignment to take "charge of Herefordshire Conferences, as heretofore, also Garway, etc."
28. Spiers, "Reminiscences," 2.
29. Spiers, "Reminiscences," 2–3.
30. Spiers, "Reminiscences," 3.
31. Spiers, "Reminiscences," 3 (25 September 1840).
32. Spiers, "Reminiscences," 5 (21 December 1840).
33. Job Taylor Smith, "Job Smith Autobiography, circa 1902," 3, MS 4809, Church History Library, Salt Lake City.
34. Allen, Esplin, and Whittaker, *Men with a Mission*, 251.
35. Parley P. Pratt, "Prospectus of the Latter-day Saints Millennial Star," M205.1 M646p 1840, Church History Library, Salt Lake City.
36. Allen, Esplin, and Whittaker, *Men with a Mission*, 252.
37. Smith, "Autobiography," 3.
38. Levi Richards, "Levi Richards Papers, 1837–1867," MS 1284, box 1, folder 1, Church History Library, Salt Lake City. Levi Richards arrived in Ledbury on 10 December 1840.
39. Palmer, "Reminiscences," 14.
40. Spiers, "Reminiscences," 29 (16 September 1841); Palmer, "Reminiscences," 30.
41. Barnes, "Diary," 7–13 (September–October 1840).
42. Needham, "Autobiography," 21 (3–8 December 1840).

43. Brigham Young, "News from the Elders," 239; Barnes, "Diary," 20–21 (6 December 1840); *Wilford Woodruff's Journal*, 2:58–9 (8 March 1841).
44. Needham, "Autobiography," 22 (12 or 13 December 1840).
45. Needham, "Autobiography," 22 (17 December 1840).
46. Spiers, "Reminiscences," 8 (29 January 1841).
47. Spiers, "Reminiscences," 8 (1 February 1841). He actually says they "hotly opposed my going out to preach the gospel so much so that my Brother would not speak at all comfortably to me and by some it was said that he threatened my life howbeit I hardly think that to be true."
48. Brigham Young, "News from the Elders," 239.
49. "General Conference," *Millennial Star* 3, no. 2 (June 1842): 29.
50. The numbers come from the transcription of the Cheltenham Branch Records, found at the Family History Library, Microfilm #86991, items 5–8. This transcription formed part of the database described in the appendix.
51. Spiers, "Reminiscences," 9 (8 February 1841).
52. Spiers, "Reminiscences," 9–10 (12 February 1841).
53. Spiers, "Reminiscences," 11 (16 February 1841).
54. Barnes, "Diary," 5 (possibly September 1840)
55. Spiers, "Reminiscences," 13 (9 March 1841).
56. John Spiers mentions the baptism of Mrs. Mary Tunks on 17 August 1841. Spiers, "Reminiscences," 26.
57. Palmer, "Reminiscences," 19, 21, 25, 26, to name but a few of his visits.
58. Palmer, "Reminiscences," 50. Mary Ann Price was baptized 18 September 1841.
59. When James Palmer went back to serve a mission in the Three Counties in 1857, he visited his sister-in-law, Elizabeth Knight, on several occasions, but said that she was not as kind to him as she had been. One example is on page 164 (1–2 March 1857) where he said he had "quite a disagreeable time with Mrs. Knight," on account of her greediness in not giving her sister Mary Ann much of the "handsome property" from their Uncle Daniel Price's will and testament.
60. Palmer, "Reminiscences," 63 (14 March 1842).
61. Spiers, "Reminiscences," 4 (26 November 1840). John Spiers said that in Kemerton, he visited many houses searching for a place to preach but was unsuccessful. On a different occasion, he mentioned that in Dilwyn, the missionaries gathered a congregation in the street, like

a "Methodist Camp Meeting" in the hope that more people would be drawn to listen to them. Spiers, "Reminiscences," 20 (13 June 1841).
62. Needham, "Autobiography," 20–21 (30 November 1840).
63. Spiers, "Reminiscences," 38 (3 January 1842).
64. Spiers, "Reminiscences," 43 (25–26 March 1842). This story is corroborated by the application for a licensed place to preach, held at the Herefordshire County Record Office. It states that John Spiers applied for a license for a place to preach in Leominster at the "Corn Square" at a house "now in the holding and occupation of Isaac Tunks and others" on 26 March 1842.
65. Palmer, "Reminiscences," 6 (April 1840).
66. Palmer, "Reminiscences," 6 (April 1840).
67. Palmer, "Reminiscences," 16 (27 December 1842); Spiers, "Reminiscences," 2 (3 April 1840); Barnes, "Diary," 21 (11 December 1840); Gailey, "Reminiscence," 23 (October 1841).
68. William Williams, "William Williams Reminisce, 1850," 6, MS 9132, Church History Library, Salt Lake City.
69. *Wilford Woodruff's Journal*, 1:516–17 (16 September 1840).
70. Palmer, "Reminiscences," 17–18 (December 1840).
71. Palmer, "Reminiscences," 17–18 (December 1840).
72. Spiers, "Reminiscences," 32 (9 November 1841).
73. "Proceedings at Dymock," *Hereford Times* (14 November 1840).
74. Spiers, "Reminiscences," 39–40 (31 January–1 February 1842).
75. Gailey, "Reminiscences," 15–16 (July 1841).
76. Palmer, "Reminiscences," 21–23 (no date, but probably January 1841).

The Harvest of Converts

A MAJOR FOCUS OF THIS RESEARCH was to document, insofar as possible, information about the converts to the Church in the Three Counties from the 1840s. Most previous research of the harvest of converts from the time of Wilford Woodruff's first arrival in the area has been based on the perspective of the missionaries who went to the Three Counties. This chapter will focus on how other documents can help us understand the converts as individuals and families. In particular, we were interested in learning more about their economic and demographic backgrounds, their conversion and emigration stories, their family relationships, and the growth and development of the Church as a whole in the Three Counties over time.

To learn more about the converts, we used both personal sources, including journals and reminiscences, and public sources, particularly membership records from The Church of Jesus Christ of Latter-day Saints, emigration records, census records, and family records found on FamilySearch.org. Several of the early converts left journals or personal histories recording their conversions and subsequent journeys through life as Latter-day Saints in the nineteenth century. We consulted written histories by individuals who emigrated to Nauvoo or to Utah whose writings have been deposited at libraries or archives in the Intermountain West. We found fewer records available for those who did not make the journey to America in the nineteenth century. We have included more information on the details of our research methods in the appendix.

This chapter and the next describe research carried out to learn more about the early converts' individual lives and experiences as members of the Church. The first aspect of this research was to identify as many converts from the early 1840s as possible, searching to understand more about the many different reports of baptism numbers found in the writings of Wilford Woodruff and other Church leaders. Church record keeping in that time period was not complete or accurate, so the majority of the convert names used in this study come from journals and reminiscences written by missionaries and members from that area.

The second focus of this research was to learn more about the lives and experiences of these early converts, including how many emigrated or stayed behind in England. By finding the individuals in a variety of records, we learned more about who they were and if they were able to remain active in the Church throughout their lives. This chapter will focus on the converts as they first joined the Church, including their stories of conversion and their demographic circumstances. Along with trying to identify individuals and families who joined the Church, we also wanted to understand more about where the branches were located and how they were organized or disbanded. Chapter 6 will consider what happened to the converts after they joined the Church, particularly whether they remained faithful to the gospel and whether they emigrated to America to join the body of Saints or stayed behind in England.

Identifying the Early Converts in the Three Counties

Later in his life, Wilford Woodruff often mentioned the great success he had had in sharing the gospel in Herefordshire, Gloucestershire, and Worcestershire, including converts who had been members of the United Brethren. Depending on the circumstances of his reminiscences and the purpose of his discussion, his reflections on the success of the work did not always contain the same details. Some individuals may question the accuracy of his words, in part because he used phrases that could be seen

Countryside in the Three Counties. (Photo by Cynthia Doxey Green.)

as contradictory. For example, when he spoke about his time in the Three Counties, on one occasion he said that all but one of the six hundred United Brethren were baptized.[1] In another circumstance he talked of "1800 people" who joined the Church in the first year the gospel was preached in the Three Counties.[2] In another instance, Wilford Woodruff stated that he "baptized 600,"[3] but his "Baptismal Record 1840" shows that he baptized just over 300 people himself.[4] Further research seemed necessary to reconcile these different statements.

There are several possible explanations for the various statements regarding the baptisms and membership of the Church during the year Wilford Woodruff was in England. One obvious reason for the changes in baptism numbers is the possibility that over time Wilford Woodruff may not have remembered precise details of his experiences and thus provided a round figure in his descriptions. Simply stating that 600 people joined the Church is easier to say than a number such as 572. The number of converts from the United Brethren congregations was most likely very close to 600, because other descriptions about the United Brethren state that there were about 600 members of the group.[5]

Another possible explanation for the disparity among Wilford Woodruff's comments about numbers of baptisms might be the precision of the words and specificity of the details that he was using at the time. He did not always state whether he was referring to the number of people he personally baptized or the number of people who were baptized in the Three Counties area. These numbers should be quite different, because soon after Wilford Woodruff performed the initial baptisms, other American and British missionaries began teaching and baptizing. If Wilford Woodruff was describing the number of people baptized in the area during the first year the gospel was preached, there could easily have been about 1,800 baptisms.

Method of Identifying Names of Converts. Because the Church in the 1840s did not keep records as carefully as in the twenty-first century, there is no feasible way to find the exact number of baptisms and names of those baptized in that time period. We found very few Church membership records from the Three Counties available after 160 years.[6] In the absence of a comprehensive list, we used the names found in missionary and member journals, though these sources are sporadic and incomplete. The writers did not always write the names of their converts, and there were many more missionaries and priesthood holders baptizing their friends and neighbors for whom there are no records.[7]

Many of these journals, diaries, or reminiscences are located in their original form in various record repositories in Utah; some are available in published form as autobiographies in Mormon pioneer collections.[8] In all instances, we used only firsthand accounts rather than secondary accounts, such as personal histories written by children or descendants of the original converts. While autobiographical writings can be affected by the ability of individuals to recollect their past accurately, these sources are not tainted by the embellishments of individuals of later generations who, not knowing the story from their own experience, may add to or take away from the history in order to focus the stories of their ancestors for their own purposes.

One of the most important sources for the names of converts in the Three Counties was "Wilford Woodruff's Baptismal Record 1840," a notebook with the subtitle "W. Woodruff's list of the number baptized in Herefordshire England 1840."[9] Wilford Woodruff listed the names, dates, and places for many of the baptisms in the area from 6 March through 22 June 1840, when he left the area for a conference in Manchester. After that time he no longer kept a detailed report of the baptisms, but in his journal he often mentioned individuals who were baptized or ordained to priesthood offices, noting also members he visited.[10] In addition to Wilford Woodruff, many of the converts and missionaries wrote of people they visited and baptized, which added significantly to the journal database we created. We have a name, partial name, or baptismal information in the journal database for 775 individuals. All of the baptisms in this database occurred sometime between 6 March 1840 and 5 February 1843, when the last of the missionaries for whom we had journals were no longer in the Three Counties area.[11]

After compiling the names of the converts mentioned in the journals, we searched for these individuals on other Church or public records to learn more about their movements or later involvement with the Church. Our record search included censuses in both Britain and the United States, marriage and death records, the ships' passenger lists on the Mormon Migration website, the company records found on the Mormon Pioneer Overland Travel website, and genealogies and histories found on FamilySearch.org.[12] Although the journals contained names of converts, they did not always provide other identifying information, such as gender, age, marital status, or place of residence. In many of the missionaries' journals, we found baptismal dates and places that helped us identify the converts in public records. On rare occasions, the journal writer included familial relationships or information on age. For example, John Spiers wrote that he baptized Ann Weaver, the ninety-five-year-old mother of Mary Fox, in Dilwyn, Herefordshire. The 1841 census in Dilwyn shows Ann Weaver, ninety-five years old, living with the Thomas and Mary Fox family. Without such information, we sometimes had difficulty identifying the converts;[13] however, we did positively identify 73 percent of the 775 people on the database.

Number of Baptisms in the Early 1840s. Finding the number of converts baptized in the early 1840s in the Three Counties area can be difficult because personal and official Church membership records are scarce. However, during the first year of the Church in the Three Counties area, Wilford Woodruff recorded membership numbers in conference reports in his journal, which were later published in the *Millennial Star*. Unfortunately, names were not included with the numbers. The journal reports the minutes of the conferences held at Gadfield Elm on 14 September 1840 and at Stanley Hill on 20 September 1840, including the number of Church members from each of the branches of the two conferences.[14] These reports provide a total membership for the Three Counties of 1,007 in September 1840, just over six months after Wilford Woodruff first arrived in the area. When Wilford Woodruff recorded the conference meetings in March 1841, he wrote that the Gadfield Elm Conference had 408 members and the Fromes Hill Conference had 1,008 members, adding in the newly created Garway Conference with 134 members. Thus by the end of March 1841 there were at least 1,550 members in the Three Counties.[15] The reports also mention that some converts had died, emigrated, or been excommunicated by the time of the conferences, meaning that the number 1,550 does not include such individuals.

There are no complete records of how many people had emigrated from the Three Counties by March 1841, but records show at least seven ships with Mormon emigrants leaving from England between September 1840 and March 1841.[16] Several of those ships did not have complete passenger lists, so we cannot know how many individuals were on them. Although not all of the emigrants in those ships would be from the Three Counties, over fifty of the converts from our journal database were on the ships, including the Benbow, Kington, and Holmes families, who had left England before the March 1841 conferences. Possibly quite a large number of the early converts from the Three Counties had already emigrated to Nauvoo by March 1841, when Wilford Woodruff noted there were 1,550 Church members in the area.[17]

Simply stated, we may never find a definitive answer to the question of how many people joined the Church from the Three Counties during Wilford Woodruff's service there. However, evidence supports there were between 1,500 and 2,000 converts.

While there is no comprehensive list of individuals who were baptized during the preaching of the early missionaries in the area, Wilford Woodruff's recollection of about 1,800 converts is likely to be very close to the correct number, although we may never know all of their names.

Understanding People Through Stories of Conversion

While we cannot know the stories of all 1,800 members of the Church, a number of journals and autobiographies of these early Saints help us glimpse the way the people in the Three Counties were prepared to hear and accept the message of the fullness of the gospel. Because we could not begin to tell the stories of all these converts, we focused our research on the first-person accounts we could locate.

Seekers. Many of the converts from this part of England were members of the United Brethren sect, a break-off from the Primitive Methodists. The United Brethren were searching for a purer form of Christianity than they had found in other churches. Many of those who were members of the United Brethren could be classified as "seekers," or people who had belonged to more than one religious group because they were looking for something different than their earlier experiences with religious worship. Thus, when they heard the gospel preached by Wilford Woodruff and other missionaries, they were prepared to accept it and be baptized.

Thomas Steed's family was among the seekers. Thomas was a young boy in 1835 when he and his parents joined the United Brethren and opened their home for preaching. In addition to participating in those meetings, his parents continued to send Thomas to the Church of England Sunday School at the Abbey Church in Malvern.[18] While attending Sunday School, Thomas "asked [his] teacher if anybody knew if God lived, and if Jesus was the Redeemer crucified 1800 years ago." The teacher answered, "My boy, you ought not to ask such question, you ought to believe; I don't know and I don't know who could tell you!" Thomas asked the same question of other people, and he received the same answer. He stated, "That caused me to think that there was

Thomas Steed and his wife. (Church History Library.)

nothing in religion, if nobody knew anything about these things, and I made up my mind to have nothing to do with it."[19] Thomas Steed's desire to learn answers to questions of eternal worth and the inability of local religious leaders to supply these answers provided fertile ground for the seeds of the gospel when Wilford Woodruff arrived in 1840.

One of the places Elder Woodruff preached at in the summer of 1840 was the Steed family home at Pale House, in Great Malvern. Thomas wrote that prior to the meeting with Wilford Woodruff, his sister Rebecca had informed him that the Apostle had the same authority that the ancient Apostles had held. Thomas attended the meeting and later wrote that he "heard the first prin-

Jonathan Lucy's home in Colwall, Herefordshire. (Photo by Cynthia Doxey Green.)

ciples of the Gospel, a Gospel sermon preached in all simplicity and plainness, for the first time in my life. I was convinced in my mind that the principles he advanced are true."[20] Right away his parents and five of his eight siblings were baptized. Thomas and his two younger brothers were baptized during the next few months, as were several aunts and uncles. Thomas had only one sibling—an older married sister—who did not join the Church.[21]

Fourteen-year-old convert Thomas Steed experienced a marvelous spiritual manifestation while at a gathering of Saints at the home of Jonathan Lucy in Colwall. Thomas recorded it later in his life.

> All at once a power put me on my feet, the Spirit of prophecy rested upon me. . . . The house was filled with the Spirit and the power of God, and every one present was thrilled with the convincing power of the Holy Spirit and which I could feel through my whole system like fire shut up in my bones. It was then plainly made known unto me that God lives, that Jesus is

the Redeemer and that Joseph Smith was a prophet of the Most High God. Of the truth of this a doubt has never crossed my mind from that day to this.[22]

Although a young man, Thomas received the gift of tongues on that occasion, enabling him to prophesy of things to come for the group of Saints, including their eventual travel to Nauvoo along with other events to occur in England.

Another truth seeker with an early interest in eternal principles was John Gailey. His desire to find truth began as a young boy.

> When I was young I was deeply concerned about eternity and the coming of the Son of God, but I told no one any thing about it for some time. After awhile some Preachers visited us calling themselves Primitive Methodists, holding forth Salvation through Christ by faith alone. I attended to their preaching for some time, and at last joined their Church. . . . Soon after I left the first and joined the united brethren as a local preacher that was to preach on Sundays which I continued to do one year and ten months. Thomas Kington who was then our leader, desired me to give myself wholy to the ministry which I did. This was in 1836. . . . I continued to preach amongst them till in 1840 when it pleased God to send Elder Wilford Woodruff to Castle Frome with the fulness of the gospel.[23]

Similarly, John Spiers's early views on religion led him to become a seeker, join the United Brethren when he was young, and become involved in teaching and preaching. The coming of Wilford Woodruff changed John, along with the entire group of United Brethren. John said:

> When quite young I had very serious thoughts of religion and was zealously attached to the Church of England. When I was about 15 years I began to view the abominations of the Church of England (more particular the character of her ministers than her doctrine) and shortly attached myself to a body of Methodists who had seperated from the Primitive Methodists under a

Mr. Thos. Kington, and others and taken the name of United Brethren. I was appointed class leader of the Redmarley class . . . and before I was 17 years old was appointed a local preacher which appointment I at first refused but afterwards accepted.

Early in the year 1840, Elder Wilford Woodruff of the twelve Apostles of the Church of Jesus Christ of Latter-day Saints came from America, and shortly came into Herefordshire and introduced the principles to some of the leading men of our society who fell in with them and was baptized. Mr. Kington after much debate with him, embraced the work and then introduced elder Woodruff all through his society most of which embraced it and those who would not were scattered so that the society was broken up, on the 3rd of April (1840).[24]

Dreams. Spiritual preparation takes many forms. Some individuals were prepared for the gospel or guided onto a path toward it through dreams. John Needham related a dream that he heard from a Sister Smith, a former member of the United Brethren living in Herefordshire who had joined the Church before Needham arrived on his mission to the area in November 1840.[25] Sister Smith told him that in February 1837, before the first missionaries arrived in England, she had a dream in which she saw a high hill, and on the summit was a beautiful building that looked like a church with a narrow white path leading to it. The whole scene was the most beautiful thing she had ever seen, and she felt a great desire to climb the hill. However, she was told that to ascend the hill she must first go down to the garden where she would learn what to do. She entered the garden and found five men standing in a circle, each holding an open Bible. She was told that these men would tell her what to do. They said they were sent from Jesus Christ to "put everyone in the way" before individuals could ascend the hill.[26] While she visited with them, they all sang a hymn, "The Spirit of God like a fire is burning."[27] They then prayed in a way she had never before experienced, bringing to her a feeling of happiness beyond anything she had so far felt in her life. After she awoke, she often wondered about the meaning of the dream. In March 1840, when she met Wilford Woodruff in Herefordshire, she recognized him as one of the men in her dream. When she attended a meeting a week or so later, she heard him sing "The Spirit of God Like a Fire is Burning." Later, when she met Elder Brigham Young and Elder Willard Richards, she recognized them as being two of the other men she had seen in the garden in her dream.[28]

A dream his mother received led William Williams to join the United Brethren, resulting in opportunities for William, his family, and work associates to hear the restored gospel. William described how his family attended the Church of England because his mother taught Sunday School classes, but at times they would go to hear other preaching because they were not satisfied with the Church of England's teachings. He related that his mother had a dream that he (William) could get a shoemaking apprenticeship with a Samuel Jones in Malvern Hills.

> She went immediately [to see Mr. Jones]. This I Pressed her to do She Loved me to well not to go she went that day I was engaged to go on the next monday I mearly mention this that whoever Reads may See the hand of the Lord in it. . . . My Boss was a Preacher amongst the United Brethren they Believed nearly the Same as the Methodists he Pressed me hard to go and hear them I went I thought them a People that were Sincere in their devotions I soon found that Spirit was catching I knew not what to do I went amongst others I had lost all relish for the Church of England and my Prayer was Lord lead me in the right way. . . . My Master urged me to attend their Prayer meetings I went one night with him.[29]

William felt that the United Brethren "tried to love truth and embrace it whereever found," so he began attending their meetings. He recounted how John Benbow, a member of the group, told them "of some strange men [that] had come from America who preached without money & had made considerable Stir in the Potteries Manchester &c all these things seemed to be subjects of thought and talk."[30]

William Williams was not convinced of the truth of Elder Woodruff's teachings upon first hearing them. He described that some of his fellow preachers of the United Brethren, including his boss, Samuel Jones, were concerned about the effect this Amer-

Malvern Hills. (Photo by Cynthia Doxey Green.)

ican was having upon their associates. Samuel Jones organized five of the preachers to fulfill preaching tasks that some of their newly converted Latter-day Saint preachers had given up. He was fighting against this new doctrine and resisting "all encroachments on our liberty by Strangers."[31] This they did for nine weeks, and William confessed that although they had opposed these men and their new religion, they all secretly wished to hear them. William went to his preaching appointment one Sunday, and he found that John Cheese, a former very zealous member of the United Brethren who had become a Latter-day Saint, was also there. William slunk to the back of the room, refusing Cheese's invitation to preach. As described in chapter 4, Williams found that Brother Cheese proceeded to preach the restored gospel with authority and in a plain style so unlike his previous teaching manner that Williams was left feeling abashed, puzzled, confused, and distressed.[32]

On the following day, while at work with fellow United Brethren preachers, William told them of his defeat at preaching. His colleagues told him to try again the following Sunday. They told William that if he were crossed again, he should take Cheese to

Colwall, where the boss (Samuel Jones) would "fight them himself and we could listen."[33] On the following Sunday, John Cheese was there again to spend the whole day with William at his preaching appointment. Cheese preached and baptized several of their best members, and so William pressed him to go to Colwall on Monday evening. William returned home, not in triumph, but in hope that his fellow brethren would feel as he had. Cheese preached the following evening, and five people, including William, were baptized. Soon after this experience, Williams reported that Wilford Woodruff came to visit his boss, and Samuel confessed that he believed the gospel and desired baptism.[34]

Impressions. Mary Ann Weston's experience shows the effect Wilford Woodruff's presence and inherent goodness had on some of the young converts. Mary Ann was an apprentice dressmaker living with a young couple, William and Eliza Phelps Jenkins, in The Leigh, Gloucestershire. Wilford Woodruff had baptized William Jenkins while Jenkins was visiting friends in Herefordshire. Soon after arriving home, Jenkins told his wife and Mary Ann about his experience and baptism. Mary Ann recounted that she was the only one at home when Wilford Woodruff first visited the Jenkins home. She was greatly affected by Woodruff's demeanor as he sat by the fire and started to sing a hymn. She recalled that "while he was singing I looked at him. He looked so peaceful and happy, I thought he must be a good man, and the Gospel he preached must be true."[35] She was soon baptized by Elder Woodruff in the pond in the middle of the village at midnight for fear of persecution.

Charles Sansom, like many early converts to the Church, was quickly impressed by the feelings he had when he encountered the missionaries and the gospel. He recalled his first connection with Latter-day Saint beliefs:

> In the fall of the year 1844 I became acquainted with a young woman of the Mormon faith, Pamela Knight. I went with her to hear the Mormons preach. I was soon convinced of the truths of the doctrine they taught. I received the glad news with a joyful heart. At New Year's holiday I went home to visit my mother and soon found that Mormonism had found its way there since I left.

During my stay I was baptized at Avening, January 3, 1845, and confirmed at Chalford by Brother Webb.[36]

Charles's mother did not join the Church, but he did not lose his enthusiasm. "It was truly a happy time for me to realize that I was living at a time when the true gospel was again on the earth; when apostles and prophets and the gifts of the gospel had been restored. I used to wish I had lived in the days of the Savior and his apostles."[37]

Learning the Gospel Through Family Relationships

While identifying the converts in the journal database, we found that a number of them shared family ties.[38] Because many of the converts in the Three Counties were already closely connected through their membership in the United Brethren, the doctrine spread easily among them, and they joined the Church together. Many were also related through blood or marriage ties.

The conversions of the Benbow family demonstrate the strength of such ties. Wilford Woodruff would not have gone to Herefordshire if William Benbow, who had been baptized in Staffordshire, had not invited Elder Woodruff to visit his brother John Benbow in Herefordshire. John and Jane Holmes Benbow were the first to hear Wilford Woodruff preach in the Three Counties, and they offered their home and the pond on their property for preaching and baptizing. The Benbow family and several of their family connections were baptized: twelve individuals with the last name Benbow are listed in Wilford Woodruff's baptismal record. FamilySearch Family Tree and other records show that these individuals included John Benbow's mother and several of his siblings and their spouses, along with some nephews and nieces. Not all of the Benbow relations carried that surname. Woodruff's baptismal record also includes Jane Holmes Benbow's nephew Robert and his wife, Elizabeth Cole Holmes, who were baptized on 9 March 1840.

Wilford Woodruff's record also lists several of the Holmes relatives and connections. Not only did Robert and Elizabeth Holmes have immediate family members and cousins who joined

Site of William and Elizabeth Collett's home in Frogmarsh, Eldersfield, Worcestershire. The Thomas Oakey family lived with William according to the 1841 census. (Photo by Cynthia Doxey Green.)

the Church, but some of the spouses' families were also baptized. Elizabeth Cole Holmes's father, William Cole, was baptized on 1 June by Wilford Woodruff. Francis Holmes, another of Jane Benbow's nephews, was married to Hannah Gittens, whose mother and siblings were baptized by John Gailey in 1840.

Another family group of new converts was the Thomas and Ann Collett Oakey family and their relatives. Both Thomas and Ann Oakey were listed on the "United Brethren Preachers' Plan" as preachers for the Bran Green and Gadfield Elm Branch.[39] Ann's parents (William and Elizabeth Bromage Collett), her brother Daniel Collett, and her sister Elizabeth Collett Ruck were all baptized by Wilford Woodruff or by Thomas Oakey. Brother Oakey also had many family members who joined the Church, including a sister, Esther Oakey Harris, and several cousins: Robert Harris, Dianna Harris Bloxham, and Elizabeth Harris Browett. Robert Harris's wife, Hannah Maria Eagles, had several siblings who joined the Church. Her mother, Ann Sparks Eagles, had married

Samuel Roberts after her first husband died; many of the Roberts children and their families were also baptized.

As the Benbows, Holmes, Oakeys, and others heard the gospel and joined the Church, they invited their family members and connections to learn more about their newfound faith.[40] Thus we found that the early converts to the Church were connected not only by their religious faith but also by ties of family and friendship. The converts generally were not individuals who *just happened* to be in the neighborhood to hear Wilford Woodruff preach. Certainly, when the gospel was first preached in the area, the United Brethren congregations had a significant role in bringing people together. In addition to their previous religious affiliation, the converts were also family members, neighbors, and friends. The gospel net spread out quickly to their kindred and connections.

Exploring the Demographic Background of the Early Converts

One of the purposes of our research was to learn as much as possible about the people and the growth of the Church in the Three Counties in the first twenty years after Wilford Woodruff came into the area. We wanted to learn more about the type of people who were joining the Church in that area in the mid-1800s, including their occupations, social status, gender, and age. Past researchers who have examined the socioeconomic status of the early Church members in England have found that typical British converts were urban and of the lower social classes.[41] In fact, a study of the Mormon emigrants who left England during the years 1850–62 stated that the overwhelming majority came from towns, with nearly 90 percent of them having occupations associated with the lower classes.[42] Similarly, one of the early United Brethren converts, Job Smith, described the United Brethren as including a "great many very poor people as its members, and few working men in fairly good circumstances, and one man who might be called wealthy, he being a farmer and owner of some land."[43] Information in the database enabled us to go beyond mere anecdotal data and reminiscences to examine more specific

Home in Brand Green. (Bran Green is now called Brand Green.) (Photo by Carol Wilkinson.)

information regarding the socioeconomic conditions of the converts in these counties.

To add to the information from the journal database, we examined Church membership records from the Bran Green and Frogmarsh branches to learn more about Church growth after the initial missionaries left in the 1840s. Although the membership records for the local branches in the Three Counties are not complete, we chose to do a case study of the membership records from the Bran Green Branch and Frogmarsh Branch, some of the first branches organized in 1840 for which actual records are still in existence.[44] These branches encompassed the area in and around the Gadfield Elm Chapel.[45]

Our database for these branches was much smaller than the journal database because we used only the records from the Frogmarsh and Bran Green Branches. Although they may have originally been separate branches, the records appear to have been blended. We found them collected together on microfilm, with many duplicates on the pages of both branch records. After

Home in Frogsmarsh. (Frogmarsh is now called Frogsmarsh.) (Photo by Cynthia Doxey Green.)

deleting the duplicate names, we identified 118 unique individuals listed in the membership records between 1840 and 1856.[46] Later references to the "branch database" refer to both the Bran Green and Frogsmarsh Branches. Because some of the membership records included information about parents' names, birth years, and birth places, we could positively identify 86 percent of the database names in the other record sources.

Occupations and Social Status. During the time of Wilford Woodruff's mission, the Three Counties were largely agricultural, as they are today. Although several large cities were nearby, including Cheltenham, Bristol, Worcester, Hereford, and Gloucester, Elder Woodruff rarely mentioned going to them. He spent his time teaching and preaching in the villages. Many of the early converts would likely have been agricultural laborers. When Wilford Woodruff described the converts in the Three Counties, he noted that there were people from "most all classes & churches, 46 Preachers one clark [*sic*] of the Church of England, one constable & a number of wealthy farmers."[47] According to this

View from Brand Green north to Pauntley Court. (Photo by Carol Wilkinson.)

statement, there was a wide spread in the economic and social status among the early members of the Church, ranging from poor laborers to wealthy farmers.

Accounts by Job Smith and other journal authors noted that a number of converts struggled financially. For example, John Spiers's father had died when John was about six years old, and John's mother provided for the family as a dressmaker. As John's elder brother grew older, he became an apprentice to a tailor and was able to help with the family finances. Their mother gave them all the education she could, which consisted of reading, writing, and some arithmetic. John worked for masons and bricklayers when he was old enough to be employed.[48]

Living in Bristol, Frederick Weight described the difficult circumstances of having an unemployed father in nineteenth-century England:

View of Hill Farm, home of John Benbow. (Photo by Cynthia Doxey Green.)

When I was about sixteen or eighteen years of age, my father was out of work a good deal and as it happened I was in work most all the time and poor people in England know very well what it means to be out of work. It means to be out of everything, house and home. I was getting thirteen shillings per week at this time and this enabled us to just keep the wolf from the door. I gave my mother my wages every week. She could just pay the rent and buy us bread from week to week and a little bacon and a peck of potatoes each day. This was all we had to live upon from week to week for about eight of us. My wages just kept us from running debt and from starving.[49]

While the parish clerk and the constable that Wilford Woodruff mentioned are not identified in database sources, we do know that two of the wealthy farmers were John Benbow and Edward Ockey. As a tenant farmer, John Benbow had a lifelong lease on his farm. After his baptism, the landowner apparently made life difficult enough for him that he chose to leave his home and farm.[50] John Benbow used his wealth to help others. For example,

Moorend Farm, home of Edward Ockey. (Photo by Cynthia Doxey Green.)

he and Thomas Kington were able to provide significant money to help with the publication of both the Book of Mormon and a Church hymnbook. When he emigrated to Nauvoo in September 1840, John Benbow paid for the passage of forty of the other Latter-day Saints.[51] When Edward Ockey emigrated to Nauvoo, the advertisement for the sale of his possessions at Moorend Farm shows that he had been prosperous.[52]

Autobiographies and journals of missionaries and early converts provide stories of a number of other converts from the Three Counties who were also financially well off. Some of them were merchants or skilled artisans or laborers; others were individuals born into wealthy families. Not all the new Church members were just eking out a living as unskilled laborers, as is sometimes reported.

For example, Mary Ann Weston Maughan's father was financially stable as a merchant owning a shop on the High Street in Cheltenham, along with other properties in nearby villages. The family lived in Corse Lawn, near Eldersfield, Worcestershire, and employed servants. Mary Ann described her grandmother's relatives as part of the high gentry, meaning that they did not have to work for a living.[53] Similarly, Emily Hodgetts Lowder's father owned a great deal of land, and she was educated in a private school. Her father retired from business when she was very young, and she remembered many pleasant trips with him. Emily had her own pony to ride back and forth to the school she attended. The family was wealthy enough to have its own cook.[54]

Anecdotal data are helpful in showing the various socioeconomic levels among the converts in the Three Counties, but only a few examples are available. By looking at the occupations of the converts in our databases, we were able to see a more accurate

Corse Lawn Hotel, dating from the 1700s. (Photo by Carol Wilkinson.)

picture of the group as a whole. This examination helped us find out whether this group of converts was made up primarily of poor people, as described by Job Smith, or by people from all classes, as noted by Wilford Woodruff.

The information for occupations in the databases came from the 1841 census for those living in the Three Counties on the date of the census, or from the Mormon Migration Index for those who left the area at an earlier date.[55] Although later censuses also listed occupations, so many changes might have occurred in that ten-year time period that we were not confident that later censuses reported the occupations of the converts at the time they were baptized. In addition, when the converts emigrated to Nauvoo or to Utah, the United States censuses often listed different occupations from those occupations the individuals had in England, because life on the frontier was not the same as life in a well-established society. These changes in occupation might also have shown that many people were able to change their status upon emigrating to a country where they were likely to own land and have more control over their situation.

In mid-nineteenth-century England, social status was determined by type of work, not necessarily by earnings or financial situation. For example, a poorly paid teacher or a clerk would be a social superior to a more highly paid shoemaker or carpenter, who performed manual labor.[56] The website *A Vision of Britain Through Time* analyzed England's censuses using three categories or classes for occupations of working-age males to create an atlas of occupations in each county over time.[57] The first category, the middle-class group, included professionals and managers, along with farmers in rural counties. The second category was a mixed group of clerical workers and artisans or skilled laborers such as shoemakers, blacksmiths, and carpenters. The third category was composed of the semiskilled or unskilled working-class laborers, including domestic servants or farm laborers. We used similar categories in analyzing occupations in our databases. The appendix includes a more detailed analysis of the occupations our databases include.

Like Wilford Woodruff, we found a variety of occupations among the converts in our databases. In the middle-class category, we found several farmers, shopkeepers, school mistresses, and an innkeeper—although some were probably not as wealthy as others. We also found a number of people in the mixed-class group of skilled laborers or artisans, including shoemakers, carpenters, stone or brick masons, miners, blacksmiths, tailors, dressmakers, milliners, or glove makers. Among the unskilled laborers, agricultural laborers made up the largest percentage of converts, as expected, along with servants and laundresses—most of whom were women. In the journal database, we found that 13 percent of the families would have been considered part of the middle class; 29 percent of the families were skilled laborers. The unskilled workers and their families comprised 58 percent of the database. In contrast, the branch database showed only one farmer, with 71 percent of the members of the branch as agricultural laborers or servants. The skilled laborers in the branch database were involved in occupations similar to those found in the journal database, including carpenter, shoemaker, baker, miner, and saddler. One unique occupation in the branch database was a midwife.

Consistent with earlier research, these databases showed that the majority of the early Saints in these counties were working-class laborers. However, they were not the poorest of the poor; most of them appeared to have work of some kind. On the 1841 census, none of the converts were listed as a "pauper," or one receiving help from the parish or government. While they may not have been rich, these Saints were able to manage to survive in spite of hardships. In fact, nearly half of the people in the journal database were working as artisans, skilled laborers, or even in what might be considered middle-class occupations. These results may be due in part to the rural nature of the Three Counties and to the fact that the early missionaries appeared to focus their efforts in the smaller villages and hamlets where many of the congregations of United Brethren were already established. According to the 1841 census, fewer than twenty-five individuals in the journal database were living in the towns of Ledbury, Leominster, and Great Malvern, and no one in the database lived in the larger towns of Hereford, Worcester, Cheltenham, or Gloucester.[58]

Gender Ratio. Gender was determined by looking at the first names or descriptions such as "brother" or "sister" used in the journals or membership records, since the journal writers very rarely specified whether a person was a man or a woman. Most of the first names in the databases were very traditional ones, such as Jane, Mary, Elizabeth, Charlotte, Charles, John, or William, so we assumed the gender of these individuals based on their names. There were five individuals for whom we could not determine gender because the first names were (1) not provided, (2) not legible, or (3) happened to be Francis or Frances. While most people might assume *Francis* referred to a male and *Frances* to a female, we could not make that assumption, in part because spelling was not standardized. In one instance, Wilford Woodruff wrote that Francis Brush was baptized in Shucknall Hill, presumably a male. However, we found the only Frances Brush living in Shucknall Hill in 1841, and she was recorded in the census as a

View from Shucknall Hill. (Photo by Cynthia Doxey Green.)

seventy-year-old female. We found that 57 percent of the converts listed in the journal database were women, while 43 percent were men. The branch records database showed more gender imbalance, with 62 percent women and 38 percent men.

Age. Previous research about the early Saints in England has stated that the majority of converts in Britain during the nineteenth century were in their twenties and thirties, because that age group would be most likely to have the freedom to accept a new religion and to be able to emigrate.[59] Older people would presumably have more established careers or families and would be less likely to uproot their families by changing religious affiliation and emigrating to America. We looked at the birth years for the individuals in the journal database using the census or FamilySearch.org as the source.[60] Over five hundred of the converts in the journal database were baptized in 1840, with the latest baptismal dates in 1843. The ages at baptism ranged from eight to ninety-five years old. We found that 35 percent of the converts were age forty or older at baptism, and 17 percent were under age twenty. Many of those younger than twenty were probably children of the older converts, as frequently a whole family was baptized. However, a number of the teenagers were baptized without their parents. Hence, those who would be in their twenties and thirties at baptism consisted of less than half of the people in the database.

The branch records database was a little more difficult to analyze because of the nature of the records, which included baptismal records, excommunication dates, and baby-blessing records. Eleven people were identified in the database with no baptismal date. Using the names of people for whom we had birth years and baptismal dates, we calculated the age at baptism for ninety-five individuals. We found that only 32 percent of the converts were in their twenties or thirties at the time of their baptism. As in the journal database, a number of families were listed, so we found that 25 percent of the converts were children and teenagers when they were baptized, and 43 percent of them were forty or older. The oldest person in the branch records was eighty-two at the time of baptism.

Unlike the findings of earlier studies, we calculated that the majority of the early converts from the Three Counties were not in their twenties and thirties. Although these findings are slightly different from demographics of converts in other parts of the British Isles, they may be explained by the particular characteristics of the United Brethren. Many of the United Brethren had been meeting together for several years prior to being introduced to the teachings of Wilford Woodruff. Some perhaps had joined the United Brethren in their twenties and thirties, ages at which they were more open or enthusiastic toward changing their religious affiliation. As they had continued meeting together and forming strong bonds of fellowship, making the change to another new religion with their friends and family did not cause as much disruption to their lives as it would for older people who had never changed religions. Another age-relevant characteristic of this convert group was that many families were baptized in which the parents were older and the children younger than the average convert in other parts of England.

Recognizing Blessings and Opposition

Life was not always easy for the new converts of the Church in the Three Counties. They had their share of tribulation, but they also received many blessings because of their newfound faith. For example, some of the young adults who joined the Church who had not yet married were able to find partners among other converts. As described in chapter 4, James Palmer met his future wife, Mary Ann Price, because her uncle allowed the missionaries to stay numerous times at his home, the Pigeon House, in Orcop Hill. James eventually baptized Mary Ann.[61] In his journal, William Williams described in rapturous detail how he met and fell in love with Mary Brooks, a girl he met several times at church meetings.[62]

Other great blessings occurred as remarkable spiritual experiences. As a young man, Francis George Wall worked in a blueing factory. Indigo blueing is poisonous, and the dust that collected in his lungs made him extremely ill, confining him to bed for months. As his condition worsened, the doctors did all they could for him, but finally they told his mother they did not expect him to live until the next morning. That night, the missionaries who were living with the family administered to Francis and gave him a blessing, promising that he would live to a great age and go to America, where he would help build towns, church buildings, and temples. The following morning, the doctor was astonished to find Francis sitting up in bed. Years later, ninety-five-year-old Francis wrote that all in the blessing had come to pass.[63]

Church members sought to move the missionary effort forward, even as they worked at their places of employment. Although not officially called as a missionary, Thomas Steed did his best to stand as a witness of Christ and share the gospel among those in his sphere of influence. He secured a job at a mansion named The Lodge in Malvern to earn money so he could emigrate to America with the Saints. When the owner, Mr. Campbell, discovered a Book of Mormon in his room, he tried to dissuade Thomas from his beliefs by furnishing him with anti-Mormon literature. Campbell also had the local minister visit Thomas to persuade him that his beliefs were wrong. But the attempt was

View of the area known as The Leigh, Gloucestershire. (Photo by Cynthia Doxey Green.)

unsuccessful. During Thomas's first year working at The Lodge, the cook was converted to the restored gospel.[64]

Along with the blessings, these early Saints experienced tribulation and opposition. Many were the only members of their families who joined the Church, and some experienced direct family opposition. John Spiers's brother persecuted him so much that John went to live with Daniel Browett in The Leigh, Gloucestershire. John's mother was saddened by the rift between her sons, and she decided that the Church was the root of the sibling problem. Consequently, she also opposed the Church and its missionary work.[65]

In 1850, Jane Ann Fowler also experienced great persecution from her family as she investigated the Church in Herefordshire and became convinced of the truth of the gospel message. She recalled,

> My parents and all my relatives persecuted me very much. My Father in particular. He thought I should obey him, he forbid me

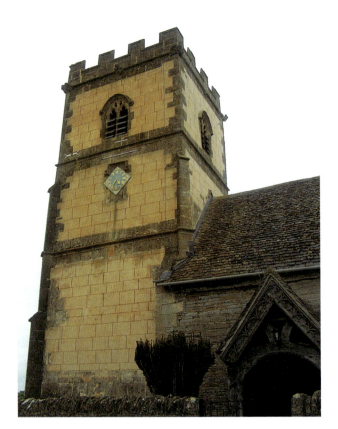

The Leigh parish church in Gloucestershire. (Photo by Cynthia Doxey Green.)

to go inside a Mormon meeting. I spent all the time I could reading and praying, and was convinced by the Spirit of the Lord that it was right, and the more I was persecuted, the more I felt I must be baptized. Father got so bitter he would not talk to me nor answer me. *Then I would get a whipping.*[66]

At last Jane Ann's father told her that if she was going to continue with the Mormons she should leave home, which she did. Ultimately, he told her not to call him Father again. After many trials, blessings followed. Over twenty-five years after Jane Ann had emigrated to America, her mother and father traveled to join her in the Bear Lake Valley in Idaho, an answer to her many prayers for her family. The summer after his arrival in the valley, her father was baptized.[67]

Mary Ann Weston Maughan described her sadness, because none of her family joined the Church: "My relatives did not obey the Gospel but they did not oppose me. This made me sorrowful and lonely. I attended all the meetings I could, often walking many miles alone to and from them."[68] Unfortunately, loneliness was not the only suffering she endured due to her membership in the Church. Mary Ann Weston was married on 23 December 1840 to another convert, John Davis of Tirley, Gloucestershire, who was a cooper and carpenter. They were the only Latter-day Saints in Tirley and were instructed by Elders Woodruff and Richards to open their house for meetings. At the second meeting in their home, a mob arrived, beating and kicking John, who was injured internally. He was never well after this event, and soon afterward he had a fall. His health deteriorated until he died on 6 April 1841. Mary Ann's physician advised her to leave and travel for the sake of her health, predicting that if she did not do so, she would shortly follow her husband to the grave. She stated, "The next day I left my home a sad lonely widow, where less than four months before I had been taken a happy bride. I did not go home, for I felt that my parents would try to stop me from gathering with the Saints. I had many homes offered me by friends, but I went to board with Mr. and Mrs. Hill of Turkey Hall. They were getting ready to go to Nauvoo."[69]

Turkey Hall, Eldersfield, Worcestershire, home of Benjamin and Mary Hill. (Photo by Cynthia Doxey Green.)

Although the persecution of the Saints was not always in the form of physical abuse, quite often the temporal well-being of these new converts was put in jeopardy. For example, Francis George Wall, while working as a chore boy in the kitchen of a gentleman, began sharing Church books, including the Book of Mormon, with a servant girl who was also a Latter-day Saint. One day the lady of the house found the girl reading the Book of Mormon and asked where she got the book. As a result of sharing the gospel, Francis lost his job.[70]

Similarly, some of the Church members suffered by being deprived of temporal help or opportunity. William Williams wrote that he expected opposition from the world, but not from the Christian people around him. He explained that the clergy, landowners, and aristocracy would often give food and clothing to the poor, but they would withhold future help if they heard that those individuals or families had become associated with the Latter-day Saints. William's family experienced this type of persecution.

In 1841 William went to visit his family who lived in Madresfield, Worcestershire. His father had worked on a farm there for over forty years, and his mother was a teacher at the Sunday School for the Countess of Beauchamp. William's mother and brother had been baptized, and while William was visiting they often spoke of the gospel with friends and neighbors. A young girl in the neighborhood overheard their conversation and informed her mother that they were Latter-day Saints. The information was spread until it reached the vicar, the Reverend Thomas Philpotts, who wrote to the Earl of Beauchamp. By that same evening William's father had orders to leave the home in six months' time, and William's mother was dismissed from teaching the Sunday School. One of their friends, Hannah James, lost her position as the lodge keeper for the estate when the vicar found that she too had joined the Church.[71]

According to William, the Reverend Philpotts went around the parish informing the people that the Lord punishes those who listen to the message of the Latter-day Saints and telling people not to rent a home to the Williams family. When he saw that the family would have no place to live, Philpotts approached William's father and promised to help the family if they would cast off William. The father refused to do this, choosing to support his son.[72] The family must have moved eventually; they were listed in Madresfield in the 1841 census (about the time of the conflict with Reverend Philpotts), but by 1851 William's widowed mother was a school mistress living in Leigh, Worcestershire.

Tracing Church Growth in the Early 1840s

One of the purposes of studying the history of the Church in the Three Counties was to learn more about the growth of the Church over time. As is widely known, the first year the gospel was preached in the area was a time of extraordinary growth. According to Wilford Woodruff's reports of the conferences held in the area during September 1840, over forty branches had been organized in the first six months of preaching.[73] The available journals are not very specific about the continued growth of branches and conferences after the first year. Sources such as the *Millennial Star* and the *British Mission Manuscript History and Historical Reports*, along with results of the case study of the Bran Green and Frogmarsh branches, provide a little more insight into Church growth in the Three Counties.

One of the regular features published in the *Millennial Star* was the periodic report of regional and national conference meetings, which included membership numbers provided by representatives from branches and conferences. These reports are a fairly reliable source for the numbers of people participating in the branches at each conference, but they do not account for the number of people who had emigrated, apostatized, or moved to another area of the country in the first few years of their publication. Due to the way the information was reported, there may not be any way to know how many people left or were baptized between the reports.

According to these conference reports, many changes took place during the first few years of the Church in Britain. Table 5.1 compares the number of members in the British Isles and the Three Counties area between 1840 and 1854.[74] By 15 April 1840, just over a month after Wilford Woodruff first arrived at John Benbow's farm in Herefordshire, there were 160 members in the Herefordshire area, constituting 9 percent of the entire Church membership in the British Isles. Membership in this area increased dramatically from 1840 to 1843, reaching a high of 1,838 members in June 1842. This number comprised 24 percent of the overall membership in the British Isles for that time period. Yet by 1849, the members in the Three Counties area decreased to

Table 5.1 Church Membership in the British Isles and the Three Counties, 1840–1854

Date	Number of members in the British Isles	Number of members in the Three Counties	Three Counties percentage of overall membership in British Isles
15 April 1840	1,671	160	9%
6 July 1840	2,513	534	21%
6 April 1841	5,814*	1,550	26%
1 June 1842	7,514	1,838	24%
4 June 1843**	7,975	1,620	20%
December 1849	26,012	1,409	5%
1 June 1851	32,226	2,382	7%
31 December 1854	29,441	1,933	6%

* Conference minutes noted that nearly 800 had emigrated from the British Isles.
** From 1843 to 1849, the conference minutes did not list membership by conference, only as an overall number for the British Isles.

1,409, accounting for only 5 percent of the members in the British Isles, probably due to greater emigration and apostasy during the later 1840s. The lower percentage of members in the Three Counties compared to the rest of the British Isles in 1849 may be because other areas began to grow at faster rates while the majority of the United Brethren and its connections had been baptized earlier in the decade.

Branches and conferences changed with the fluctuation of Church membership in the area. On 14 June 1840, a number of branches were assigned to the Bran Green and Gadfield Elm Conference of The Church of Jesus Christ of Latter-day Saints, and a week later the Fromes Hill Conference was organized with over twenty branches.[75] Determining specific numbers of new members proved to be difficult in those very early days of the Church, as evident in the report by Wilford Woodruff from the June 1840 conferences. He wrote, "The different Branches in this region are so scattered, that it has not been possible to ascertain the number of members connected with each individual Church, but the whole number of the Churches connected with the Bran Green and Gadfield Elm, and the Froome Hill Conferences, together with a small Branch of 12 members, 1 Priest, and 1 Teacher at Little Garway, is 33 Churches; 534 Members; 75 Officers, viz.–10 Elders, 52 Priests, and 13 Teachers."[76] The Church continued to grow rapidly in this area. When Brigham Young reported the conference meetings he held in December 1840, the Garway Branch had become the Garway Conference, with 95 members, and he stated that the total membership number was 1,261 for the Garway, Gadfield Elm, and Stanley Hill conferences.[77] The "Table of Nineteenth Century Church Units in the Three Counties" included in the appendix contains a detailed list of the branches and conferences.

The Cheltenham Conference is a good example of how the branch or conference boundaries changed over time. Sometime in 1841 or 1842, the name of the Gadfield Elm Conference was changed to the Cheltenham Conference, and changes in conference and branch boundaries continued from time to time.[78] During the next few years, the number of branches in the Cheltenham Conference fluctuated from seven to twenty, as some branches were reassigned to other conferences or new conferences were created. For example, in 1847, the following branches from the Cheltenham Conference were assigned to the new Edgehill Conference: Edgehill, Bran Green, Pouncel, Littledean, Woodside, and Vineyhill. Only Cheltenham, Apperley, Norton, Frogmarsh, Caudle Green, Compton, and Gloucester were left in the Cheltenham Conference.[79] By June 1848, however, the conference boundaries changed again, with the Edgehill and Chalford Conferences subsumed under the auspices of the Cheltenham Conference, bringing in the previous branches and adding the Kingswood, Cam, Tetbury, Avening, Chalford Hill, and Cirencester branches.[80]

Branch boundaries also changed over time as the number of members was continually increasing or decreasing due to baptisms and emigration. When Wilford Woodruff recorded the minutes from the first conferences in the Three Counties held in June 1840, the recorded branches were very similar to the congregations listed on the "United Brethren's Preachers' Plan," showing that the creation of the branches naturally reflected the prior organization of the United Brethren.[81] These congregations may have been gatherings of family connections, friends, and neighbors, which could account for branches being located in small hamlets, sometimes within the same parish. For example, the Kilcot and Bran Green Branches were both located within the Newent parish boundaries, but they were far enough apart that the United Brethren had two different meeting places. Most branches were quite small, perhaps not including much more than an extended family group. In the report of the twenty-three branches of the Frome's Hill Conference on 20 September 1840, only six branches had over fifty members, and eleven of them had fewer than twenty members. [82]

Many branches were in existence for only a short time, probably while a group of members were living in the area. If large numbers of people were not continually being converted, the branches would usually disband after a number of their members emigrated to America. The Bran Green and Frogmarsh Branches are examples of the influence a strong family can have in maintaining the Church in a certain area. The branch record lists the Robert Ruck and Thomas Oakey families, all of whom were children and grandchildren of William and Elizabeth Bromage Collett. The Colletts and their descendants accounted for 16 percent of the individuals in the branch records. The Oakeys and the Rucks were obviously influential in the branch. We found that 52 of the 118 members were baptized by either Robert Ruck or Thomas Oakey. The last ordinance listed in the branch records was recorded in 1856, the same year that Thomas Oakey's family left for Utah.

Robert Ruck home in Hawcross, Redmarley D'Abitot, Worcestershire. (Photo by Cynthia Doxey Green.)

Examining the lives of the early converts in the Three Counties has provided insight into several aspects of Church growth in that area. Although the baptismal records for the mid-nineteenth century are not complete, the information from the available membership records, the journals of missionaries and converts, and the conference reports found in the *Millennial Star* combine to paint a fuller picture of Church growth in the area. The added information from other public records, such as the census, emigration records, and civil registration, provide a greater understanding about the people who joined the Church. Although the exact number of Wilford Woodruff's baptisms cannot be verified, the current estimates are very similar to those he reported. Obviously, Elder Woodruff's work among the United Brethren and others living in the Three Counties area bore unanticipated fruit.

Notes

1. Wilford Woodruff, in *Journal of Discourses*, 18:124. Edward Phillips, "Biographical Sketches of Edward and Hannah Simmonds Phillips, 1889, 1926, 1949," 1, MS 11215, Church History Library, Salt Lake City. In the typescript of his autobiography, Edward Phillips stated that the one United Brethren preacher who did not join the Church was Philip Holdt.
2. Wilford Woodruff, in *Journal of Discourses*, 15:343.
3. Woodruff, *Leaves from My Journal*, 128.
4. "Wilford Woodruff's Baptismal Record, 1840," in *Wilford Woodruff's Journal*, 1:377–95. The "Baptismal Record" has no entries after 23 June 1840, when Wilford Woodruff left the area for a conference in Manchester. He continued to baptize people in Herefordshire, but he did not record their names, so he could have easily baptized six hundred people before he left England in 1841.
5. John Gailey, "History of John Gailey, Undated," 1, MS 11009, Church History Library, Salt Lake City. See also Woodruff, *Leaves from My Journal*, 126.
6. Branch and conference membership records from the nineteenth century are available on microfilm at the Family History Library and the Church History Library in Salt Lake City. There are thirty-three different branch or conference records from the nineteenth century from the Three Counties. However, the *British Mission Manuscript History and Historical Reports, 1841–1971* (LR 1140 2, Church History Library, Salt Lake City) lists over 125 branches or conferences in the Three Counties during the nineteenth century. The table of branches in the appendix has more information about the branches. The manuscript history is also online at churchhistorycatalog.lds.org.
7. For example, Wilford Woodruff's baptismal record mentions that from 1–15 May 1840, "Elders Richards and Kington had Baptized 50." *Wilford Woodruff's Journal*, 1:387. Additionally, John Spiers, James Palmer, John Needham, John Gailey, and James Barnes wrote of Henry Glover, Martin Littlewood, and William Kay, who preached with them at various times and for whom we have no written record. Presumably, many other priesthood leaders were also baptizing people without recording the information.

8. Examples of published materials would be the autobiographies found in Kate B. Carter, comp., *Heart Throbs of the West*, 12 vols. (Salt Lake City: Daughters of Utah Pioneers, 1939–51), or Carter, *Our Pioneer Heritage*.
9. Wilford Woodruff, "Baptismal Record 1840," in *Wilford Woodruff's Journal*, 1:377–95. According to Kenney's note on page 377, "The Baptismal Record is a small notebook attached by a string to the inside of the second manuscript journal."
10. Not every name mentioned in Wilford Woodruff's journal was included in the database unless there was some identifying information, such as a full name and dwelling place, or a place and date of priesthood ordination.
11. By 1843, the missionaries for whom we have record either had emigrated to Nauvoo or were preaching in areas other than Gloucestershire, Worcestershire, and Herefordshire. We did not follow their records after they left the area.
12. All of these sources are on the Internet. Censuses are found on Family Search.org or Ancestry.com. Birth, marriage, and death records for England are on Freebmd.org.uk or Ancestry.com. The ship passenger lists and other information for Mormon Migration is found at mormonmigration.lib.byu.edu. The Mormon Pioneer Overland Travel information is found at history.lds.org/overlandtravels. FamilySearch.org has both user-contributed and Church-contributed information on Family Tree, including histories, photos, genealogies, and baptismal dates.
13. John Spiers, "John Spiers Reminiscences and Journal, 1840–77," 16, 16 April 1841, MS 1725, Church History Library, Salt Lake City. Spiers wrote that Mary Fox was baptized on 31 March 1841.
14. *Wilford Woodruff's Journal*, 1:513–14, 517–19. At those conferences, the Bran Green and Gadfield Elm Conference had seventeen branches, with a total membership of 253. The Fromes Hill Conference reported twenty-three branches, with a total membership of 754.
15. *Wilford Woodruff's Journal*, 2:61–62, 66–69.
16. Mormon Migration Index, http://mormonmigration.lib.byu.edu. The ships which had left England before the conferences in March 1841 were the *North America* (September 1840), the *Isaac Newton* (October 1840), the *Alliance* (December 1840), the *Caroline* (January

1841), the *Sheffield* (February 1841), the *Echo* (February 1841), and the *Alesto* (March 1841).

17. "Conference Minutes," *Millennial Star* 1, no. 12 (April 1841): 302. The minutes state that nearly eight hundred people had emigrated from the British Isles in the previous season, which number had not been included in the calculation of the number of members of the Church. We do not know if the emigration number includes children or only baptized members of the Church. The number of individuals could be greater than eight hundred. The *Caroline* originated from Bristol rather than Liverpool. In all likelihood, most of the passengers were from the Three Counties. Unfortunately, there is no passenger list to provide the number of emigrants.

18. Thomas Steed, "The Life of Thomas Steed From His Own Diary 1826–1910," 2, BX 8670.1 .St32, L. Tom Perry Special Collections, Harold B. Lee Library, Brigham Young University, Provo, UT. Also online at https://books.FamilySearch.org.

19. Steed, "Life of Thomas Steed," 4.

20. Steed, "Life of Thomas Steed," 4–5.

21. Steed, "Life of Thomas Steed," 5.

22. Steed, "Life of Thomas Steed," 5–6.

23. John Gailey, "John Gailey, Reminiscence and Diary, ca. 1840–41," 7–8, MS 1089, Church History Library, Salt Lake City.

24. Spiers, "Reminiscences," 1–2.

25. John Needham, "John Needham Autobiography and Journal, 1840 August–1842 December," 53–54, MS 25895, Church History Library, Salt Lake City. Unfortunately, on page 53, when he was describing the family, Needham gave no identifying information about Sister Smith other than the fact that she had a married daughter named Sister Taylor, who lived in West Bromwich, Staffordshire. We were not able to identify Sister Smith in our list of converts.

26. Needham, "Autobiography," 55–56.

27. Needham, "Autobiography," 57. The hymn "The Spirit of God" was written for the Kirtland Temple dedication on 27 March 1836. Sister Smith would not have known the song except through her dream, because the first missionaries to England did not arrive until the summer of 1837.

28. Needham, "Autobiography," 57.

29. William Williams, "William Williams reminiscence, 1850," 3–4, MS 9132, Church History Library, Salt Lake City. Spelling and punctuation are in the original.
30. Williams, "Reminiscence," 4.
31. Williams, "Reminiscence," 5.
32. Williams, "Reminiscence," 5–6.
33. Williams, "Reminiscence," 6.
34. Williams, "Reminiscence," 6–7.
35. Mary Ann Weston Maughan, "The Journal of Mary Ann Weston Maughan," in *Our Pioneer Heritage*, 2:353–54.
36. Charles Sansom, "Journal of Charles Sansom, 1826–1908/prepared by great-granddaughter Doris Barber Smith; addendum research by grandson Howard and wife LaVon Sansom," 2, M270.1 S229s, Church History Library, Salt Lake City.
37. Sansom, "Journal," 3.
38. FamilySearch.org's Family Tree often provided relationship information that is not always available in the journals or branch records. Just over half of the branch members had parents' names listed in the records, but the journals very rarely mentioned family relationships. Because Family Tree is a compilation of genealogies submitted by descendants and researchers, the records have not been verified. However, in spite of the possibility of error, there is more information about the converts submitted by their family members than can be found in other public records. Thus, when identifying the converts' names in FamilySearch, we also looked at other family members connected to them, searching for relationships with others that might be in our database.
39. "United Brethren Preachers' Plan of the Frooms Hill Circuit, 1840," 248.6 U58p 1840, Church History Library, Salt Lake City.
40. FamilySearch.org's Family Tree helped us identify these family relationships, although sometimes we found the families living near each other on censuses. We also found many of the families listed together on the Mormon Migration website or on the Mormon Pioneer Overland Travel website.
41. Ronald W. Walker, "Cradling Mormonism: The Rise of the Gospel in Early Victorian Britain," *BYU Studies* 27, no. 1 (Winter 1987): 29.
42. Philip A. M. Taylor, "Why did British Mormons Emigrate," *Utah Historical Quarterly* 22, no. 3 (July 1954): 260–62.

43. Job Smith, "The United Brethren," *Improvement Era*, July 1910, 819.
44. While Bran Green and Frogmarsh were separate branches in 1840, their records were combined at some point during the period from 1840 to 1856. The *British Mission Manuscript History* shows that the Bran Green Branch disbanded in 1848. With the number of duplicate individuals listed on both sets of branch records, it appears that the branches became one or at least their records were combined at some point. The membership records for these two branches are available in the Family History Library: Film #86991 Items 15–16, and Film #86998 Items 17–18.
45. Bran Green and Frogmarsh are spelled different ways, depending on the record. Bran Green is written as Brangreen, Brand Green, or Brandgreen. Frogmarsh is sometimes spelled Frogsmarsh. We will consistently use Bran Green and Frogmarsh unless the record to which we are referring spells the names differently. Today, the maps show these hamlets as Brand Green and Frogsmarsh.
46. One important note about this database is that not all the names on the branch records have a corresponding baptismal date. Some individuals are listed in the records because they were blessed as children or they moved into the area or they were excommunicated. Hence, no baptismal date is listed.
47. *Wilford Woodruff's Journal*, 1:440 (16 April 1840).
48. Spiers, "Reminiscences," 1.
49. Frederick Weight, "A Brief History of the Life of Frederick Weight by himself," 4–5, MSS SC 3200. L. Tom Perry Special Collections, Harold B. Lee Library, Brigham Young University, Provo, Utah.
50. V. Ben Bloxham, "The Apostolic Foundations, 1840–1841," in *Truth Will Prevail*, 139–40. Wilford Woodruff also wrote that when he went to visit the Benbows on 10 April 1840, he "found Broth John Benbow had sold his possessions & entirely left the Hill farm and taken up his abode of a season at Frooms [sic] Hill." *Wilford Woodruff's Journal*, 1:433 (10 April 1840).
51. *Wilford Woodruff's Journal*, 1:490–91 (11 August 1840).
52. The advertisement of the auction of all his farm implements and possessions shows that he wanted to sell cattle, farming utensils, sacks of grain, and casks of cider. "Moorend Farm, Castle Frome, Herefordshire, To Sell By Auction," *Hereford Times*, 27 March 1841.
53. Maughan, "Journal," 348–49.

54. Emily Hodgetts Lowder, "Emily Hodgetts Lowder—103 years," in *Our Pioneer Heritage*, 7:424.
55. When possible, we used the occupation listed in the 1841 census rather than the Mormon Migration Index because the census was more likely to reflect the social status of the family in England. The ships' lists were more likely to be self-reported data, allowing someone to state the occupation as something that was not reflective of their social station. For example, John Cheese and Thomas Kington both listed their occupations on the passenger list as "preacher." However, an itinerant preacher for the United Brethren probably did not receive the same level of respect from society as a minister from the Church of England. Similarly, another emigrant, Richard Lilley, was an agricultural laborer on the 1841 census, but on board the *Chaos* in late 1841, his occupation is listed as "farmer." Agricultural laborers performed farming work, but he was probably not in the same social class as John Benbow, a gentleman farmer who hired agricultural laborers. When the only record of occupation was from the Mormon Migration Index, we had to use the label "farmer" with caution, knowing that perhaps those individuals were not in the same social class as farmers in the 1841 census in England.
56. Susan L. Fales, "Artisans, Millhands, and Labourers: The Mormons of Leeds and Their Nonconformist Neighbors," in *Mormons in Early Victorian Britain*, ed. Richard L. Jensen and Malcolm R. Thorp (Salt Lake City: University of Utah Press, 1989), 163.
57. *A Vision of Britain Through Time*, "Statistical Atlas, Social Structure," www.visionofbritain.org.uk/atlas/.
58. According to the manuscript history and the branch records held at the Family History Library (Salt Lake City), branches were established by 1841 in the larger towns listed, but apparently, the missionaries whose diaries are available did not baptize many people there. See "Nineteenth-Century Church Units in the Three Counties" in the appendix for the dates of branch organization.
59. Walker, "Cradling Mormonism," 29.
60. In FamilySearch.org, the birth years are actually christening years because there were no birth records at the time. Christenings might not have occurred when the child was an infant. If there was no birth date, we did not know if the year was correct. When there were census records to corroborate the dates, we were more confident in the

birth years listed. If the only age we had was from the 1841 census, we knew that the individual could have been older than listed, but we used the birth year listed in the census. The 1841 census usually rounded down to the fives for anyone over the age of sixteen, so that the age of a twenty-four-year-old was usually recorded as twenty.

61. James Palmer, "James Palmer Reminiscences, ca. 1884–98," 50, MS 1752, Church History Library, Salt Lake City.
62. Williams, "Reminiscence," 14–18.
63. Francis George Wall, "Francis George Wall–Pioneer of 1863," in *Our Pioneer Heritage*, 7:363–64.
64. Steed, "Life of Thomas Steed," 6–7.
65. Spiers, "Reminiscences," 2.
66. Jane Ann Fowler Sparks, *Jane Ann's Memoirs*, comp. Marsha Passey (Montpelier, ID: M. Passey, 2004), 4; emphasis in original.
67. Sparks, *Memoirs*, 13.
68. Maughan, "Journal," 354.
69. Maughan, "Journal," 356.
70. Wall, "Journal," 363.
71. Williams, "Reminiscence," 11–12.
72. Williams, "Reminiscence," 12–13.
73. *Wilford Woodruff's Journal*, 1:519.
74. Initially we wanted to examine Church growth in the Three Counties for the twenty-year period of 1840–60, but we found that there were no statistical reports listed in the *Millennial Star* from 1856–60 for this area.
75. "Minutes of the Conference Held at Gadfield Elm chapel, in Worcestershire, England, June 14th, 1840," *Millennial Star* 1, no. 4 (August 1840): 84–85. "Minutes of the Conference Held at Stanley Hill, Castle Frome, Herefordshire, June 21st, 1840," *Millennial Star* 1, no. 4 (August 1840): 86–89.
76. "Conference at Stanley Hill," *Millennial Star* 1, no. 4 (August 1840): 88–89.
77. Brigham Young, "News from the Elders," *Millennial Star* 1, no. 9 (January 1841): 239. The Fromes Hill Conference met at a home in Stanley Hill, and Brigham Young called it the Stanley Hill Conference. However, according to the *British Mission Manuscript History*, the Fromes Hill Conference was still in existence until 1844.
78. "General Conference," *Millennial Star* 3, no. 2 (June 1842): 29. This is the first time we see the name "Cheltenham Conference" instead

of Gadfield Elm Conference. Possibly, the name changed because by that time the Gadfield Elm chapel had been sold.

79. "Conference Minutes: Edgehill Conference, Cheltenham Conference," *Millennial Star* 9, no. 12 (15 June 1847): 188–89.

80. "Conference Minutes, General Conference held at Music Hall, Camp Field, Manchester, Sunday August 13, 1848," *Millennial Star* 10, no. 17 (1 September 1848): 267.

81. "Conference at Gadfield Elm," *Millennial Star* 1, no. 4 (August 1840): 84–85. "Conference at Stanley Hill," *Millennial Star* 1, no. 4 (August 1840): 86–89. Only six of the meeting places listed in the preachers' plan were not listed as branch names for these conferences.

82. *Wilford Woodruff's Journal*, 1:517–19.

Emigrating or Remaining in England

CHAPTER 5 DESCRIBED THE CONVERTS' STORIES as the Church began its development in the Three Counties. This chapter focuses on what they did after they joined the Church: whether they emigrated to America or remained in England, and whether they remained faithful to the Church throughout their lives or eventually became less active, inactive, or even hostile as their lives continued. Many descendants of these converts from the Three Counties have anecdotal data about their own ancestors, but our journal database and branch database provide more information about the group as a whole. Another useful source has been the conference reports from the *Millennial Star*, which supply additional data regarding the rate of emigration from the Three Counties. The first part of the chapter will describe the database findings about the converts' emigration to America, as well as whether they followed the body of the Latter-day Saints to the western United States. The second part will look at converts who stayed in England, including possible reasons why they chose to stay, along with information from journals and the databases concerning apostasy among them.

At the funeral for William Pitt in 1873, Wilford Woodruff described the converts from the Three Counties: "There has been less apostasy out of that branch of the Church and kingdom of God than out of the same number from any part of the world that I am acquainted with."[1] As examples, he mentioned some of his friends and companions from the Three Counties who had emigrated to Nauvoo and later traveled and settled in Utah. Thomas Kington, John Benbow, and William Pitt left England within the first year of hearing the gospel and made their way to Nauvoo, eventually becoming part of the exodus from Nauvoo and crossing the plains to settle in Utah. Other former United Brethren members, including Edward Ockey, John Spiers, James Palmer, Edward Phillips, and Robert Harris, also left England for Nauvoo in the early 1840s, and followed the path of the Saints to Utah and Idaho. While Wilford Woodruff may have seen that most of the people he remembered from the Three Counties remained faithful to the Church, his statement cannot be verified without comparing the lives of all the converts. However, there is no way to know who all the converts were, let alone to identify them in other records sufficiently to make a judgment on their faithfulness as a group. The journal and branch databases do allow us to trace the movements of the converts to get a general sense of how many emigrated or stayed in England. These databases, considered along with other records and journals, provide greater insight about their strength and faithfulness to the restored gospel as praised by Wilford Woodruff.

Following Those Who Emigrated to America and Trekked West

Because of the stories of many pioneers who joined the Church and then traveled to join the Saints in Zion, Latter-day Saints may think that emigration was the norm for the early members of the Church in England. However, the databases developed for this study and the emigration reports in the *Millennial Star* demonstrate that the call to gather to Zion was heeded by some and not by others. Some were full of zeal, as evident at the 12 March 1848 Worcester Conference: "Elder Butler then arose and stated that he was happy to state that the long-wished for time had arrived when the Saints were called upon to gather home unto Zion, and if we cannot get the people to believe by precept, the time will soon arrive when we will teach them by example, by going out from their midst unto a land of refuge, whilst the overflowing scourge passes over the nations."[2] From the perspective of Church leaders in the mid-1800s, the choice to emigrate to Zion appears to have been a part of the measure of Church members' faithfulness.

The *Millennial Star* began recording emigration statistics in 1848. Table 6.1 shows the number of emigrants from the Cheltenham Conference listed in the reports from 1848 to 1854. After 1854, the emigration statistics were for the British Isles overall, rather than for each individual conference. The table demonstrates that from 1848 onward, the members from the Cheltenham Conference were not emigrating in large numbers; the largest number of emigrants from this conference for a six-month period was 25 in 1849. As there were 606 members in the conference, 25 emigrants would be a small percentage of the whole. The conference report for 30 June 1853 shows that during the first six months of 1853,

Table 6.1 Cheltenham Conference Emigration Statistics, 1840–1854

Date	Number of branches	Number of members	Number who emigrated
25 Feb 1849	20	545	23
4 Jun 1849	19	564	8
18 Dec 1849	19	606	25
1 Jun 1850	20	731	10
1 Jun 1851	20	861	22
1 Dec 1851	19	902	0
1 Jun 1852	20	902	8
31 Dec 1852	22	842	0
30 Jun 1853	23	809	19
31 Dec 1853	21	739	0
30 Jun 1854	21	765	23
31 Dec 1854	21	786	18

only 19 members emigrated from Cheltenham, but 114 emigrated from Herefordshire and 48 from Worcestershire. The total from all three counties who left during that six-month period was 181.[3] Obviously, the *Millennial Star* reports are inadequate for understanding the emigration rate or the situation of the Three Counties. Adding information from the databases enabled us to gain a more accurate perspective of emigration in the Three Counties, along with some details of emigration that occurred before the *Millennial Star* began reporting it in 1848.

The journal database reveals that of the 577 people who were positively identified, 34 percent were listed on ships' passenger lists found on the Mormon Migration website. Often, the emigrants were traveling on the same ship with family members and friends from the Three Counties. The *North America*, one of the first ships of Mormon emigrants, left Liverpool in September 1840 with 28 passengers listed in our journal database. Although children younger than eight are not listed in our databases, the passenger list includes many children and other relatives of those 28 people, increasing the number from the Three Counties on that

Statue on a Liverpool dock commemorating the emigration of Latter-day Saints. (Photo by Cynthia Doxey Green.)

ship. In fact, Wilford Woodruff recorded in his journal that John Benbow generously paid the expenses for 40 of the local Saints to emigrate to America.[4] When we added in the family members of those in the database who are also on the passenger list, we found 43 total emigrants from the Three Counties, some who probably paid their own way.

Mormon Migration lists several ships in the early 1840s that did not have complete passenger lists.[5] For some of these ships, the only way we know there was a group of Church members on board was because of the diaries or autobiographies that are available. For example, there were three trips in 1841—one voyage of the *Harmony* and two voyages of the *Caroline*—embarking from Bristol, Gloucestershire, which would have meant that most of the passengers probably came from the Three Counties. Unfortunately, the only passengers' names listed for the *Harmony* are the twenty-nine individuals who happened to be mentioned in the diaries of two passengers, James Barnes and Mary Ann Weston Maughan. Similarly, while Edward Phillips's history stated that there were one hundred in their company on the *Caroline* traveling from Bristol to Quebec in August 1841, Phillips only mentioned himself and the group leader by name.[6] The other voyage of the *Caroline* in January 1841 recorded no passenger names, but the *Millennial Star* reported that a group from Herefordshire and the surrounding area left Bristol at that time.[7]

Several other ships in the early 1840s likewise had no complete passenger lists. Because of the lack of official listings, we had to assume that if FamilySearch showed places of marriage or death in America, or if the United States census or the Mormon Pioneer Overland Travel website included these individuals, they must have emigrated to America. These other records were particularly helpful for identifying the converts who married or died in Nauvoo, Illinois, the intermountain west, or any place in between. In addition to those individuals listed on Mormon Migration, we found another 81 individuals from the journal database for whom there is evidence of emigration based on their later life events, although their names did not appear on a passenger list. The total percentage of emigrants for the journal

Pastoral scene in Newent, Gloucestershire. (Photo by Cynthia Doxey Green.)

database came to 49 percent, or almost half of all those individuals noted in the journals.

Unlike the journal database, the database for the Frogmarsh and Bran Green Branches showed an emigration rate of only 30 percent. Several possibilities may explain why fewer people listed in the branch records emigrated. If the individuals were still in England by the time the branch records were written in the mid-1840s, these individuals may have been too old, too infirm, or too poor to leave earlier, or they may have had family concerns or other issues that were keeping them in England. Perhaps by the time they were able to deal with the difficulties that prevented them from emigrating in the early 1840s, they may have decided they could not leave home for other reasons. The earliest emigrants listed in the branch records were the Thomas and Comfort Boulter family, who left in 1849, while the rest of the emigrants from the branch left from 1855 to the 1880s.[8]

The Thomas and Ann Collett Oakey family left from the Frogmarsh Branch. Their daughter, Sarah Ann Oakey Ludlum, later recounted the family's experience as they left their home in Eldersfield, Worcestershire, and sailed to New York City in 1856

Dovecote, Pigeon House Farm, Eldersfield, Worcestershire. (Photo by Cynthia Doxey Green.)

aboard the *Thornton*. The family traveled with their fellow emigrants to Iowa City where they became part of the ill-fated Willie handcart company. Sarah and most of her family miraculously survived the ordeal of the trek, but her eleven-year-old sister Rhoda perished as they were about to enter the Salt Lake Valley.[9]

Family Trials. Personal histories of the Latter-day Saints from the Three Counties show that many of them desired to gather to Zion, first in Nauvoo and later in Utah. Carrying out this desire was sometimes difficult because a large number had to leave their families and friends. However, despite all the trials associated with leaving England and undertaking a hard journey, they also had a sense of happy anticipation. Jane Ann Fowler Sparks described her experience when she was seventeen years old and traveling without her family:

> To travel to Utah with no means and only my heavenly father for a friend, but I never felt happier in all of my life than I did at the time. My saddest grief was in leaving my dear mother and my only sister. . . .We were four green horns, as they would call us in this country [America], but we were full of faith and did not realize the trials we were going to pass through before we reached our journeys [sic] end.[10]

The previous chapter shared the sad story of Mary Ann Weston Maughan, whose first husband had been brutally beaten by a mob soon after their marriage. After his death soon thereafter, Mary Ann settled her business, and in May 1841, she left with a group of Saints bound for Nauvoo. As she bade her family farewell, her mother was brokenhearted, and her two little sisters "clung around my neck, saying 'We shall never see you again.'" She recorded that she could "never forget" the grief and sorrow that she experienced at parting with her family.[11] While she and her party were preparing to sail from Bristol, Mary Ann's father sent lawyers to find the "young widow dressed in black" on board the ship to persuade her to come home. Having been warned previously that the lawyers were coming, she laid aside her black clothing for more cheerful attire, and in so doing she went undetected.[12]

Emily Hodgetts Lowder came from a wealthy family, all of whom, with the exception of her father, joined the Church. In 1856, their mother thought it best for them to emigrate without her husband's knowledge. The plan was for the wife and daughters to travel to Liverpool while their father was away from home for a few days, leaving William Ben, who was recovering from an illness, to stay at home to tell the father about their emigration. Emily recounts the events that transpired:

> When Father received the news he hastened to Liverpool with officers. He followed us, as we were still in the Irish Channel and not yet on the open sea. Father paid the captain of the vessel one hundred sovereigns to cast anchor for one hour. We all hid. His time was about expired when Mother finally gave herself up. He did not force Mother to go back but, through kind

Albert Dock in the port of Liverpool. (Photo by Cynthia Doxey Green.)

she went home with him. I was fifteen and my sister, *Maria*, was seventeen. We came on alone to Boston.[13]

Apparently, the emigration of the Hodgetts family was sensational enough that it was described in the newspapers. The newspaper account was somewhat different from the daughter's recollection, however, indicating that Mrs. Hodgetts had taken a great deal of cash and portable property with her when she left home.[14] After recovering from his illness, Emily and Maria's brother William Ben arrived in Boston ahead of them by taking a fast steamer. Emily continued:

William Ben brought a letter from Mother telling us what to do. This letter I kept until it fell to pieces, reading it often and crying. . . . In the letter she said, "Maria, come home and take care of your mother in the hour of trial, my days are short. Emmie, my loved one, go to Utah with your brother and keep faithful, work in the house of the Lord. William Ben, be a guide and protection to your sister, tenderly watch her footsteps." Maria stayed in Boston two weeks then returned to England. My brother and I came on to Utah. Mother only lived a few months after Maria's return home.[15]

Emily and William Ben made their way to Salt Lake City in a wagon train following the Willie and Martin handcart companies in 1856, suffering much from the harsh winter weather. In 1860, when she was only nineteen years old, Emily married, and her brother William died.[16]

Travel Trials. Even when people were on their way to Zion, they were not free from difficulty, often suffering sickness, deprivation, and death on the voyage across the ocean and the journey to Nauvoo or Utah. Francis George Wall arrived in New York with his parents and two sisters in 1863. While the family was on a train from New York to Missouri, one of the train cars caught fire, burning much of the passengers' luggage. The train officials received five thousand dollars from the railroad company to cover the loss, but when the Saints tried to get money for their losses, the train officials refused to give them any compensation.[17]

Mary Field Garner tells of being seasick during the whole voyage across the Atlantic, which took seven weeks because the ship was driven off course.[18] Illness was often a problem for the travelers because they lived close together in cramped quarters on board the ship. Sarah Davis Carter recalled: "While crossing the ocean on the ship *Windermere*, smallpox broke out. My two brothers, Rhuben and Levi, both died from this dreadful disease and were buried in the sea. It almost killed my mother to see those two darlings, with weights attached to their feet, slide into those shark-infested waters."[19]

Sarah said that when they arrived in New Orleans, an elder of the Church escorted those Saints who had recovered from the smallpox but were left with ugly scars on their bodies to an emigrant home. Not wishing to be associated with them, he made them walk on the other side of the road and instructed them not to speak to him. Sarah's grandmother was so upset at his behavior that she predicted that he would "die in a ditch." Sarah confirmed that he later became a drunkard and died in a gutter.[20]

George and Mary Bundy, Job Smith's uncle and aunt. (Church History Library.)

Home Connections. As the English Saints from the Three Counties arrived in Nauvoo, many of them settled near to their acquaintances from England. For example, Edward Phillips said that he "boarded with an old friend by the name of Jenkins." There he met his future wife, Hannah Simmonds, also from Gloucestershire, who was living with Benjamin and Mary Hill, formerly from Eldersfield, Worcestershire. Hannah and Edward were married in the presence of Benjamin and Mary Hill by Heber C. Kimball in 1842.[21]

Similarly, George Bundy and his nephew Job Smith from Redmarley, Worcestershire, lived with Daniel Browett from the Leigh, Gloucestershire, for the first six weeks they were in Nauvoo. Then they lived with Charles Price, a former United Brethren preacher, and then with John Newman, who was originally from Deerhurst, Gloucestershire. Some of the English converts used this network of friends to obtain employment. George Bundy and Job Smith secured jobs working at the Nauvoo brickyard for a dollar a day under superintendent Frank Pullen from Ledbury,

Gloucestershire. They finally settled on a quarter section of land where several families of their English acquaintances also lived.²²

Job Smith eventually left Nauvoo and traveled west with the Latter-day Saints to Salt Lake City. Soon after arriving, he was called to return to England on a mission where he labored in the Norwich Conference. While in England, he visited many of his relatives who were still living in Hawcross and Redmarley, Worcestershire. While on this mission, he met his future wife Adelaide Fowles in Bedfordshire, England.²³

William Pitt had been a musician in the Dymock, Gloucestershire, Anglican parish church before he was baptized by his brother-in-law, Thomas Kington, on 13 June 1840. In Nauvoo, Pitt was able to use his musical abilities for the good of the community as he became leader of the Nauvoo Brass Band. The Nauvoo Brass Band played at significant occasions in Nauvoo, including the procession as the bodies of Joseph Smith and Hyrum Smith arrived in Nauvoo from Carthage Jail. As William Pitt traveled west with the Saints, he and his brass band often played concerts in small settlements in Iowa to provide money and provisions for the pioneer trek. Along the way west and upon arrival in the Great Salt Lake Valley, music from the band, under the direction of William Pitt, was an important way to enliven the spirits of the weary pioneers and to provide beauty for Church meetings and other events.²⁴

William Pitt. (Church History Library.)

As a young man, Thomas Steed emigrated to America, arriving in Nauvoo on 13 April 1844. Some of his relatives had already arrived and were available to greet him. He recalled his arrival:

> The prophet Joseph Smith was at the pier. At first glance I could tell it was him, by his noble expression. He came on board to

shake hands and welcome us by many encouraging words, and express his thankfulness that we had arrived in safety. As he could not stay with us, he sent Apostle George A. Smith to preach on board. "What did you come here for?" asked he. "To be instructed in the ways of the Lord," answered someone. "I tell you, [Elder Smith said] you have come to the thrashing floor, and after you have been thrashed and pounded you will have to go through the fanning mill, where the chaff will be blown away and the wheat remain." (The troubles in Nauvoo were just coming upon them.)[25]

Thomas immediately joined the Nauvoo legion, belonging to the company captained by John Cheese, who was also from the Three Counties.[26] After Joseph Smith's martyrdom and the Saints' expulsion from Nauvoo, Thomas made his way to Utah with some of his relatives, finally arriving in 1850 and settling in Farmington.[27] Thomas served as part of the rescue party that went out to help the struggling Willie and Martin handcart companies in 1856. His twenty-year-old niece Sarah Steed was in the handcart company and survived the ordeal.[28] Thomas's father never emigrated to America, possibly due to his ill health, but he died in the faith in Malvern, Worcestershire, in 1855. Thomas's mother began her journey to Utah in 1857 after her husband died, traveling with her married daughters, Rebecca and Ann. The ocean voyage was too much for her, and she died an hour after disembarking in Boston.[29] In 1875, Thomas went back to England on a mission and experienced a joyful reunion with several of his family members, many of whom had joined the Church when he did but had stayed in Malvern, Worcestershire.[30]

Faithfulness Amidst Suffering. The story of the Field family from Stanley Hill, Herefordshire, reflects the tragedies and suffering the early Saints faced after they arrived in Nauvoo and were then forced to leave for the West in order to remain faithful to their convictions. Mary Field Garner recorded that her father did not have enough money to buy a home when they arrived in Nauvoo, so they rented one from a fellow Latter-day Saint. Mary faced the sadness of having her father and two sisters die in Nauvoo, leaving her mother with six children to rear. They were very poor and survived on one pint of cornmeal per day for the seven of them. She lamented, "OH! How hungry we were for something else to eat. The children cried for a piece of white bread, and mother, oft times, would cry with us, as she was unable to give us the bread or get enough food to satisfy the hungry cries of her children. The Saints were very kind to us and tried to help us the best they could."[31]

The sadness of destitution was sometimes accompanied by spiritual blessings. After the death of Joseph Smith in 1844, Mary was present at the meeting where Brigham Young took on the appearance and voice of Joseph Smith, showing the people that the mantle of Joseph Smith had fallen on him. She recounts, "I had a baby on my knee who was playing with a tin cup which fell on the floor just after [Brigham Young] arose to speak. Mother stooped over to pick it up. We were startled by hearing the voice of Joseph. Looking up quickly we saw the form of the Prophet Joseph standing before us. Brother Brigham looked and talked so much like Joseph that for just a minute we thought that it was Joseph."[32] Edward Phillips from Gloucestershire, corroborated this experience: "I . . . heard with my own ears and saw with my own eyes. We all thought Joseph had come back to us although we knew he was in his grave."[33]

In September 1846, the Field family crossed the Mississippi River as the Saints were forced out of Nauvoo by the mob. They were too destitute to travel west with the Saints, so they lived with several other families who were in a similar desperate situation on Nickerson Island in the middle of the river. During that winter, the mob sent word that the stranded people could return to their homes so that they had decent shelter. They continued to live in this quiet, deserted town for two more years. One night in 1848, Mary's mother witnessed a heartbreaking event as she went to the pump to get water.

> She heard a terrible crackling of timber. Looking up she saw the beautiful Nauvoo Temple in flames. She ran back into the house, waking us children and also the Lee family [with whom they stayed] and several neighbors to watch it burn to the ground. It is impossible to describe our feelings to see our sacred tem-

ple, which we were so proud of and which had cost the Saints so much hard work and money to build, being destroyed. The anti-Mormons were also angry about it, as they were proud to have this beautiful structure in the community.[34]

The next spring, the Field family started west, staying two seasons at Council Bluffs, Iowa. As they journeyed west, an Indian chief was attracted to Mary, who had red, curly hair hanging in ringlets down her back. He offered many ponies for her, but her mother refused and later hid her under a feather mattress as the chief followed the camp for several days. The mother informed the chief that Mary was lost. He hunted through the wagons to find her and even felt the mattress but failed to detect her. After staying all day to see if she came back, he finally left when night came. Mary and her family arrived in the Salt Lake valley, and the chief managed to find her there sometime later. He was again rebuffed and finally left for good after three days.[35] In spite of all her trials, at the end of her life Mary Field Garner stated, "I am glad my parents embraced the Gospel in England and came to Zion."[36] Mary died at the age of 107 in 1943, true to her beliefs. At her funeral, her previously-written testimony was read:

> It is said I am the only living witness to have actually seen and known the Prophet Joseph Smith and I want to bear my testimony to the world and especially to every Latter-day Saint to the truthfulness of this Gospel as revealed through the Prophet Joseph, that Jesus Christ is the Savior of mankind, that Joseph Smith was a true and living prophet of God, that he was divinely called of God to establish His true Gospel on this earth in this last dispensation, that he was a true and faithful leader of the Saints and that the principles he advocated were true and correct beyond a doubt, that he lived the Gospel as he taught it to his people, that he did seal his testimony with his blood, that I was in Nauvoo at the time of the martyrdom and I did see their bodies returned to Nauvoo to be prepared for burial, that I did view the bodies before they were buried.[37]

Many Latter-day Saints who emigrated from the Three Counties lived in the Nauvoo area at first. The journal database affirms that 65 percent of the 282 emigrants arrived in America prior to 1846, at which time the body of the Saints left Nauvoo and began to move west. The rest of the emigrants represented in the database were part of the Mormon pioneer migration to Utah. The majority (61 percent) of all the emigrants from England were listed either in the Mormon Pioneer Overland Travel website, having traveled west before 1869, or in reports or narratives of their later life events in Utah or Idaho. We found 137 of the people in the database listed on Mormon Pioneer Overland Travel, with evidence of another 40 who traveled west either in an unrecorded pioneer company or on the train after 1869. Sixty-three of the English emigrants from the database did not arrive in Utah because they had died (1) while they were en route on the ship, (2) in either Nauvoo or Missouri before their trek west began, or (3) somewhere on the plains as they traveled with the Saints. We assume these individuals were true to the gospel because they were following the Saints, even though they did not reach their intended destination.

Nearly half of the converts from the Three Counties demonstrated their faithfulness by following the prophets and staying true to their convictions as they emigrated to Nauvoo and the western United States. These Saints contribute evidence to support Wilford Woodruff's statement that those he taught in England remained fully involved in the Church. However, not all of those who arrived on the American continent made it all the way to Nauvoo or later to Utah.

Different Destinations. Twenty-five of the individuals in our database crossed the ocean to join the Saints but did not finish the journey to Nauvoo or to the Salt Lake Valley. Their names were on censuses or other records in the Midwest in the 1860s or later. Some emigrants may have stopped either because they needed to work or because they gave up their quest when faced with the trials of the journey. William Clayton was on the *North America* in 1840 with the first group of converts from the Three Counties. His description of the journey to Nauvoo related that after arriving in New York, the emigrants had to travel over land

and by boat on lakes, rivers, and canals through New York, Ohio, and Illinois. Several families decided to stay for a time in other communities, some to work to make enough money to continue the trip. Clayton stated that some in his group were tired and sick, but others became disgruntled, "inclined almost to wish they had not left England." Several families decided to leave the group and stay in Kirtland, Ohio, for a season, "cheerful and rejoiced in the prospect of soon having a place to rest." William Clayton wrote that all of them dropped out of the group receiving a letter of recommendation to go to Kirtland, except for Thomas Hooper from Herefordshire, "whose conduct has been very bad."[38] Thomas and his wife, Hannah, were both baptized by Wilford Woodruff in England, but aside from being mentioned in William Clayton's journal, they cannot be found on other records associated with the Latter-day Saints. Either they both died soon after leaving the group or they stayed in Ohio or another area and did not rejoin the Saints.

Some people listed in the journal database lived in Nauvoo but never left Illinois to go west with the Saints. One of these was the widow of John Cheese. John was one of the first to join the Church in Herefordshire, and although there is no death record for him, he most likely died in Nauvoo. Mary Cheese had remarried and was recorded as living in Nauvoo in the 1850 census with two of her children, both of whom had come from England with her.[39] Mary could not be found on later census records, but her children married and stayed in Hancock County, Illinois. Those who stayed in the midwestern states may have apostatized from the Church or they may have been merely too tired or too poor to move west. Without details from their own lives or their family stories, there is no way of knowing their reasons for not following the body of the Church west.

We were surprised to find that six of the Saints from our database who lived in Nauvoo returned to England. The public records cited in our database do not provide enough information to discern whether their return was a result of disillusionment and apostasy from the Church or due to family or economic situations that would have affected their choice. John Spiers's journal mentioned the William and Susanna Margretts family as being apostates who returned to England from Nauvoo.[40] In contrast, John and Lydia Pullen Fidoe lived in Nauvoo after they left England in 1841, were back in Bishops Frome, Herefordshire, in the 1851 and 1861 censuses, but eventually died in Ohio in the 1880s. The obituary for John Fidoe in the *Deseret News* in Utah in 1881 mentions that because John had been in the Navy earlier in life, he enjoyed traveling, perhaps accounting for the return to England. The obituary states, "He died in full faith of the gospel," in Ohio.[41]

Those Who Remained in England

Many people may assume that converts who emigrated were more faithful to the gospel than those who did not. Evidence demonstrates that emigration may not be the only proof of a convert's strength of testimony, and lacking desire to follow the call of the prophets to gather in Zion was not the only reason individuals may not have emigrated. The database by itself cannot answer the question of whether those who stayed in England were still committed to the Church, but one should not discount the faithfulness of those individuals who stayed in England.

Without knowing their hearts and minds, those in the present day cannot say whether those who stayed behind were less faithful to their baptismal covenants than those who emigrated. On his mission to England in 1851, Job Smith traveled to the Three Counties to visit relatives. He recorded that his grandfather, William Smith, was still living in Deerhurst and was an elder in the Church, but that he was over seventy years old and in very poor circumstances.[42] William Smith had obviously remained active in the Church but had not been able to join the Saints, likely due to poverty, age, or health concerns. This example demonstrates reasons that at least some of those who were faithful to their covenants remained in England. Additional reasons might have included caring for a sick family member or being married to someone who was not a member of the Church, as well the possibility of individual apostasy. Converts dealing with any of these situations except apostasy might have remained faithful to the gospel throughout their lives, even if they did not join the Saints in America. The public records and anecdotal information from journals and autobiographies of missionaries and members provide examples of all of these reasons for staying in England.

Reasons for Not Emigrating. Some families who joined the Church early in the 1840s were not able to emigrate as soon as they desired or not at all because of poverty. Some converts from the early years had to wait many years before they had a chance to join the Saints in Utah. William and Elizabeth Bishop Davis, who had been members of the United Brethren, were baptized by Wilford Woodruff in 1840. Their daughter Sarah recollected, "My father's wages were small and . . . his family was large. . . . We knew if we emigrated to Utah, which was the great desire of our hearts, we would have to save every penny that we possibly could."[43] They worked for many years and were finally able to save enough money to emigrate in 1854.

Samuel Eames. (Church History Library.)

Another stalwart member who had to wait and work was Samuel Eames of Garway Hill, Herefordshire, who was not able to emigrate until the end of his life. Many years earlier Samuel had "sold all [he] had and devided [sic] the money and . . . sent 4 of [his] Children to America."[44] Samuel, his wife, and their son John stayed behind in England for over twenty-five years. In a letter to his children in America, Samuel expressed his desire to die in America. He was finally able to travel over the sea and across the plains to Utah in 1868. He died two months after his arrival.

Home of Samuel Eames in Garway, Herefordshire. (Photo by Carol Wilkinson.)

Being poor and unable to emigrate did not prevent converts from continuing active membership in the Church. William G. Davis was a missionary in the Three Counties in the 1880s, some forty years after Wilford Woodruff had first preached the gospel there. He met several people who had been baptized in 1840, including some who are listed in our journal database.[45] His journal details his experiences with the Saints, confirming some of the assumptions we had made about those who remained in England after being converted. For example, he described some of the Church members he visited as being "in a very poor condition," but generous to the missionaries.[46]

Some members who might have had finances sufficient to emigrate did not do so because of family problems and responsibilities. The Pritchard family had responsibilities that kept them from emigrating. They had been members of the Church for several years when Davis arrived. Davis wrote that they desired to emigrate, but their elderly father lived with them: "The family will not emigrate while he lives. Although they could raise the means. They think he will not live to get through."[47]

William Davis described a different form of family responsibility that kept some of the early members from emigrating: a spouse who was not a member of the Church. When there was not a large concentration of Church members in an area, many young people had a hard time finding someone to marry who shared their faith. William Davis stated that Brother Roberts's two daughters "both married out of the church which they regret very much."[48] Some of the individuals who married out of the Church may have been faithful in their hearts, but found it difficult to participate in Church meetings, or to provide opportunities for their children to learn the gospel. Emigration might not have been a possibility.

Because not everyone who might have desired to emigrate was able to do so, we tried to look at other options for examining the faithfulness of the people who stayed in England. Some of the people who could not emigrate had family members who did manage to join the Saints in America. In the instances that FamilySearch.org showed a full pedigree and family group record for converts who remained in England, we could usually trace other family members, often finding that someone in the family had emigrated. This pattern helped us account for the William and Margaret Lane Crook family of Apperley and Deerhurst, Gloucestershire. According to FamilySearch Family Tree, William and Margaret died in England in the 1870s, but three of their adult children emigrated to join the Saints in Utah. At least twelve individuals listed in the database who died in England had spouses, children, or grandchildren who emigrated to Utah or Idaho. Although these records alone do not prove that these twelve people remained active in the Church until they died, their emigrant family members perhaps reflected the faithfulness of those who remained in England.

The situation of Elizabeth Tringham provides a contrasting example. Wilford Woodruff baptized Elizabeth in 1840. Her grandson, Charles Smith, left a diary in which he stated that both his grandfather and grandmother joined the Church in early 1840 and he was baptized in August 1840. He wrote that his grandfather, Lindsey Tringham, left the family in 1841 to go to Nauvoo, but his grandmother stayed in England because she did not

Pond in Apperley, Gloucestershire. (Photo by Cynthia Doxey Green.)

want to travel on the sea. After a short time in Nauvoo, Lindsey Tringham became somewhat disillusioned about the Church and returned home to his family. Charles noted that when he decided to emigrate to Nauvoo in 1842, his grandmother "tied up my clothes in a bundle and told me to go and never return."[49]

Individuals Not Clearly Tracked. Sometimes while searching Family Tree for the converts, we found there was very little information about their lives, and their ordinances all occurred within the last forty years, probably due to the Church extraction or indexing programs. While this finding does not indicate that the early converts were disaffected from the Church in England, it is possible that the descendants of these converts did not remain involved in Church activity and had not provided genealogical data for their ancestors. For example, Jonathan Lucy did not emigrate, but in the *British Mission Manuscript History*, he is named as the leader of the Colwall Branch through 1847.[50] While he is not named again as the branch leader, there was a Colwall Branch in existence through 1854,[51] so he might have been actively involved in the Church during that time. Because there are no other Church

Deerhurst, Gloucestershire. (Photo by Cynthia Doxey Green.)

records of the Lucy family, there is no evidence of his continued activity after the branch disbanded. The Lucy family's records on Family Tree appear to have been extracted from Colwall parish records. Thus, even though Jonathan and his wife might have been faithful throughout their lives, the next generation may not have been active in the Church.

The Lucys and others may have had difficulty remaining active in the Church if the branch in their village dissolved and they had to travel many miles to attend meetings. The *Millennial Star* conference reports and the *British Mission Manuscript History* provided data showing how branches and conferences grew, changed boundaries, and disbanded as time went on.[52] One of the patterns we noticed was that many of the small branches in rural villages were in existence from 1840 until the mid-1850s and were then either dissolved or subsumed into larger branches in bigger towns and cities. Only 10 percent of the branches in the Three Counties listed in the *Manuscript History* continued beyond 1860. Branch membership probably changed due to new baptisms, emigration, inactivity, or death, so branch boundary

Home of Jonathan Lucy, Herefordshire. (Photo by Cynthia Doxey Green.)

changes often reflected the locations of the bulk of the Saints. While these changes may have been important for building a strong base for the Church in larger towns and cities, they could have caused difficulty for people in the small villages who might not have been able or willing to walk several miles to Church every Sunday to join with the Saints in other towns. Those people might not have left the Church in their hearts, but they may have felt that the Church left them.

Because branch boundary changes might have affected the Church activity of many in our databases, we looked at how many of the people died in England before the 1861 census, during the time when the likelihood of having a nearby branch of the Church was higher. Of the 295 people in the journal database not listed on the emigration websites, 26 percent died in England prior to the 1861 census. Similarly, of those in the branch database, 30 percent of those who did not emigrate also died before 1861.[53] The individuals who died earlier than 1861 may have continued activity in the Church until they died since there was a local branch to attend. We consider it likely that some who lived beyond those twenty years without emigrating may not have had the means or opportunity to remain actively involved in the Church because relocated branches were too far away.

William G. Davis's missionary journal from the 1880s contains examples showing the impact branch boundary changes had on Church activity. As he visited the branches and members of the Church, Davis found individuals who had been members for many years. Davis was welcomed by the Chambers family in Shucknell Hill. They said they had been members of the Church since 1850, "but the branch being broken up about 1855 they had not met with the saints since that time."[54] Some families listed in the journal database from the 1840s were participating in their local Church branches when Davis met them in the 1880s. For example, Jonathan Davis, who was baptized by Wilford Woodruff on 13 March 1840, was still faithful to the gospel in 1881. William Davis visited with him several times and learned that the family was waiting to hear from friends in Utah who had promised to help them emigrate.[55] Unfortunately, the Jonathan Davis family was still in Bishops Frome, Herefordshire, during the 1891 census and could not be found in emigration records. William Davis also wrote about a few people who were not exemplary members of the Church; for example, he met the president of one of the branches coming home after spending his wages at the "publick house according to the usual custom."[56]

Those who Fell Away. Not all the converts from the Three Counties in the 1840s were stalwart in their new beliefs. William Williams recorded that in the early days of the Church the Saints "seemed to have forgot there was a Sifting time to come That the Net when it was cast into the Sea gatherd good & bad fishes we were astonished that Some as Soon as Persecuton were offended and would go no more with us I soon began to See why this was and asked the Lord for Strength to keep me faithful to the End That I might be Saved."[57] Trials and persecution motivated some like Williams to pray for strength to stay the course, but such difficulties led others to leave their newfound faith.

Because the available public records for the databases do not give specific information about each person's faithfulness to the Church, we relied on anecdotes about some families to enlighten us

about their Church activity. Both the Castree and Holley families from Garway Hill had family members who emigrated to Utah, but some of those who stayed behind may not have been strong in their faith. A local history book about Garway Hill, Herefordshire, mentions some of the early Church members who lived in the area, including the Castree and Holley families. This history states that three of John and Anne Cecil Holley's sons left for Utah in 1856, while the rest of the Holley family stayed in England.[58] Because no Church records are now available for the Garway area, there is no record of whether the Holley family in England remained faithful to the Church in their lifetime. However, the history of Garway Hill provides information that some members of the Castree family had difficulties in remaining true to their faith. Several of the Castrees are described as "colourful," having been written up in the *Hereford Times* because of some criminal activity.[59]

When Thomas Steed went back to the Three Counties as a missionary in 1875, he visited Henry Jones, whom he described as an "apostate" living near Malvern Link, Worcestershire. He visited him several times, trying to convince him of the error of his ways, and Thomas finally told Henry that "he was a miserable, unhappy man." Henry's daughter corroborated that remark, saying, "Father, you know you are a miser-

Countryside around Garway, Herefordshire. (Photo by Carol Wilkinson.)

able, unhappy man." A few days later, Thomas went again to see Henry Jones, afterwards writing, "How great his darkness! That man once enjoyed the light of the Holy Spirit, but now denies the power thereof."[60]

In addition to anecdotal data for individuals, the conference reports published in the *Millennial Star* can give a perspective on overall faithfulness of the members in the Three Counties. For example, in 1859, the *Millennial Star* referred to some of the Church members in the Cheltenham, Worcestershire, and Herefordshire Conferences as "dull and sleepy."[61] The dullness, or lack of interest and enthusiasm, may have come as the members had been in the Church for many years but had not yet joined in emigration. On a more positive note, laudable things must have occurred soon thereafter; later that same year the *Star* recorded, "Cheltenham Branch, which *was* the dullest in the Conference, but is *now* flourishing. . . . The old suspicious spirit is almost defunct."[62]

While investigating apostasy versus faithfulness in the Three Counties, we found a few sources with information regarding members in the British Isles being cut off (excommunicated) during the early days of the Church. Little information on excommunication is available through the journal database because journals are not official records of the Church. Only a handful of people in that database are listed as "cut off" because their excommunication was specifically mentioned in journals. One example, mentioned earlier, is the Margretts family, whom John Spiers described as apostates acting in opposition to the missionaries.[63] Another example, taken from the journal of James Palmer, mentions that in a January 1841 meeting at the Kitchen (Brother Thomas Arthur's home) in Garway, Philip Castrey, a member of the Castree family mentioned earlier, was cut off. In spite of his disaffection from the Church, he must have repented because about a year later, Palmer noted that he baptized Philip Castrey.[64]

Unlike the journal database, the branch database, coming from official Church membership records, contains excommunication data for thirty-five individuals. Four of those thirty-five have a rebaptism date listed, and another five people are recorded in the emigration records, signifying that they proba-

The Kitchen, Garway, Herefordshire. (Photo by Carol Wilkinson.)

bly rejoined the Church. The majority of those excommunicated were not mentioned in later Church records, but they could have been rebaptized even though the early records are lacking that information.

Starting in 1847, the *Millennial Star* conference reports began to record the number of members who had been excommunicated (cut off) since the previous conference. A report of people being cut off in the Three Counties gives us insight into excommunication decisions. At the 29 August 1847 Mars Hill Conference in Herefordshire, the president of the conference "observed that the number cut off might seem great, but he could say with assurance, that there had not been one cut off, or even one suspended, during the last fourteen months that he had been there, that was in good standing when he came; those that had been dealt with were some that had not been known as Saints for years past, and he was glad to see their names erased."[65] This Church leader apparently thought it was important to remove from the Church records the names of people not participating regularly in meetings.

In 1853, the *Millennial Star* reported that Church membership numbers for the first half of 1852 were incorrect in many parts of the British Isles because of errors in recording those who had emigrated, been cut off, or died, as they found "many members unaccounted for."[66] Church leaders at the national level suspected that conferences had been dropping off the names of people who could not be found.[67] This problem evidently continued for several years; in 1859, members were being cut off without the knowledge of the president of the conference,[68] and sometimes without the knowledge of the Church member. In July 1860, a *Millennial Star* editorial mentioned, "Out of the many thousands who have been cut off from the Church in these lands, a large portion have retained the spirit of the work. Indeed, many of them have not known that they were cut off from the Church until some months afterwards."[69]

As implied by the statements from British Church leaders in the mid-1800s, some were excommunicated as punishment for not attending meetings regularly with the Saints. Mary Philpotts of Cradley, Herefordshire, received a letter declaring, "The Officers in the Ridgway Cross branch met in Council July 6th . . . and it was declared that you had neglected your Duty according to the covenant you made, in not assembling with the Saints. It was proposed and carried in this Council that you be notified to appear with the Saints on Sunday, July 13th or you must expect to be dealt with according to the law of the Church of Jesus Christ of Latter-day Saints."[70] Apparently, Mary Philpotts did not make it to Church that day; according to a history of Cradley, she returned to the Church of England.

Table 6.2 shows the report of excommunications for the Cheltenham Conference during the years 1849 to 1854, the only years for which the *Millennial Star* reported these statistics for each conference in the British Mission. The table shows that a number of excommunications occurred in that conference during these years with similarities to those of Mary Philpotts and those reported in the 1860 editorial in the *Millennial Star*.

Table 6.2 Cheltenham Conference Excommunication Statistics, 1849–54

Date	Number of branches	Number of members	Number excommunicated
4 June 1849	19	564	7
18 Dec. 1849	19	606	19
1 June 1850	20	731	11
1 June 1851	20	861	24
1 Dec. 1851	19	902	32
1 June 1852	20	902	61
31 Dec. 1852	22	842	97
30 June 1853	23	809	34
31 Dec. 1853	21	739	63
30 June 1854	21	765	68
31 Dec. 1854	21	786	22

In conclusion, without further study and comparison of all other areas of the Church and more complete records from the Three Counties, Wilford Woodruff's statement that fewer converts apostatized from the Three Counties than from any other area may never be verified. The incompleteness of the records for the Three Counties suggests that records of Church membership in other areas might be somewhat lacking as well. Thus, such a study would be extremely difficult.

Another difficulty we encountered in this study is that the databases and the public records we used provided very little information about those who left the Church. In the branch database, results are limited to what was available about the Church members in the Bran Green and Frogmarsh area. While this study cannot give an accurate number of the early converts to the Church in the Three Counties who actually remained actively involved in the Church, it does show that nearly one-half of the members in our databases emigrated to join the Saints in America. Many of those who stayed in England may have remained faithful, at least while there were active branches in their area. Further research using additional branch and conference records might provide more accurate rates of activity and apostasy during the mid-nineteenth century in England.

Notes

1. Wilford Woodruff, in *Journal of Discourses*, 15:345.
2. "Conference Minutes: Worcestershire Conference" *Millennial Star* 10 no. 11 (12 June 1848): 168.
3. "Statistical Report of The Church of Jesus Christ of Latter-day Saints in the British Isles," *Millennial Star* 15 no. 31 (30 July 1853): 510.
4. *Wilford Woodruff's Journal*, 1:490 (11 August 1840).
5. *Mormon Migration*, https://mormonmigration.lib.byu.edu. In 1840 and 1841 alone, there were four ships where there were fewer than fifty passengers' names listed, but there could have been many more on board. The ships were the *Alliance* (Possibly Liverpool to New York, 23 December 1840—four passengers listed), the *Caroline* (Bristol to Quebec, leaving 31 January 1841—no passenger list), the *Harmony* (Bristol to Quebec, 10 May 1841—twenty-nine passengers listed), and the *Caroline* (Bristol to Quebec, 8 August 1841—three passengers listed, but 100 Saints were on board).
6. Edward Phillips, "Biographical Sketches of Edward and Hannah Simmonds Phillips, 1889, 1926, 1949," 1, MS 11215, Church History Library, Salt Lake City.
7. "Emigration," *Millennial Star* 1, no. 10 (February 1841): 263.
8. The finding that no one emigrated from the branch before 1849 provides evidence that in all likelihood the branch records were kept in earnest starting in the mid to late 1840s. If the records had started when the branch was first created in 1840, they would have included the names of individuals from the journal database who left England in the early 1840s.
9. Sarah Ann Oakey Ludlum, "Her Journey West," in *Treasures of Pioneer History*, comp. Kate B. Carter (Salt Lake City: Daughters of the Utah Pioneers, 1956), 5:257–58. Sarah's description does not mention

where her sister Rhoda Rebecca died, but FamilySearch Family Tree provides a death date of 9 November 1856, with the place being Emigration Canyon in the mountains east of Salt Lake City. According to the Mormon Pioneer Overland Travel website, the Willie handcart company arrived in Salt Lake City on 9 November 1856, the same day as Rhoda's death.

10. Jane Ann Fowler Sparks, *Jane Ann's Memoirs*, comp. Marsha Passey (Montpelier, ID: M. Passey, 2004), 6.
11. Mary Ann Weston Maughan, "The Journal of Mary Ann Weston Maughan," in *Our Pioneer Heritage*, 2:357.
12. Maughan, "Journal," 358.
13. Emily Hodgetts Lowder, "Emily Hodgetts Lowder—103 Years," in *Our Pioneer Heritage*, 7:425; emphasis in original.
14. "Disgraceful Elopement," *The Times* (London, England), Friday, 4 April 1856, 11.
15. "Emily Hodgetts Lowder—103 Years," 425.
16. "Emily Hodgetts Lowder—103 Years," 426; William B. Hodgetts Company 1856, found on https://history.lds.org/overlandtravels.
17. Francis George Wall, "Francis George Wall—Pioneer of 1863," in *Our Pioneer Heritage*, 7:364.
18. Mary Field Garner, "Mary Field Garner autobiographical sketch, ca. 1940," 2, MS 10472, Church History Library, Salt Lake City.
19. Sarah Davis Carter, "She Came in 1853," in *Our Pioneer Heritage*, 12:227.
20. Carter, "She Came in 1853," 227–8.
21. Phillips, "Biographical Sketch," 2.
22. Job Taylor Smith, "Job Smith Autobiography, circa 1902," 5, MS 4809, Church History Library, Salt Lake City.
23. Smith, "Autobiography," 18, 21, 27.
24. "The Nauvoo Brass Band," *Contributor* 1, no. 6 (March 1880), 135–36.
25. Thomas Steed, "The Life of Thomas Steed From His Own Diary, 1826–1910," 8–10, BX 8670.1 .St32, L. Tom Perry Special Collections, Harold B. Lee Library, Brigham Young University, Provo, UT (parentheses in original). Also online at https://books.FamilySearch.org.
26. Steed, "Life of Thomas Steed," 10.
27. Steed, "Life of Thomas Steed," 11–17.
28. Steed, "Life of Thomas Steed," 22.
29. Steed, "Life of Thomas Steed," 25.

30. Steed, "Life of Thomas Steed," 33, 36.
31. Garner, "Autobiographical Sketch," 3.
32. Garner, "Autobiographical Sketch," 5.
33. Phillips, "Biographical Sketch," 2.
34. Garner, "Autobiographical Sketch," 8.
35. Garner, "Autobiographical Sketch," 9–10.
36. Garner, "Autobiographical Sketch," 13.
37. Garner, "Autobiographical Sketch," 13.
38. William Clayton, "William Clayton Diary, 1840 January–1842 February," 29 October 1840, MS 2843, Church History Library, Salt Lake City.
39. 1850 census, Hancock County, Illinois, "United States Census, 1850," database with images, FamilySearch (https://familysearch.org/ark:/61903/1:1:M85T-B49).
40. John Spiers, "John Spiers Reminiscences and Journal, 1840–77," 30–31 (29 October 1841), MS 1725, Church History Library, Salt Lake City.
41. "Obituary: John Fido," *Deseret News*, 7 September 1881, 512.
42. Smith, "Autobiography," 21.
43. Carter, "She Came in 1853," 227. Although Sarah Davis Carter recalled in her history that the Davis family traveled in 1853, the passenger list for the *Windermere* on Mormon Migration, shows that the family traveled in 1854, leaving Liverpool 22 February 1854.
44. Samuel Eames, "Samuel Eames correspondence 1861," MS 9490 Church History Library, Salt Lake City, 3. Transcription is by Jay G. Burrup.
45. William George Davis, "William G. Davis Diaries, 1880–1882," 31 (4 December 1880), MS 1689, Church History Library, Salt Lake City.
46. Davis, "Diaries," 50 (4 February 1881).
47. Davis, "Diaries," 42 (10 January 1881).
48. Davis, "Diaries," 51 (7 February 1881).
49. Charles Nephi Smith, "Diary and Reflections of Charles 'Nephi' Smith, son of Thomas and Mary Smith," 2, https://familysearch.org/photos/documents/4972727?pid=KWJ8-Z8G. This document is attached to Charles Nephi Smith on FamilySearch.org Family Tree. We recognize that documents attached to Family Tree are provided by family members and may not be correct.. This diary is written in autobiographical form, however, lending credence to its origin. As a verification of Charles's writings, we found Lindsey Tringham listed as a passenger of the *Chaos*, leaving Liverpool 8 November 1841, Mormon Migration.

50. "First Division of Mars Hill Conference," *Millennial Star* 9 no. 6 (15 March 1847): 83.
51. "Home Intelligence: Herefordshire Conference," *Millennial Star* 16, no. 42 (21 October 1854): 665.
52. For more information on Church units in the Three Counties, see the table in the appendix.
53. Over 100 people could not be identified on the 1851 or 1861 censuses for whom we have no death date or place, so we cannot be sure if they died, or if they had moved to another county.
54. Davis, "Diaries," 63 (18 March 1881).
55. Davis, "Diaries," 33 (13 December 1880), 102 (9 May 1881).
56. Davis, "Diaries," 31, (5 December 1880).
57. William Williams, "William Williams Reminiscence, 1850," 9, MS 9132, Church History Library, Salt Lake City. Spelling and punctuation are in the original.
58. Joan and Brian Thomas, *Garway Hill Through the Ages* (Almeley, Herefordshire: Logaston Press, 2007), 127–29. FamilySearch Family Tree shows that the temple ordinance dates for the Holley and Castree family members who settled in Utah took place during their lifetime, while those for the people who stayed in England were not completed until after their deaths. That finding, however, may only reflect the fact that there was no temple in England at the time.
59. Joan and Brian Thomas, *Garway Hill Through the Ages*, 134.
60. Steed, "Life of Thomas Steed," 33–34.
61. "Minutes of the Special Council," *Millennial Star* 21, no. 6 (5 February 1859): 96.
62. "Correspondence: Cheltenham Pastorate," *Millennial Star* 21, no. 24 (24 June 1859): 384–85, emphasis in original.
63. Spiers, "Reminiscences," 30–31 (29 October 1841).
64. James Palmer, "James Palmer Reminiscences, ca. 1884–98," 20, 60, MS 1752, Church History Library, Salt Lake City.
65. "Conference Minutes: Mars Hill," *Millennial Star* 10 no. 3 (4 February 1848): 37.
66. "Half-yearly Statistical Reports, and Records," *Millennial Star* 15 no. 5 (29 January 1853): 73–74.
67. "Half-yearly Statistical Reports, and Records," *Millennial Star* 15, no. 5 (29 January 1853): 74.

68. "Minutes of the Special Conference," *Millennial Star* 21, no. 8 (19 February 1859): 130.
69. "Editorial," *Millennial Star* 22, no. 28 (14 July 1860): 441.
70. Wynnell M. Hunt, *Cradley: A Village History* (Trowbridge, England: W. M. Hunt & Cradley Village Hall Management Committee, 2004), 19.

From Then until Now

OUR FOCUS SO FAR IN THIS BOOK has been on the history of the Church in the Three Counties in the mid-1800s. This final chapter shifts focus to the situation of the Latter-day Saints in these counties from that time until the present, including ways members have connected with past events. To better demonstrate those connections, we offer a brief background of events that occurred in Britain in these intervening years.

The Interim Period

Between 1840 and 1900, many British Saints emigrated to the United States. Starting in the 1880s, deep prejudices against the Church developed in England as former Church member William Jarman was delivering anti-Church lectures. A calm period followed the 1890 manifesto, which officially ended polygamy. But during the period from 1910 to 1914, various ministers and former LDS members mounted another anti-Church campaign, claiming that the missionary program was a front to enslave British girls and take them to the United States as polygamous wives. After World War I, this campaign influenced politicians, who subsequently denied the Church's application for missionary visas. However, appeals from Utah's congressional delegation were successful, and in 1920, American missionaries were once again on British soil.[1]

Seventeen years later in 1937, President Heber J. Grant and other Church leaders from the States joined local leaders to celebrate the centennial of the Church in the British Isles. During the first one hundred years, 126,593 persons had been baptized, and 52,000 of those had emigrated to the United States. During two weeks of festivities, President Grant dedicated chapels in Burnley, Bradford, Rochdale, Merthyr Tydfil, Liverpool, Southwest London, and North London. Two years later, World War II began, and American missionaries were evacuated, leaving local members to perform missionary work.[2]

After the war, plans and construction began on a temple south of London, and on 7–9 September 1958, approximately 12,000 members attended the dedication services of the London Temple, conducted by President David O. MacKay. Two years later, on 17 June 1960, the Manchester Stake became the first stake in England. During the early 1960s, the Church called building missionaries and began a program to construct several meetinghouses. The Cheltenham chapel, dedicated on 13 December 1964, was the first in the Three Counties area.[3] On 21 March 1982, this chapel became the home of the new Cheltenham Stake. In 2015, this stake consisted of the Cheltenham, Gloucester, Hereford, Stroud, Swindon, Worcester, and Yate Wards and the Evesham and Forest of Dean branches.

Three Counties Connections with the Past

Sesquicentennial Celebrations. From 24–26 July 1987, along with other Latter-day Saints throughout the British Isles, Church members in Herefordshire, Worcestershire, and Gloucestershire commemorated the 150th anniversary of the first missionaries' arrival in England. The British Isles Advisory Committee had three objectives for the Sesquicentennial celebrations:

Objective 1: To create a greater public awareness of the Church and, in particular, its British dimension.

Objective 2: To bring about a greater interest in the Church and encourage vigorous and productive missionary and member-missionary activity.

The dedication of Hill Farm pond by Elder Russell M. Nelson at the sesquicentennial celebrations in 1987. (Photo by Carol Wilkinson.)

Objective 3: To stimulate a pride in the Church and Church history in British Latter-day Saints.[4]

As part of the celebrations, in 1987 a history of the Church of Jesus Christ of Latter-day Saints in the British Isles titled *Truth Will Prevail* was published by University Press, Cambridge. British Saints involved in the organization of the celebratory events felt strongly that to reach the market of the British public, the book should be published in Britain.[5] In addition, James and Lavelle Moss wrote a guidebook to historic sites in Britain,[6] and Church leaders gathered oral histories of British members of the Church.[7]

Six regional conferences took place throughout the British Isles, including one in Cardiff. The Church had purchased a small piece of land at Hill Farm, where John Benbow had lived, and erected a public marker commemorating Wilford Woodruff's mission in the Three Counties; Elder Russell M. Nelson dedicated this memorial on 25 July 1987. The land includes the area around the pond where Wilford Woodruff baptized so many people, along with a walking path from the parking site.

Hill Farm pond marker placed in 1987 at the place where Wilford Woodruff first performed baptisms. (Photo by Cynthia Doxey Green.)

Among the celebrations, a British musical with the title of the new book *Truth Will Prevail* was performed in Bristol during 1987. The Church also produced *A Story of Strength*, a video which portrayed the early missionary exploits of Wilford Woodruff in the Three Counties area. Many local Church members participated as extras in the film. During this celebratory year, "Harvest in Herefordshire," an article chronicling the early missionary success, was published in the January 1987 *Ensign*.

Restoration of Gadfield Elm Chapel. The Gadfield Elm chapel was sold in 1842 to provide funds to help the new British converts emigrate to America. Neglect over the next 152 years made it an unsightly ruin. Prior to the celebrations in 1987, Elder Neal A. Maxwell had looked into the possibility of the Church's purchasing the old Gadfield Elm chapel but felt the asking price was too high.[8] Over the years it was occasionally used as a shelter for farm animals, but in 1994 the land and chapel came up for sale at an auction.

Noticing the auction poster, Wayne Gardner, a local member of the Church, approached another member, Simon Gibson,

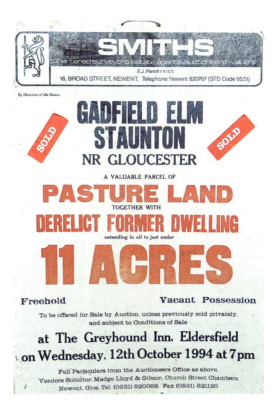

Right: Gaðfielð Elm auction poster. (Courtesy of Gaðfielð Elm Chapel.)

and the two of them discussed the idea of purchasing the property. One dark night in the pouring rain, Wayne and Simon drove out to visit the dilapidated building to decide whether to buy it. Surveying the appalling condition of the ruin, which had only three intact walls, Simon had the feeling that the building was beyond repair. Then he had the following experience:

> It was pitch black. . . . Wayne left me in there and I remember thinking, "This is beyond repair." And I must admit I just stood there in the pouring rain and I did have this spiritual prompting, no doubt about that at all, telling me, "Do it." Yes, definitely. Because I didn't have the time or the inclination to really want to do it. And I remember all I could visualize in my mind was Wilford Woodruff's eyes. Have you ever seen his eyes? Oh, I just saw those eyes and then I thought of Brigham Young. . . . Once I'd had that spiritual witness that I needed to do it, I thought, "There's no way I'm going into the next life not having done it and have to face those two very formidable gentlemen." . . . That's exactly what it was. I could visualize it. I mean it was just like there's no way I'm not doing this now. I've got to do it because I think it would be important to those men and to the Church.
>
> So there I was standing in the pouring rain and then I got back into the car absolutely soaked. As I sat in the car I thought, "At least the fireplace was intact . . . so you could imagine where

Gadfield Elm chapel ruin. (Photo by Alec Mitchell.)

the lectern had been." And I thought, "This has got to be the only place, certainly the only place I could think of in Europe, where you could, once it was restored, bring youth to. . . . They could sit in that chapel and you could say, "On this spot Brigham Young, Wilford Woodruff and Willard Richards all preached the message of the restored gospel." This one spot could act as a focal point for this wonderful story. And I thought that would be a big deal for a lot of people, imagine holding a testimony meeting here and inviting the kids to bear their testimonies on the same spot that Wilford Woodruff and Brigham Young testified to those people. You know it would be powerful, which is what is happening right now.[9]

A group of local members got together and came up with sufficient money to purchase the chapel at the auction.[10] Stones were missing from the chapel, but only a few yards away lay a dilapidated barn built of stone from the same time period and the same quarry, so the members purchased some of that stone from the owner of the barn. Work on rebuilding the chapel began immediately.[11] When the walls were up, Church headquarters

Reconstruction on Gadfield Elm chapel. (Photo by Wayne Gardner.)

made a donation to help pay for a new roof. To provide sufficient financial aid for the project, members created the Gadfield Elm Trust. The aims of the Trust were (1) to preserve the chapel, (2) to restore the chapel to its former nineteenth-century condition when occupied by the early Latter-day Saints, (3) to raise awareness of nineteenth-century LDS history in the British Isles, and (4) to create a recreational site for public use.[12] The Trust obtained some pews from a non-conformist chapel in Wales that had been built during the same time period as the original Gadfield Elm chapel. Restoring the old well outside provided the chapel's new water supply. The restoration was completed in time for the new millennium.[13]

During the time the chapel was being restored, local saints held a Church pageant in June 1995 to commemorate the 155th anniversary of the first conference in the British Isles at the first LDS chapel in Britain. Local members in period costumes represented Thomas Kington, Willard Richards, Wilford Woodruff and others as they reenacted the conference.[14] During this time the Gadfield Elm Trust began to produce literature to help educate the public.

The Gadfield Elm chapel was rededicated on 23 April 2000, by Elder Jeffrey R. Holland of the Quorum of the Twelve, who had direct ancestors from the area: Ellen Benbow Carter from Castle Frome and William Carter of Ledbury. Elder Holland had been an area president for the area fifteen years earlier and was delighted to be involved. He described the circumstances leading to his presence that day:

> I'm supposed to be today in Fukouka, Japan, with President Hinckley starting the first of four temple dedications that would have taken us from Fukuoka, Japan, to Adelaide, to Melbourne, Australia, to Suva, Fiji and a quick side trip to Bangkok, Thailand (laughs). Those are his [President Hinckley's] kind of side trips. That's where I'm supposed to be today. But in the broken-hearted prayers of the night when I said, "Surely, surely they won't dedicate Gadfield Elm without me," suddenly there was a strike in Adelaide and all temple dedications were put on hold for a month. And President Hinckley said, "Well you might

Elder Jeffrey R. Holland speaking at the dedication of the restored Gadfield Elm Chapel in 2000. (Photo by Gerry Matthews.)

President Gordon B. Hinckley plants an oak tree at Gadfield Elm in 2004 after the chapel is donated to the Church by members of the Gadfield Elm Trust. Left to right, Simon Gibson, Brian Bliss, Craig Gardner, Peter Gardner, President Hinckley, Wayne Gardner, Cheryl Gardner (background). (Photo by Gerry Matthews.)

as well go to England." And don't tell me that prayers of children and apostles aren't answered.¹⁵

The members of the Gadfield Elm Trust felt that should the Church leaders wish to take ownership of the chapel, they would donate it. In 2004 the Church accepted the offer, and on 26 May 2004, President Gordon B. Hinckley received the keys and deed of the chapel and planted an oak tree to commemorate the occasion. The building, which now contains historic displays and literature informing visitors of the history of the Church in this area, is used for special events such as firesides, Relief Society meetings, and seminary graduations. People are allowed to camp on the property next to the chapel, allowing youth groups and families to travel and learn about the history of the area.¹⁶

Other Significant Events. Local Church members in the Three Counties have engaged in a number of activities that connect them to the history of the Church in the United States. In 1997 local Church members received media coverage as they dressed in pioneer clothing and trekked the six miles from Ledbury to Dymock to mark the passing of 150 years since the arrival of Mormon pioneers in the Salt Lake Valley in 1847.[17] In 2002 the local Ledbury and District Historical Society published a booklet titled *The Mormons in the Three Counties, 1840* to create interest in the Mormon role in their local history including its link with the pioneer days of the United States. In 2005, local Church members pulled handcarts from Malvern town center up Worcestershire Beacon to celebrate the 175th anniversary of the founding of the Church.

Several types of connections were involved with an event that occurred from 4 to 11 August 2011, when saints from the Cheltenham Stake traveled to Salt Lake City and joined with members of the Salt Lake Glenmoor stake to perform *Faith: The Musical* at the LDS Conference Center. The play was written by David Markham of the Cheltenham Stake, who had written *Truth Will Prevail* in 1987. It follows the story of the Thomas Oakey family, baptized by Wilford Woodruff in 1840, including the family's journey of faith to America, where they suffered great deprivation and death while crossing the plains with the ill-fated Willie handcart company before finally arriving in Salt Lake City.[18]

Some more recent events have focused specifically on the work of Wilford Woodruff and on the Benbow family. From 31 July to 10 August 2013, over 300 Church volunteers performed in The British Pageant in Chorley, on the Preston England Temple grounds in a large marquee that seated 1,500.[19] Part of the pageant chronicled the 1840 conversion of John and Jane Benbow and Ellen Benbow Carter to the message of the gospel restoration.[20] In 2015 local members of the Cheltenham Stake congregated at Gadfield Elm chapel and celebrated the 175th anniversary of the June 1840 conference that was held in the chapel establishing the organization of the Church in that area. The celebration consisted of a dramatic retelling of the events of Wilford Woodruff's mission to the Three Counties area.[21]

Right: Castle Frome map.

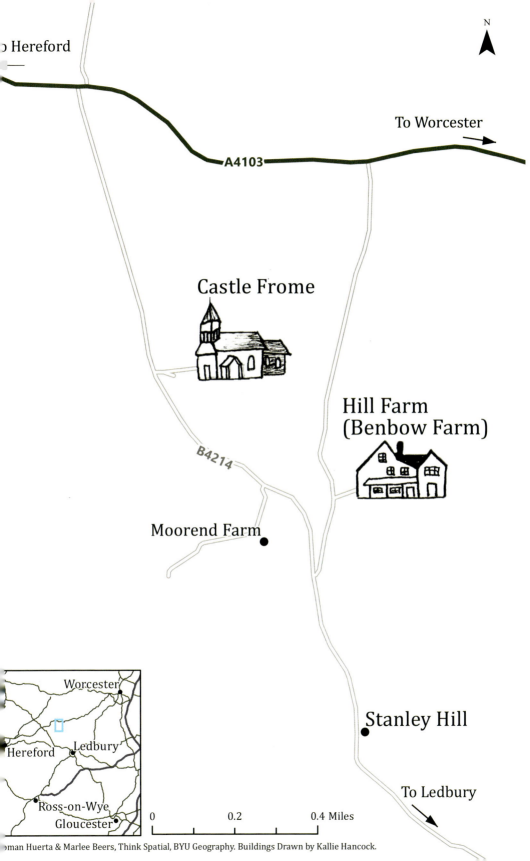

Current entrance to Hill Farm, Herefordshire, where John and Jane Benbow lived. (Photo by Carol Wilkinson.)

Historic Sites

Sites of important events of early Church history in the Three Counties link Church members and other interested people of the twenty-first century to their nineteenth-century roots. The remainder of this chapter will focus on these locations of so much Church progress and individual member and missionary growth. We hope this will be useful in providing geographical and historical contexts, especially for people desiring to visit the area.

Hill Farm and Pond. As discussed in chapter 3, Wilford Woodruff arrived at Hill Farm in March 1840 in company with William Benbow. William introduced Elder Woodruff to his brother John Benbow and his wife Jane, who were tenant farmers at Hill Farm. Two days later John, Jane, and three of their friends were baptized in the pond on the farm. On the following Sunday, Elder Woodruff preached three sermons in three different locations to a combined total of almost one thousand people. The last sermon was preached at the Benbow's home.[22] This sermon may have

Top: Attached barn at Hill Farm. (Photo by Carol Wilkinson.) Right: Interior of attached barn at Hill Farm. (Photo by Carol Wilkinson.) Bottom: The pond at Hill Farm where Wilford Woodruff baptized his first converts. (Photo by Cynthia Doxey Green.)

been preached in an attached barn, as this was the only building on the farm that could accommodate a large number of people. During the next few weeks, Elder Woodruff preached in the area, and many converts were baptized in the pond.

Castle Frome Church. On the Sunday following the baptisms of John and Jane Benbow, the local parish rector of the church in Castle Frome, being disconcerted at the numbers attending two sermons preached earlier that day, sent a constable to Hill Farm with a warrant to arrest Elder Woodruff before his final address. The constable agreed to let Elder Woodruff preach before making the arrest, but he was so moved by the teaching of Elder Woodruff that he was converted. Two parish clerks attending another sermon were similarly touched and also requested baptism.

Moorend Farm. Moorend Farm was the home of Edward Ockey, a member of the United Brethren and a friend of John Benbow. He sold all of his stock and property in March 1841 to provide money so that he and other Church members could emigrate to America.[23]

Dymock. Thomas Kington, the superintendent of the United Brethren, lived in Dymock. In this village on 18 May 1840, Mary Pitt, who had not walked without crutches for eleven years and

Moorend Farm was the home of Edward Ockey, a member of the United Brethren. (Photo by Cynthia Doxey Green.)

Top to bottom: The exterior of Castle Frome Parish Church. Right: The Norman font in Castle Frome Parish Church. Bottom: Interior of Castle Frome Parish Church. (Photos by Cynthia Doxey Green.)

Above: Dymock village. (Photo by Carol Wilkinson.) Below: Dymock map.

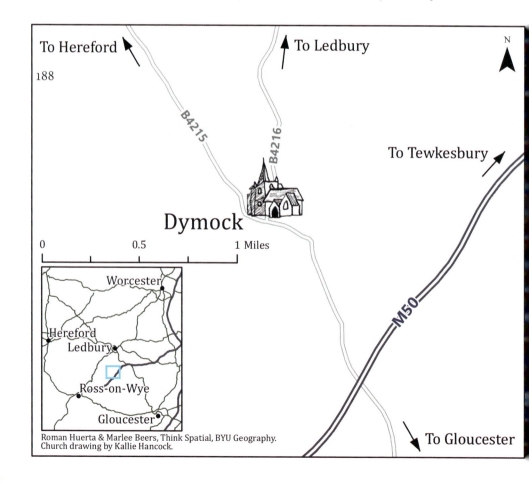

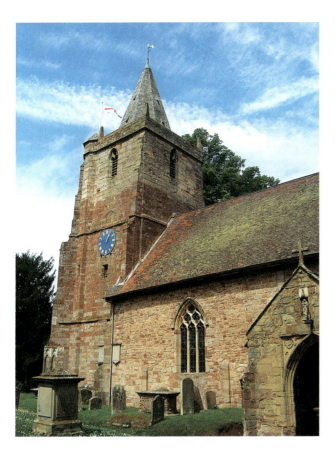

Above: Dymock Parish Church. (Photo by Cynthia Doxey Green.)
Below: Interior of Dymock Parish Church. (Photo by Cynthia Doxey Green.)

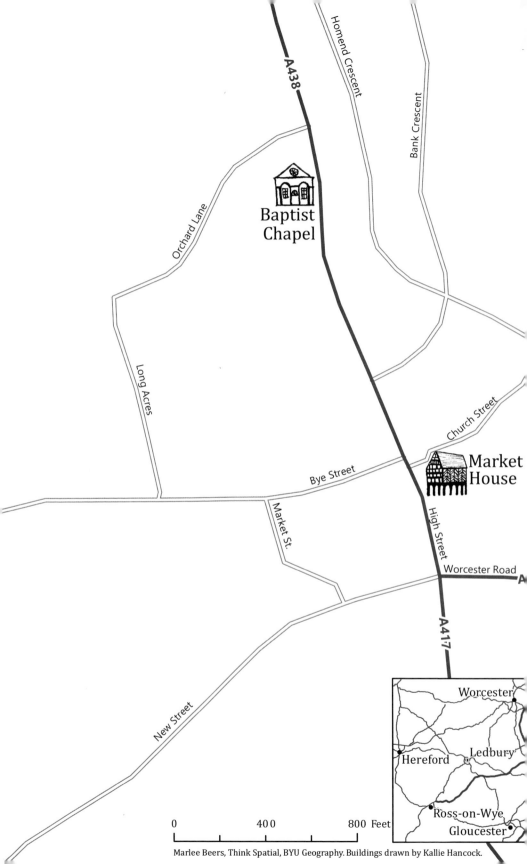

Covered marketplace in Ledbury. (Photo by Carol Wilkinson.)

had been confined to bed for six years, was healed of her infirmity by a blessing from Brigham Young, Wilford Woodruff, and Willard Richards.[24] By September, opposition to the Church was mounting, and as Elder Woodruff preached in Dymock, a mob pelted the home with anything they could lay their hands on. They smashed windows and roof tiles, creating a raucous noise to attempt to stop the sermon, which they were not able to do.[25]

Ledbury Baptist chapel. (Photo by Cynthia Doxey Green.)

Ledbury. The market town of Ledbury was a base for the missionaries in 1840. Brigham Young stayed there for a week. Wilford Woodruff was approached by the minister of the Baptist Church in Ledbury and invited to preach in the chapel. As a result of Elder Woodruff's preaching, several members of the congregation were baptized in the font of the chapel.[26]

Left: Ledbury map.

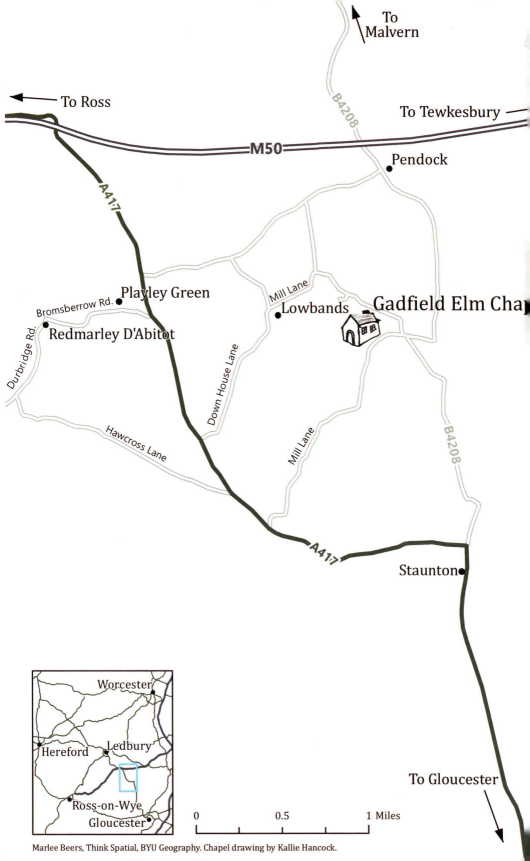

Marlee Beers, Think Spatial, BYU Geography. Chapel drawing by Kallie Hancock.

Top: Restored Gadfield Elm chapel. Right: Interior of restored Gadfield Elm chapel. (Photos by Carol Wilkinson.)

Gadfield Elm Chapel. On 4 March 1836, two of the United Brethren, Thomas Kington and John Benbow, both of the parish of Castle Froome, purchased the land known at the time as Gatfields Elm in the parish of Eldersfield for the sum of twenty five pounds, for a chapel for the use of the Society of the United Brethren.[27] In 1840, Elders Woodruff, Young, and Richards all spoke in the chapel and conducted conferences there. In September of 1840, former members of the United Brethren who had since joined the Church gave the Gadfield Elm chapel to The Church of Jesus Christ of Latter-day Saints. It was the first chapel the

Left: Gadfield Elm map.

Top: The restored well at Gadfield Elm chapel. Right: Stone in the restored Gadfield Elm chapel commemorating the original chapel. (Photos by Cynthia Doxey Green.)

Church could claim title to in Britain. In 1842, the chapel was sold to help finance emigration of Church members to America.[28] As the decades passed, the building fell into disrepair, until it was purchased and restored by local Church members in 1994 and given to the Church in 2004. (See description of the purchase and restoration of Gadfield Elm chapel earlier in this chapter.)

Hawcross. William Simmons was a member of the United Brethren who lived in Hawcross. On 8 April 1840, Wilford Woodruff and Thomas Kington preached at his home, and after the meeting, many requested baptism. As a "body of water [was] situated at the bottom of the garden," they got ready, assembled there,

Top: William Simmons home, Hawcross. Left: A pond in Hawcross near the home of William Simmons. (Photos by Cynthia Doxey Green.)

and the baptisms began. However, a group of individuals began to throw stones at Elder Woodruff, several of them striking him, so that the remainder of the baptisms had to be deferred. On this occasion, Job Smith received direct confirmation from Wilford Woodruff that the latter was an Apostle and had the authority to baptize. Job was later baptized by Thomas Kington on 18 May 1840, in Dymock.[29]

Currently there is no pond situated at the bottom of the garden of William Simmons's home on Hawcross Lane, but early maps show several small ponds near where William Simmons lived.

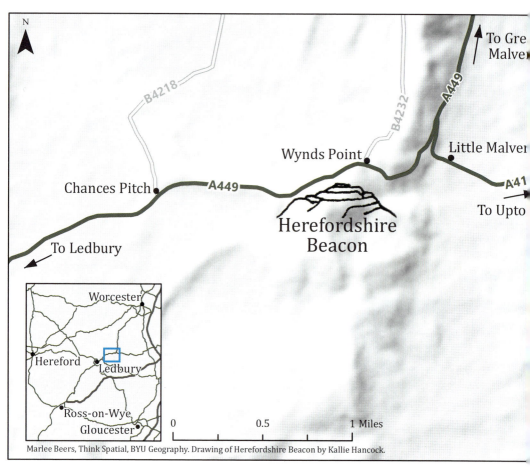

Above: Herefordshire Beacon map.

Baptisms might have taken place in the pond pictured, which is situated on Hawcross Lane approximately 300 meters west of the junction with Innerstone Lane, next to the road on the right hand side. It is on private property, but is visible from the road.

Herefordshire Beacon. This hill, part of the Malvern Hills area, was the site of an Iron Age hill fort (as shown in the photograph). Elder Woodruff would often retire here to contemplate the work of the restoration. On 20 May 1840, he went to Herefordshire Beacon accompanied by Brigham Young and Willard Richards; after they held a meeting, they decided to publish the Book of Mormon and a hymnbook in England. Brigham Young immediately traveled to Manchester to start the publications. Both John Benbow and Thomas Kington made financial contributions to help in accomplishing this goal.[30]

Top: Malvern Hills; Herefordshire Beacon on the far left. Right: Iron Age fort ruins on Herefordshire Beacon. (Photos by Cynthia Doxey Green.)

Conclusion

The historical events described in this book have shown that when Wilford Woodruff arrived at Hill Farm in March 1840, the ground had been prepared and the field was white, ready for the great harvest of souls that took place over the next few years. In addition to the missionary work of Elder Woodruff, other Apostles and missionaries labored in this critical endeavor to bring the message of the restored gospel to a people seeking further light and knowledge.

While records are inconsistent and incomplete, from the available information we know that many converts emigrated to the United States soon after baptism while others stayed behind for a time. Of those who did not leave with the early groups, some eventually emigrated, and others remained in England. As with any group of people who experience change, some converts remained faithful to their newfound beliefs and some drifted away from the Church. Wilford Woodruff called particular attention to the faithfulness of the converts who went to America. The events of this time of great harvest have provided a legacy for local Church members from the Three Counties, often joined by members from across England and across oceans, to engage in a variety of performances and activities to remind themselves and others of the roots of the kingdom they are continuing to build today.

Notes

1. "Country Information: United Kingdom," *Church News*, 1 February 2010.
2. "Country Information: United Kingdom," *Church News*, 1 February 2010.
3. "Country Information: United Kingdom," *Church News*, 1 February 2010; "A Heritage of Love: An Account of the History of the Church of Jesus Christ of Latter-day Saints in the Cheltenham, England Stake, Written and Researched by Members of the Cheltenham Stake, ed. Jennifer Mason," M274.2 C516c 1987, Church History Library, Salt Lake City, 24.
4. 1987 British Sesquicentennial Celebrations: Report of the British Isles Advisory Committee, March 1985, Office of the Europe Area Presidency, 4.
5. V. Ben Bloxham to James R. Moss, 21 March 1986.
6. James Moss and Lavelle Moss, *Historic Sites of The Church of Jesus Christ of Latter-day Saints in the British Isles* (Salt Lake City: Publishers Press, 1987).
7. David Cook, personal communication, Solihull, England, 2006.
8. Wayne Gardner, interview by Carol Wilkinson, 31 May 2005, Gloucestershire, England, in author's possession.
9. Simon Gibson, interview by Carol Wilkinson, 13 September 2006, Monmouth, in author's possession.
10 Carol Wilkinson, "The Restoration of the Gadfield Elm Chapel," in *Regional Studies in Latter-day Saint Church History: The British Isles*,

ed. Cynthia Doxey, Robert C. Freeman, Richard Neitzel Holzapfel, and Dennis A. Wright (Provo, UT: Religious Studies Center, 2007), 48–51.
11. Wayne Gardner, personal communication, 31 May 2005, Gloucestershire, England.
12. The Gadfield Elm Trust, *"The Gadfield Elm Trust"* (brochure, 1996).
13. Simon Gibson, interview by Carol Wilkinson, 11 August 2005.
14. Head, R. J. "Creating a Mormon Mecca in England: The Gadfield Elm Chapel," *Mormon Historical Studies* 7, no. 1–2 (2006): 93–94.
15. Jeffrey R. Holland, address at dedication of Gadfield Elm chapel, 23 April 2000, videotape in possession of author Carol Wilkinson, transcribed by Carol Wilkinson.
16. Wilkinson, "The Restoration of the Gadfield Elm Chapel," 55–57.
17. England Bristol Mission Alumni Website, http://www.mission.net/england/bristol/ensign/1998-03.html.
18. Joseph Walker, "English, U.S. Mormons join forces to create 'Faith,'" *Deseret News*, 3 August 2011.
19. "Truth Will Prevail! UK Mormons Honour British Heritage in The British Pageant," http://www.mormonnewsroom.org.uk/article/truth-will-prevail-uk-mormons-honour-british-heritage-in-the-british-pageant.
20. *"British Pageant: Truth Will Prevail,* 'Character Bios,'" http://britishpageant.org/character-bios/.
21. "Gadfield Elm at 175," http://bycommonconsent.com/2015/06/13/gadfield-elm-at-175-4/.
22. Allen, Esplin, and Whittaker, *Men with a Mission*, 124–25.
23. "Moorend Farm, Castle Frome, Herefordshire, to Sell By Auction," *Hereford Times*, 27 March 1841; Edward Ockey, "reminiscence and journal, (ca. 1857–58)," MS 11746, Church History Library, Salt Lake City, 1.
24. Woodruff, *Leaves from My Journal*, 131–32.
25. Allen, Esplin, and Whittaker, *Men with a Mission*, 199.
26. Wilford Woodruff, "Elder Woodruff's Letter [Concluded]," *Times and Seasons* 2, no. 9 (1 March 1841): 329.
27. V. Ben Bloxham, "Deed of Conveyance Between Thomas Shipton (as Grantor) of the One Part and John Benbow and Thomas Kington (as Grantees) of the Other Part Dated 4 March 1836," 9 October 1984,

1–2, transcript from a photographic copy of the copy in the Public Record Office, London.
28. "The History of Gadfield Elm Chapel," www.lds.org.uk/content/view/23/47/.
29. Job Taylor Smith, "Job Smith Autobiography, circa 1902," 1–2, MS 4809, Church History Library, Salt Lake City.
30. Allen, Esplin, and Whittaker, *Men with a Mission*, 151.

Appendix

IN ORDER TO PROVIDE MORE DETAILS about the research described in some of the chapters, this appendix explains the processes we used to identify the early converts from the Three Counties, their locations, and their families. A synopsis of the research is in the earlier chapters, but greater detail is provided here for the interested reader. We focus on how we created both the journal database and the branch database, some of which was explained in chapter 5. Next we describe the public records and the methods used to identify the individuals to learn more about their demographic circumstances and their later involvement with the Church, as explained in chapter 6. We add a more detailed analysis of the occupations found in the databases. The next section describes how we found many of the dwellings and licensed places for preaching associated with members of the United Brethren, as described in chapter 2. Finally, the appendix contains a table with the names of the branches and conferences of The Church of Jesus Christ of Latter-day Saints located within Gloucestershire, Worcestershire, and Herefordshire in existence during the nineteenth century.

Sources for Convert Names

We used several sources to find the individuals who joined the Church in the Three Counties in the mid-1800s. We began by creating two different databases. One database comes from journals of the missionaries and local converts, and one comes from Church membership records of the Frogmarsh and Bran Green Branches.

Journal Database. As mentioned in chapter 5, one of the most important sources for the names of converts from the early 1840s in the Three Counties was "Wilford Woodruff's Baptismal Record 1840: W. Woodruff's list of the number baptized in Herefordshire England 1840."[1] In order to be sure that we had correctly written the names in our database, we studied both the copy of Woodruff's own handwriting along with Scott G. Kenney's published transcription of Wilford Woodruff's journals. Additionally, we used the resource of another transcription of the notebook found in a series of five articles written by Jay Greaves Burrup called "150 Years Ago: A Look Back at Wilford Woodruff and the West Midland Mormons of 1840," published in the *Herefordshire Family History Society Journal* from July 1990 to October 1993.[2] In these articles, Burrup combined the daily journal entries with the names listed in the notebook of baptisms so that the reader can read Wilford Woodruff's daily activities, at the same time seeing the names of those who were baptized each day. Burrup also identified many of the individuals listed with some birth, marriage, and death information, along with some family relationships. Because he was using the records available at that time in the Family History Library, he was not able to identify as many people as we were, in part because the records in the 1980s and 1990s were not automated as they are today. Most of his identifications were correct and helpful to us as we began our research.

At the end of the notebook, Wilford Woodruff stated that 542 individuals were baptized in the area by 22 June 1840,[3] the last day he made notations of converts' names. He mentioned that 242 of that number had been baptized by "Elders Young[,] Richards[,] Kington[,] and others."[4] Although he recorded the number of baptisms being 542, he named only 479 people baptized from 6 March to 22 June 1840. To our database we added 30 more names of people he met, stayed with, or ordained to priesthood offices that he mentioned in his journal prior to leaving the area permanently in 1841.[5] We also assumed that if he described someone as "Brother" or "Sister," the individual probably had been baptized beforehand.

The other names in this database came from the journals, diaries, and reminiscences we found of the missionaries or local members from the early 1840s. Baptismal dates in the database ranged from 6 March 1840 to 5 February 1843, when the last of the missionaries for whom we have journals left the Three Counties area.[6] There were 98 individuals without baptismal dates, with another 24 having just a year or month listed. For example, Thomas Steed named several family members who were baptized, including aunts and uncles, but he did not provide a date of baptism.[7] The documents from which we found convert names included journals, reminiscences, or autobiographies located in the Church History Library, Brigham Young University's L. Tom Perry Special Collections or in published works.[8] Like Wilford Woodruff, many of the missionaries recorded the names of converts they baptized, along with dates and places of baptism. Although we also examined some secondary sources and biographies to clarify information about an individual, no name was included in the database unless we also found the name in one of the primary documents.[9] In all, the journal database contained the names of 775 individuals.

Branch Database from the Record of Members, The Church of Jesus Christ of Latter-day Saints. As mentioned in chapter 5, there were numerous branches in the Three Counties created during the early 1840s, but actual membership records of the Church from that time period only exist for a relatively small number of branches. Information about the branches in existence in mid-nineteenth century Britain is available from the *British Mission Manuscript History and Historical Reports, 1841–1971.*[10] In the early twentieth century, assistant Church historian Andrew Jenson and his staff at the Church Historian's Office scoured published records like the *Millennial Star* from Britain, *The Times and Seasons* in Nauvoo, and the *Deseret News* in Salt Lake City for information regarding the history of the British Mission. Jenson also traveled to Britain to learn more of the history of the branches from local inhabitants who may have had knowledge of the beginnings of the Church in their areas. He and his staff then transcribed their findings and added to the history of the local units they had identified, creating the list of branches that is in the *Manuscript History*.[11]

According to the *Manuscript History*, there were over 120 branches established at some time during the nineteenth century in the Three Counties. Most of those branches ceased to exist after fifteen to twenty years, with only a few lasting until the beginning of the twentieth century. Membership records currently are available on microfilm at the Church History Library or the Family History Library for only thirty-three of the congregations in the Three Counties. At the end of the appendix, there is a table of branches in the Three Counties with microfilm numbers and the coverage of dates found in the records.

There may be several reasons for the lack of membership records now available. One reason is because the membership records may not actually have been created at the time the branches were organized. The records vary in their completeness and accuracy. We first looked at several different branches in the Cheltenham Conference records and found that the same people were listed many times in the same branch record book, almost as if the branch clerk periodically rewrote the information for every individual in the branch. The names and ordinance dates in the records do not have an alphabetical or chronological order, perhaps because they were written at a later date as branch members recollected their baptisms. In other words, the branch clerk perhaps began recording the members and their ordinances in the later 1840s, and could only ask about the ordinances of those individuals who were still living in the area. Those who had been baptized earlier and emigrated soon thereafter are not included on the branch records, even though the records do show some baptismal dates from as early as 1840.

An earlier research study provides another possible explanation for why many branches listed in the *Manuscript History* do not currently have membership records available.[12] The study compared Church membership records and the 1851 ecclesiastical census in Britain, finding that while Church meetings recorded on the census might have taken place in several different homes or meeting places, the records of the branch sometimes were centralized in one place. By finding the addresses in the 1851 population census of the Church members listed in the branch records and comparing them with the "meeting places" listed on the 1851 ecclesiastical census, the researchers showed that although the members' records were held in one place, the branch was broken into smaller groups, meeting in several places at the same time. A similar phenomenon may have occurred in the Three Counties where several of the branches or meeting places kept their records together in one central location. Thus, in looking for the records for one of the branches listed in the *Manuscript History*, we might find that their membership records are contained within the records of another branch.

Another possible reason for the small percentage of membership records during this time period is the loss or destruction of the records before they were able to make it to Church headquarters in Nauvoo or Utah. If a branch leader emigrated but could not carry the membership records, they may have been left for others who perhaps were not as diligent in keeping the records. A further study of the 1851 ecclesiastical census in Britain showed that seventy-six meeting places recorded in the 1851 census had no corresponding membership records available today.[13] Evidently, the lack of Church records was a countrywide phenomenon, not just limited to the Three Counties.

Given that less than a fourth of the branches in the Three Counties listed in the *British Mission Manuscript History* have available membership records at the Family History Library, we chose to do a case study of two branches: the Bran Green Branch and the Frogmarsh Branch. These branches encompassed the area in and around the Gadfield Elm chapel, which was originally built by the United Brethren but was deeded to the Church in 1840 when the majority of the United Brethren were converted.[14] Bran Green, an area in the parish of Newent, is about five miles southwest of Gadfield Elm and was the meeting place for a congregation of the United Brethren, and later a branch of the Church.[15] The Frogmarsh Branch was first mentioned during the 15 March 1841 Bran Green and Gadfield Elm Conference meeting.[16] Frogmarsh is an area in the Eldersfield parish, about two miles northeast of the Gadfield Elm chapel. These two branches coexisted for several years, according to the *British Mission*

Manuscript History, but the last mention of Bran Green Branch was in 1848, while the Frogmarsh Branch continued reporting as part of the Cheltenham Conference until 1884.[17] The two branches' records appear to have become one after the Bran Green Branch dissolved, because many of the members listed in the records in Bran Green Branch are duplicated in the Frogmarsh Branch. The Church membership records for these two branches cover the period from 1840 to 1856.[18] After deleting the duplicate records listed on the branch records, the database for these branches shows 118 unique individuals in the membership record between 1840 and 1856.

Description of Public Records

Because we wanted to know more about the converts' demographic circumstances and possible emigration, we searched several types of records that would provide information regarding their gender, ages, occupations, social status, and emigration. The following is a description of each of the different types of records we used and where we accessed them:

Censuses. Although governments take censuses for reasons other than genealogical purposes, they are some of the most useful and accessible tools for historians who want to know more about individuals living in the nineteenth and twentieth centuries. England's censuses took place every ten years, starting in 1841. The 1841 census asked for names, gender, ages, occupations, and whether the individual was born in the county in which he or she was living at the time of the census. The ages listed in the 1841 census are not necessarily correct because the enumerator rounded down to the nearest five- or ten-year age if the individual was over sixteen years old. The 1851 and 1861 censuses added more information, such as the individual's age at last birthday, the relationship to the head of household, marital status, and birth parish.

The United States federal census also occurred every ten years, beginning in 1790, but only the heads of household, gender, and approximate ages of other individuals in the household were listed through the 1840 census. Beginning in 1850, the census included the names, ages, and gender of each individual in the household, along with occupation, value of real estate, and state or country of birth. Unfortunately, none of the United States censuses before 1880 provided the relationship to the head of household, which meant that we sometimes had to rely on Family Tree or other records to know how people in the household were related.

The 1841 census was helpful in identifying the individuals in the databases if the converts were still living in England when the census was taken on 6 June 1841. Unfortunately, a large number of the early Church members from the Three Counties emigrated in late 1840 through early 1841, so they are not enumerated on the census in England. Nor are they enumerated in the United States census because that census was taken in June 1840. However, if the converts continued living in the United States, we were often able to find them in the 1850 census, either in Utah, Illinois, or other places in between. In identifying the people in the databases, we searched the 1841 census first, then the 1851 and 1861 censuses to learn if the people stayed in the same area for those twenty years. If we did not find them in the later censuses, we looked for them in the United States censuses in 1850 and 1860. All of the censuses from both countries are searchable on the internet at FamilySearch.org or Ancestry.com.

Mormon Migration. The website *Mormon Migration* includes a database of voyages where Mormon immigrants traveled to the United States from 1840 through 1923. Included on the website are accounts of the voyages, culled from official ship records along with journals, diaries, and reminiscences of some of the travelers. Unfortunately, as noted in chapter 5, a number of voyages have no passenger lists currently available for searching. The website sometimes includes identifying information such as names, place of origin, family members traveling together, ages, and occupation. In searching this website, we were sometimes able to find several related families or neighbors from the Three Counties traveling together on the same ship. This website is mormonmigration.lib.byu.edu.

Mormon Pioneer Overland Travel. This website brings together information of the Mormon pioneer companies and other related records for over sixty thousand people who traveled from various places heading for the Salt Lake Valley from 1847 to 1868. The website contains records of the companies' rosters and information about the travelers based on diaries, journals, and other documents. The data about the individuals on the rosters often include names, ages, individuals traveling together, the company they were in, along with birth and death information where possible. This database is online at history.lds.org/overlandtravels.

Index of Civil Registration of Births, Marriages, and Deaths in England. Beginning in 1837, the government of England and Wales required that all births, marriages, and deaths should be registered with the local registrar. These records provide vital information, including parents' names, birth, marriage, and death dates and places. The actual certificates are accessible only by ordering them from the General Registry Office and paying a fee for each certificate. However, the index to these certificates is available online at freebmd.org.uk. While the index does not give exact dates and places for the vital events (only the quarter and registration district are listed), often one can find enough information to correctly identify the individual. As we searched the index, we often found converts' marriage and death records in England.

FamilySearch.org. FamilySearch.org is the official source for family history research provided by The Church of Jesus Christ of Latter-day Saints. While it contains many primary sources which have been indexed and are available for viewing (such as the census and other records), it also has a compiled genealogy on Family Tree. Family Tree combines data from sources like Church membership records, temple ordinance records, along with ancestral information submitted by individuals in the Church and the community. While there is much useful information found on Family Tree, there is always the possibility that the research submitted by individuals is faulty. As we researched Family Tree, we were careful not to accept everything recorded there without comparing it to other original records we searched.

Even though we knew that some of the data on Family Tree could be incorrect, it was still useful in helping us establish family relationships among the early converts. Family Tree often showed birth, marriage and death dates, family relationships, and baptismal dates that corresponded with the information we had on our databases. When we found such information, we were more confident that we had identified the people on our databases correctly. Sometimes Family Tree also provided vital information that helped us verify that the individuals emigrated and died in Nauvoo, Iowa, or Utah, especially because very few vital records exist for those areas during the 1840s to 1860s. Another important aspect of Family Tree is that many descendants have uploaded photos, stories, letters, or diaries that may not be in any other repository.

While the accuracy or validity of the information was something we kept in mind when looking at Family Tree, one of the reasons we used this source was because it helped us answer one of the questions we had about whether the convert stayed active in the Church. For example, when we found the converts on Family Tree connected to other family members, and with death dates listed in the United States, particularly Nauvoo, Iowa, Utah, or Idaho, we had confidence those individuals emigrated and stayed faithful to the Church for the rest of their lives. For many of those converts, their baptismal dates corresponded with what we already knew from the database, and their temple ordinances often occurred during their lifetime. Presumably, not only were they active in the Church but some of their children and other descendants also were members of the Church. We were able to make these conclusions because of the vast amount of information about these early converts shown on Family Tree.

On the other hand, when we found the converts' names along with only one or two events or relationships listed in Family Tree, we assumed that the information was probably community indexed or extracted from other records such as parish registers in England. As we looked further on FamilySearch.org, we sometimes found that a christening record or marriage record had been indexed for Family Tree. In these situations, we usually found that the dates for baptism and temple ordinances were more recent than forty years ago, not from the 1800s. The individuals from our databases with this small amount of information on Family Tree most likely joined the Church, but they probably did not emigrate, nor did their descendants remain actively involved in the Church. We cannot assume that they were not faithful based on this information, but we see that their names did not remain on Church records through the years.

Convert Identification in Public Records

Names, Ages, Marital Status, and Gender. Unfortunately, we encountered several difficulties as we attempted to identify the converts from the journal database in other public records. One of the foremost problems was that while most journal writers provided converts' names and often the date and place of baptism, they seldom recorded other identifying information. The journals did not record whether the individuals were male or female, old or young, married or single, or even if they lived in the area where they were baptized. For example, James Palmer wrote, "Following is a list of names of Persons that I have baptized into the church at different times and different places and I much regret to day that I did not record their names in full,"[19] He recorded several surnames, calling them "Brother" or "Sister" and provided very few baptismal dates or places. Clearly, identifying the correct "Brother Boulter" living in Herefordshire, Worcestershire, or Gloucestershire is practically impossible because there are so many males with the last name Bolter or Boulter. While preaching the gospel, James Palmer wandered through all Three Counties and Monmouthshire in Wales. Because he did not give a date for Brother Boulter's baptism, we cannot find a baptismal place, which could have provided hints for identification.

Wilford Woodruff was usually careful about writing the name of the convert, along with the date and place of baptism, but there was rarely an indication of gender, age, or marital status. For example, Wilford Woodruff recorded that Francis Hill was baptized in May 1840 at Keysend Street in the parish of Berrow, Worcestershire. With no other identifying information, the following questions arise: Was Francis a woman or a man? Was Francis an eighty-year-old or a teenager? If she was a woman, was Hill her maiden name or her married name? Did Francis live in Berrow, or did he or she travel several miles to hear Wilford

Woodruff preach before being baptized? Did Francis Hill die or emigrate before the 1841 census? There were many individuals named Francis Hill on the census, Mormon Migration Index, and FamilySearch Family Tree, so we were unable to answer these questions about gender, age, and emigration. When converts' names were common, such as Ann Jones or William Morris, identification was difficult unless there was some other information included in a journal.

A rather humorous problem of identifying the individuals whose names were recorded in missionary journals came because of the lack of standardized spelling. People often spelled the way they heard someone speak. Wilford Woodruff was an American listening to people from southwestern England, many of whom may have had varying accents. Some people in that area drop the "H" sound at the beginning of a word, saying that they live in 'erifordshire, rather than Herefordshire. In Woodruff's *Baptismal Record*, he listed the baptisms of John and Mary Allard and John Arvart in the parish of Colwall, Herefordshire. In searching the 1841 census, we found John and Mary Hallard and John Harford all living in Colwall. Apparently Wilford Woodruff wrote exactly what he heard the people say, and they probably dropped the "H" sound at the beginning of their names.

In rare instances, the missionary wrote something noteworthy about the individual, such as when the person was the parent or grandparent of someone else recently baptized, or if the person was much older or younger than the average convert. For example, on 4 April 1840, Wilford Woodruff wrote that he "baptized 11 women at Gadfields [sic] Elm & in the number was three generations a Daughter, Mother, & Grandmother. One of 8 years of age."[20] This helpful information would suggest that if two women baptized that day had the same surname, they would probably be the eight-year-old daughter and her mother; a third woman, probably with a different last name, would be the grandmother. Sadly, three pairs of women with the same last names are listed on that day in the baptismal record, and there are no ages for any of them. It is impossible to know which of the eleven women baptized that day are the three-generational group based on the journal alone.

After discussing the difficulties in finding these individuals on other records, one may wonder whether we could be certain in identifying *any* of the individuals in our database. Surprisingly, we were able to identify the vast majority of the people listed in the database on at least one of the other records we searched, which included the census, FamilySearch Family Tree, Mormon Migration Index, Mormon Pioneer Overland Travel, or on civil registration in England. In the journal database of 775 people, 73 percent of the individuals were identified on at least one of the other records, while 26 percent were not identified on any other record. Eleven of the names were categorized as "possibly identified" because their names were found on one or two other records, but we were not sure if they were the same people because of differences in some of the information.[21]

Fortunately, the membership records for the Bran Green and Frogmarsh Branches often had more identifying information available. Some of the branch record books actually had columns asking for parents' names, the converts' birth dates and places, age at baptism, and places of residence. The branch records contained parents' names for 63 of the 118 people in the database, as well as some kind of age or birth information for 96 individuals. Such information was very helpful in identifying the converts in other records because it provided maiden names for married females, along with birth years to help narrow down our choices in other records. For example, there are three women named Ann Brooks in the Frogmarsh Branch records, all of whom were baptized in 1840. The membership record gives the age at baptism for two of them and includes the parents' names and birth year for one of those. The birth information made it possible to identify those two women. We could not identify the third Ann Brooks because we did not know her age or whether Brooks is her maiden or married name.

We went through the same process of identifying the individuals from the branches on other records as we did with the journal database. The rate of identifying individuals in the branch database from other sources was quite high at 86 percent, with only 11 percent not identified at all, and 3 percent as possible identifications. We used both the journal database and the branch database to examine the information we could gather about the converts from the Three Counties.

Place-Names. One of the best ways to identify the converts was by looking first at the 1841 census. We assumed that the baptismal places were within walking distance of the convert's homes. While some people might have had another form of transportation, the majority of the converts probably did not. However, "walking distance" in that time period could possibly be up to ten miles. Wilford Woodruff wrote that he walked many miles between preaching places, but probably most of the converts did not walk as far as he did to the meetings they attended. We looked for individuals living within a radius of four or five miles from the baptismal place.

The "United Brethren Preachers' Plan" provides information about the places for many of the meetings. The meetings with the Latter-day Saint missionaries were held in homes or barns previously licensed for preaching by the United Brethren and in easy reach of the local members. The preachers' plan shows when and where meetings were to take place during the months of April, May, and June, with the assigned preachers listed. Wilford Woodruff wrote in his journal that on 10 May he met at Jonathan Lucy's home in Colwall in the morning, traveled to Pale House (Thomas Steed's parents' home in Great Malvern) in the afternoon, and then preached that evening at Benjamin Holland's home, north of Malvern Hill.[22] His eight-mile route follows the preachers' plan already established for that day. On the plan there was a meeting scheduled in Colwall in the morning, one at 2 p.m. at Pale House, and one at Malvern Hill at 6 p.m.[23] While the missionaries may have traveled long distances to their appointments, the people attending the meetings probably lived near the meeting and baptismal places.

Many of the place-names listed on the preachers' plan and in missionary journals were not parish names, but were homes, farms, or hamlets within a parish. For example, many people were baptized in Keysend Street or in Stokes Lane or in Hawcross, none of which are parish names. We used very detailed Ordnance Survey maps that are on a scale of 1¼ inch to 1 mile and found many of the hamlets or farms on the maps. However, the current Ordnance Survey maps only show county boundaries, not parish boundaries. For parish boundary information, we used FamilySearch's historical maps of *England and Wales Jurisdictions, 1851*, which are online at maps.familysearch.org. On this website, in addition to showing parish boundaries, the boundaries can be overlaid on old Ordnance Survey maps showing topography, some farm names, hamlets, and other areas within the parish. Using these tools, we found Keysend Street in Berrow, Worcestershire; Stokes Lane in Avenbury, Herefordshire; and Hawcross in Redmarley D'Abitot, Worcestershire.

Another service from this website lists the names of parishes within a five-mile radius of the parish of choice. With the location information in hand, we could then search the 1841 census for the names of the converts, looking for people that lived within a five-mile radius of their place of baptism. If the name was quite common and there were several individuals within the area, we were not able to identify the individual. When we did find individuals on the census, we used clues from the census for birth year and household members' names to look for the same individuals in Family Tree or the other records. If we found them in the other records with the same name and age, we assumed that we had identified the individual correctly.

Comparison of Journal and Branch Databases. Although we treated the journal and branch databases as separate entities in our analyses, there was some overlap between them. Because the Bran Green and Frogmarsh areas are very near Gadfield Elm, several of the early converts baptized by Wilford Woodruff or his associates in the area around Gadfield Elm chapel are also listed in the branch records. Most of the baptism dates from 1840 in the branch database actually listed the person who baptized them, among whom were Wilford Woodruff, Willard Richards, Thomas Kington, John Gailey, and James Palmer, all missionaries that we know were preaching at that time in the Three Counties.

We think the branch records were not kept as early as 1840 because, in spite of some overlap, there are relatively few people listed on both of the databases. We know that the journal database is not complete because there were many priesthood holders and missionaries baptizing in the area who did not keep journals.

If the branch records were maintained from the very beginning of the branch organization, we would expect to see more people on both databases. As we examined the people listed on the journal database who were baptized in the parishes surrounding Frogmarsh and Bran Green (Eldersfield, Redmarley, or Newent), we found that those who emigrated before the mid-1840s were not listed on the membership records. However, if an individual from the journal database either died in England or emigrated after the mid-1840s, they were often listed in the branch record as well. This finding lends credence to the idea that branch records were not kept until after the mid-1840s, at which time individuals were recollecting their baptismal dates. There were twenty-seven people listed on both databases. Where there are inconsistencies in dates and places of baptism, we assumed that the dates in the missionary journals would be correct because they were recorded at the time of the event, rather than being recollected by an individual later.

Identification of Occupations and Social Status

In order to learn more about the social standing of the converts, we turned to a website called *A Vision of Britain Through Time* (www.visionofbritain.org.uk). This website provides statistical atlases for a variety of issues such as social structure, population density, and industry and agriculture, based on the information from England's censuses from 1841 to 2001. With respect to social structure, the website used five categories or classes of occupations of working-age males to develop maps showing how these categories varied in English counties over time.[24] The atlases are created for each year of the census, providing the percentages for each occupation group by county. We used the 1841 occupation atlas to inform us regarding the typical occupations in the Three Counties at that time because these counties were fairly rural, as compared to Lancashire or other counties where there were large groups of Latter-day Saints.

Using the occupations of adult men in the censuses, the atlases divided the professions into five categories according to their social status or income. Class 1 signifies middle-class professionals, while class 2 included other middle-class occupations like managers and farmers. Class 3 is a mixture of middle-class and working-class people because it includes clerical workers and artisans or skilled laborers—such as blacksmiths, masons, weavers, or carpenters. Many such artisans could actually have higher earnings than clerical workers, but they were considered "working-class" because of the manual aspect of their work, in spite of their better income. Classes 4 and 5 constituted the lower working class, covering semiskilled and unskilled laborers, including farm laborers and domestic servants. The atlases combined classes 1 and 2, or all the middle-class occupations, and classes 4 and 5, or the lower-class occupations.

One of the reasons we used these atlases to compare the occupations in our databases was because of previous research stating the early Church members in Britain were generally poor urban unskilled laborers.[25] Because the Three Counties are more rural in nature, we wanted to compare the occupations of the converts in our databases to the occupations most likely found in the Three Counties. In our research, we found a number of farmers and artisans among the converts, with just over half of the people in the journal database being unskilled laborers. We wanted to know if those findings showed a very different group joining the Church in the Three Counties in comparison to converts in other parts of Britain, or if it was the effect of rural counties versus industrialized counties. The statistical atlases helped us compare our database findings with the social class structure in the Three Counties, showing that the early converts were a lot like their neighbors in terms of their occupations: a lot of agricultural laborers, a number of artisans and skilled laborers, and a few farmers and middle-class workers.

The overall results from our research are in chapter 5. Only 466 individuals in the journal database had some kind of identifiable occupation in the family. We used occupations listed on the 1841 census where possible. If individuals left the country before the census, we used the occupations on the *Mormon Migration* website if they were listed. Over one hundred people were excluded from the analysis because of the following reasons (1) they died or left England prior to the 1841 census,

(2) they could not be located on that census or on passenger lists (although they were located in later censuses), or (3) their occupations were either illegible or not recorded.[26] We did not use occupations listed in later censuses or in later ship passenger lists because we wanted to see the social status of the people near the time they actually joined the Church in the early 1840s.

Generally, females were less likely to have occupations listed in the census. When a woman had no occupation and was in the same household with an individual who appeared to be her husband, we recorded her occupation as "wife of" the husband's occupation. Similarly, when someone younger than eighteen on the census appeared to be living with parents or other close relations, we recorded their occupation as "child of" the parents' occupation, unless there was a specific occupation listed for the child. We used these designations for wives and children because we presumed that a wife or child of a farmer would be living a different lifestyle than a wife or child of an agricultural laborer. We viewed the people as part of a family, rather than as separate individuals. Although most of the individuals with occupations listed on the records were men, fifty-nine of the identified females had occupations such as servant, laundress, dressmaker, governess, glove maker, or agricultural laborer. There was even one female farmer. Unlike the statistical atlases, we included the occupations for women along with the men.

In the journal database, we found that 13 percent of the people could have been considered middle class, with occupations such as farmers, governesses, or ministers. Almost one-third (29 percent) of the people in the database were skilled laborers, such as shoemakers, brickmasons, or carpenters. As was expected, a large proportion of the individuals in the database—58 percent—were unskilled laborers, with the biggest occupation being agricultural laborers. The branch database only had one farmer, and 71 percent of the members were agricultural laborers or servants. The skilled laborers in the branch database came from similar occupations as those in the journal database, such as carpenter, shoemaker, baker, miner, and saddler. One unique occupation in the branch database was a woman who was a midwife.

The statistical atlas on *A Vision of Britain* shows that the combined classes 1 and 2 comprised between 15 to 20 percent of the working males in the Three Counties in 1841. There were 32 to 47 percent of the males who worked in occupations in class 3 (the skilled laborers and clerical workers). Finally, 40 to 49 percent of males in the Three Counties were in classes 4 and 5, or the unskilled laborers. The reason for the large ranges in these percentages mentioned here is because each county had different percentages. For example, the middle-class occupations comprise less than 15 percent of working males in Worcestershire, but 17 to 20 percent in Herefordshire. In Worcestershire, the atlas shows 42 to 47 percent of the occupations in class 3, but Herefordshire only had 32 to 36 percent of males working in that same class. Classes 4 and 5 were more similar for all three counties, probably because many of the men were agricultural laborers.

When we compared the statistical atlas to our databases, we found that the journal database reflects something of the general make-up of workers in the Three Counties, while the branch records show a much poorer group of people. Almost three-fourths (71 percent) of the individuals in the branch worked in unskilled occupations, much higher than the statistical atlas of 1841 shows, with only one individual that could be viewed as middle class. The journal database does have a higher percentage of unskilled manual laborers than the average listed on the statistical atlas in the Three Counties (58 percent versus 49 percent), but the difference is not quite as marked as that of the branch database. The percentage of skilled artisans (29 percent) in the journal database is close to the lower range of that class (32 percent to 47 percent) found in the Three Counties generally. With 13 percent of the journal database coming from the middle class, the rate is not far off from the Three Counties percentage for classes 1 and 2 of 15 percent to 20 percent.

We did not statistically analyze the comparisons of occupations among the converts and the average man in the Three Counties, but the percentages show that many of these early converts in the Three Counties were fairly similar to their neighbors in terms of social status. Previous studies of early British converts looked at more urban and industrialized areas such as

Lancashire, which may be why they found so many poor laborers among the converts.²⁷ The similarities between the converts and their neighbors may account for the fact that the average converts in our databases were not poor urban workers but rather they had a variety of occupations, reflecting the nature of the local economy in the Three Counties. They may have been different from Church members in northern England simply because of the economic differences between rural southwestern England and the more industrialized north.

Method of Identifying Homes of the United Brethren

In identifying the homes of the United Brethren (a process briefly described in chapter 2), we first used the names of individuals found on the "United Brethren Preachers' Plan" and in the journal of Wilford Woodruff. We did not attempt to find everyone in our databases. Rather, we concentrated on a few names that seemed somewhat prominent among the United Brethren. Most of the individuals we searched had licensed places for preaching for the United Brethren.

Many years ago, V. Ben Bloxham conducted research in the local county record offices in Herefordshire, Worcestershire, and Gloucestershire, identifying many of the individuals who had applied for licenses for preaching in their homes or barns or other buildings. We are indebted to his efforts in identifying the licensees and the names of the individuals who lived in the homes. After he passed away in 2005, we were given access to his notes and files, all of which provided us insight during the initial steps of our research of the converts from the Three Counties. Unfortunately, although Bloxham compiled a list of licensed places and had many copies of the licenses, we found no source information about where he located the licenses, other than the county record offices he visited. We began our search for the homes by using Bloxham's list of licensed places to preach, which included the name of the licensee as well as the name of the occupier of the home if it was different. For example, Thomas Kington was the licensee for several places, but those same homes had other occupiers. Because he was the superintendent of the

United Brethren, he obviously was the one who instigated and paid for licenses for a variety of properties.

We went to the county records office in Herefordshire, Worcestershire, and Gloucestershire where we searched the tithe apportionment schedules from the 1830s and 1840s for the names of the United Brethren members listed as occupiers of the licensed places for preaching. These tithe apportionment schedules provided numbers corresponding to the homes and fields on the tithe survey maps for each area. We were able to identify the homes and property on the tithe maps.[28] We then compared the tithe maps to the detailed Six-inch Ordnance Survey maps (6 inches to 1 mile) that were located in the county record offices and located the homes that we found on the tithe maps. The final step was to locate the homes on modern Ordnance Survey maps that showed 1¼ inch to 1 mile. Using these detailed maps to guide us, we then traveled to the locations and photographed the homes or fields where the homes probably stood at one time. Obviously, some of the homes on the present-day sites are newer than the 1840s, but many are from that period. The homes show that many of the United Brethren who had licensed their homes for preaching did not live in hovels.

Identification of Nineteenth-Century Church Units in the Three Counties

We created a table of all the branches or conferences that we could find from two main sources: the *British Mission Manuscript History and Historical Reports, 1841–1971* and the Family History Library's microfilm collection of Church membership records. We decided to include only the names of branches that began in the nineteenth century because branch boundaries may have changed in the twentieth century due to easier transportation, which allowed people to travel farther for church meetings.

The number of branches in the Three Counties fluctuated during the nineteenth century, as mentioned in chapter 6. Branches were formed as missionaries traveled throughout the area, baptizing and creating small branches as they went. As the members of the branch either moved from the area or emigrated to America, many of the branches were dissolved. Sometimes, as in the case of Frogmarsh and Bran Green, the branches, or their records, may have been combined with others and the names of the branches lost. As we studied the branch histories in the *Manuscript History*, we found that many of the branches on record had fewer than fifty members, and some had fewer than twenty. These small branches would have been very difficult to carry on after one or two families emigrated. In chapter 6 we talked about how the changes in branch boundaries may have affected the activity of Church members in the area, especially if they had to walk several miles to attend church after their local branch was dissolved. We created a list of the branch locations and the dates of organization to help us understand more about the development of the Church in the Three Counties.

The accompanying table shows the names of the branches or conferences in the Three Counties as listed in the *Manuscript History* and the membership records in the Family History Library. The Garway Conference was especially lacking in information. Although the conference was created in 1841 with several branches, the *Manuscript History* mentioned only two branches in Herefordshire: Garway and Ewyas Harold.

The table is an alphabetical listing of the names of the branches as found in the various records, along with their parish and county jurisdiction, if known. Then, we added in the information we could find from the Family History Library Catalog (online at FamilySearch.org) and the branches listed in the *British Mission Manuscript History* (online at churchhistorycatalog.lds.org). Quite often the branch names were the names of small hamlets or villages, so the parish location, conference, and county provide a better sense of the location of the branches. We could not locate some of the branches. On the table, the Family History Library film number and dates refer to the microfilm numbers in the Family History Library, along with the dates of coverage for the membership records held there. The *Manuscript History* dates and the Church History Library Catalog number refer to the dates the *Manuscript History* provides for the branches and the Church History Library Catalog number where one can find the branch histories.

222 The Field Is White

Nineteenth-Century Church Units in the Three Counties

Unit Name	Parish	Conference	County	FHL Film #	FHL dates	Manuscript History Dates	CHL Catalog Number*
Apperley Branch	Apperley	Gadfield Elm	Gloucestershire	86976, 86991	1840–1847	1840–1846	LR 10717 2
Ashfield Branch	Leigh?	Frome's Hill	Worcestershire			1840–1842	LR 1140 2
Avening Branch	Avening	Chalford Hill	Gloucestershire			1847–1848	LR 1140 2
Ball's Gate Branch	Leinthall Earls	Mars Hill	Herefordshire			1841–1847	LR 1140 2
Bishops Frome Branch	Bishop's Frome	Frome's Hill	Herefordshire			Jun 1840–Mar 1841	LR 1140 2
Bran Green Branch	Newent	Gadfield Elm	Gloucestershire	86998	1840–1856	1840–1848	LR 1140 2
Bringstye Common Branch	Whitbourne	Frome's Hill	Herefordshire			1841–1847	LR 1140 2
Bristol Branch		Frome's Hill	Gloucestershire			1841–1962	LR 1136 2
Bristol Conference	Worcester St. John			86999, 86991, 86987	1840–1876, 1894–1912, 1896–1947	not listed	
Broad Heath Branch		Frome's Hill	Worcestershire			1841	LR 1140 2
Bromsgrove Branch	Bromsgrove	Worcestershire	Worcestershire			1834–1848, 1913	LR 1140 2
Bromyard Branch	Bromyard	Frome's Hill	Worcestershire			1841–1842	LR 1140 2
Bury Hill Branch	?	?	Herefordshire			not listed	LR 1140 2
Bushbank Branch	King's Pyon	Frome's Hill	Herefordshire			1841–1842	LR 1140 2
Caison Hill Branch	?	Bristol	Gloucestershire			not listed	
Cam Branch	Cam	Bristol	Gloucestershire			1843–1854	LR 1140 2
Caudle-Green Branch	Brimpsfield	Cheltenham	Gloucestershire	86990, 86991	1841–1878, 1842–1856	not listed	
Chalford Branch	Chalford	Chalford Hill	Gloucestershire	86990, 86991	1842–1875, 1843–1855	1849–1865	LR 1590 2
Chalford Hill Branch	Chalford	Chalford Hill	Gloucestershire	86990	1842–1875	1845–1847	LR 1591 2
Chalford Hill Conference							

Name	Location	County		Dates		Reference
Cheltenham Branch		Gloucestershire	86986, 86991		1840–1982	LR 1630 2
Cheltenham Conference	Cheltenham	Gloucestershire	86991	1841–1901, 1840–1898	1842–1898	LR 1631 2
Chosen Branch	Apperley?	Gloucestershire	86992, 86991	1840–1901	1852–1855	LR 1140 2
Church Down Branch	Churchdown	Gloucestershire		1851–1852	1855	LR 1140 2
Cirencester Branch	Cirencester	Gloucestershire	86992		1852–1965	LR 1739 11
Cliffords Mine (Mesne) Branch	Newent	Gloucestershire	86992, 86991	1842–1855	1852–1856	LR 1140 2
Clifton-on-Teme Branch	Clifton-on-Teme	Worcestershire		1840–1856	Sep 1840–Mar 1841	LR 1140 2
Colwell Branch (Colwall)	Colwall	Herefordshire			1840–1847	LR 1140 2
Compton Branch	Compton Abdale	Gloucestershire	86992	1841–1893, 1841–1856	1847–1891	LR 1140 2
Coomesmore Branch	Byton	Herefordshire			1841–1842	LR 1140 2
Cradley Branch	Cradley	Herefordshire			1846, 1879	LR 1140 2
Cranham Branch	Cranham	Gloucestershire			Sep 1840	LR 1140 2
Crossway Green Branch	?	Worcestershire			1846–1848	LR 1140 2
Crowcroft (Crowcut) Branch	Leigh	Worcestershire			1840–1841	LR 1140 2
Deerhurst Branch	Deerhurst	Gloucestershire			1840–1844	LR 1140 2
Dinmore Hill Branch	Hope Under Dinmore	Herefordshire			1840	LR 1140 2
Dudley Branch	Dudley	Worcestershire	86995	1856–1910	not listed	
Dunsclose Branch	Mathon St James	Herefordshire			1840–1842	LR 1140 2
Durley Common Branch—at times Dealy or Darla	Tarrington	Herefordshire			1840–1841	LR 1140 2
Durlow Common Branch	Tarrington	Herefordshire			1847	LR 1140 2
Dursley Branch	Dursley	Gloucestershire	86995	1842–1878	1842–1854	LR 1140 2
Dymock	Dymock	Gloucestershire			1840–1841	LR 2390 2

Nineteenth-Century Church Units in the Three Counties (continued)

Unit Name	Parish	Conference	County	FHL Film #	FHL dates	Manuscript History Dates	CHL Catalog Number*
Earl's Common Branch	Himbleton	Worcester	Worcestershire			1842–1848	LR 1140 2
Easthampton Branch	Shobdon	Frome's Hill	Gloucestershire			1842	LR 1140 2
Edgehill Branch	Dean Forest Holy Trinity	Cheltenham	Gloucestershire			1842–1848	LR 1140 2
Ewyas Harold	Ewyas Harold	Garway	Herefordshire			1841–1846	
Fly Ford Flavell Branch	Flyford Flavell	Gadfield Elm	Worcestershire			1841–1848	LR 1140 2
Forest of Dean Branch	Dean Forest Holy Trinity	Gadfield Elm	Gloucestershire	86998	1840–1870	1841–?	LR 1140 2
Frogsmarsh Branch	Eldersfield	Gadfield Elm	Gloucestershire	86991	1840–1856	1841–1861, 1884	LR 1140 2
Froomes Hill Branch	Castle Frome	Frome's Hill	Herefordshire			1840–1850	LR 1140 2
Froomes Hill Conference						1840–1844	LR 1140 2
Gadfielm Elm Branch	Eldersfield	Gadfield Elm	Worcestershire			1840–1841	LR 1140 2
Garway Conference			Herefordshire			1841–1848	LR 1140 2
Garway or Little Garway Branch	Garway	Garway	Herefordshire			1840–1845	
Gloucester Branch	Gloucester		Gloucestershire	86999	1840–1876	not listed	
Haw Cross Branch	Redmarley D'Abitot	Gadfield Elm	Worcestershire			1840–1841	LR 1140 2
Hereford Branch	Hereford	Herefordshire	Herefordshire	87002	1847–1899	1870–1982	LR 3764 2
Herefordshire Conference				87002	1854–1902	1848–1870	LR 1140 2
Highleaden Branch	Rudford	Gadfield Elm	Gloucestershire			Sep 1840–May 1841	LR 1140 2
Hill Common Branch	?	Gadfield Elm	Gloucestershire			1841	LR 1140 2
Hope Rough Branch	Much Cowarne	Frome's Hill	Herefordshire			Jun 1840–Sep 1840	LR 1140 2
Keysend Street Branch	Berrow	Frome's Hill	Worcestershire			1840–1850	LR 1140 2
Kidderminster	Kidderminster	Worcestershire	Worcestershire	87007	1864–1948	1845–1982	LR 4434 2
Kilcott Branch	Newent	Gadfield Elm	Gloucestershire			1840–1843	LR 1140 2
Leadenhall Branch	Upleadon	Cheltenham	Gloucestershire			1854	LR 1140 2
Ledbury Branch	Ledbury	Frome's Hill	Herefordshire			1840–1854	LR 1140 2

Leominster Branch	Frome's Hill	Leominster			1842–1861, 1885	LR 1140 2
Lime Street Branch	Gadfield Elm	Eldersfield	Gloucestershire		1840–1843	LR 1140 2
Linton Branch	Cheltenham	Linton	Gloucestershire	87027	1850–1854	LR 1140 2
Little Dean Hill Branch	Cheltenham	Littledean	Gloucestershire		1850–1851	LR 1140 2
Little Dean Woodside Branch		Littledean or Dean Forest	Gloucestershire		Sep 1850–Mar 1851	LR 1140 2
Longney Branch	Cheltenham	Longney	Gloucestershire		1853–1856	LR 1140 2
Lugwardine Branch	Frome's Hill	Lugwardine	Herefordshire		1840–1847	LR 1140 2
Malvern Branch	Frome's Hill	Great Malvern	Worcestershire		1840–1841	LR 1140 2
Malvern Hill Branch	Frome's Hill	Mathon St James?	Gloucestershire		1840–1861	LR 1140 2
Marden Branch	Frome's Hill	Marden	Herefordshire		Jun 1840–Mar 1841	
Mars Hill Branch	Mars Hill	?			1844–1847	LR 1140 2
Mathon Branch	Frome's Hill	Mathon	Gloucestershire		Mar 1841	LR 1140 2
Michael Church Branch	Stanley Hill	Michaelchurch Escley	Gloucestershire		1841	LR 1140 2
Moorend Cross Branch	Frome's Hill	Mathon	Worcestershire		1841–1847	LR 1140 2
Nailsworth Branch	Cheltenham	Nailsworth	Gloucestershire	87020	1850–1947	LR 1140 2
Naunton Beauchamp Branch	Gadfield Elm	Naunton Beauchamp	Gloucestershire	1844–1879	1841–1842	LR 1140 2
Newberry Hill Branch	Cheltenham	?	Gloucestershire		1842	LR 1140 2
Nimphsfield and Uley Branch	Chalford Hill	Nymphsfield, Uley	Gloucestershire		1847	LR 1140 2
Norton Branch	Cheltenham	Norton	Gloucestershire		1840–1855	LR 1140 2
Old Storridge Branch	Frome's Hill	Alfrick	Herefordshire		1840–1850	LR 1140 2
Orcop	Garway	Orcop	Herefordshire		1843	
Pale House Branch	Frome's Hill	Great Malvern	Gloucestershire		1840–1841	LR 1140 2
Persal Green Branch	Worcestershire	?	Worcestershire		1845–1848	LR 1140 2

Nineteenth-Century Church Units in the Three Counties (continued)

Unit Name	Parish	Conference	County	FHL Film #	FHL dates	Manuscript History Dates	CHL Catalog Number*
Pinvin Branch	Pinvin	Cheltenham	Gloucestershire			1842–1848	LR 1140 2
Pinwick Branch	?	Gadfield Elm	Gloucestershire			Mar 1841	LR 1140 2
Ponsett Branch	?	Cheltenham	Gloucestershire			May 1842	LR 1140 2
Ponshill Branch (Pouncell/Pontshall)	Weston Under Penyard	Cheltenham	Gloucestershire	87027	1840–1863	1843–1856	LR 1140 2
Powyek (Powick) Branch	Powick	Frome's Hill	Gloucestershire			Mar 1841	LR 1140 2
Preisteign Branch	Presteign	Mars Hill	Gloucestershire			Jan 1847	LR 1140 2
Randon Branch	?	Worcestershire	Worcestershire?			Sep 1849	LR 1140 2
Red Marley Branch	Redmarley D'Abitot	Cheltenham	Gloucestershire			May 1842	LR 1140 2
Richards Castle Branch	Richard's Castle	Mars Hill				Jan 1847	LR 1140 2
Rock Hill Branch	Bromsgrove?	Cheltenham	Gloucestershire?			May 1842	LR 1140 2
Ross Branch	Ross-on-Wye	Cheltenham	Herefordshire			Oct 1853–Apr 1854	LR 1140 2
Ruardeans Hill Branch	Ruardean	Cheltenham	Gloucestershire			1848–1851	LR 1140 2
Shatterford Branch	Arley	Worcestershire	Staffordshire			1846–1848	LR 1140 2
Sheepscombe Branch	Sheepscombe	Cheltenham	Gloucestershire	86991	1843–1867	1850–1856	LR 1140 2
Shortwood Branch	Horsley	Cheltenham	Gloucestershire	87032		1849–1889	LR 1140 2
Shucknell Hill Branch	Weston Beggard	Frome's Hill	Herefordshire			1840–1847	LR 1140 2
Stanley Hill Branch	Bosbury	Frome's Hill	Herefordshire			1840–1845	LR 1140 2
Stoke Prior Branch	Stoke Prior	Frome's Hill	Herefordshire	87034		Mar 1841	LR 1140 2
Stoke Street Milbro Branch	?	Mars Hill	?			Jan 1847	LR 1140 2
Stokes Lane Branch	Avenbury	Frome's Hill	Herefordshire			1840–1847	LR 1140 2
Tetbury Branch	Tetbury	Chalford Hill	Gloucestershire	87036		1845–1856	LR 1140 2
Tewkesbury Branch	Tewkesbury	Cheltenham	Gloucestershire	87036		1850–1879	LR 1140 2
Thornbury Branch	Thornbury	Chalford Hill	Gloucestershire			1847, 1902–1909	LR 1140 2
Twigworth Branch	Twigworth	Gadfield Elm	Gloucestershire			Jun 1840–Mar 1841	LR 1140 2
Upleadon Branch	Upleadon	Cheltenham	Gloucestershire			1854–1856	LR 1140 2
Viney Hill Branch	Awre	Cheltenham	Gloucestershire			1846–1856	LR 1140 2

Unit Name	(Name)	County	FHL Film	FHL Dates	Manuscript History Dates	CHL Catalog Number
Walton Hill Branch	Clent or Halesowen	Gloucestershire			1841	LR 1140 2
Wellington Heath Branch	Wellington Heath	Herefordshire			Sep 1840	LR 1140 2
Whitecroft Branch	Dean Forest, St. Paul	Gloucestershire			Mar 1851–1852	LR 1140 2
Wich Bowl Branch (Wychbold)	Dodderhill	Worcestershire			Sep 1848	LR 1140 2
Widbourne Branch (Whitbourne)	Whitbourne	Herefordshire			May 1842	LR 1140 2
Wind Point Branch (Wynds Point)	Colwall	Herefordshire			Jun 1840–Mar 1841	LR 1140 2
Wolferwood Common Branch (Wofferwood Common)	Stanford Bishop	Herefordshire			Jun 1840–Mar 1841	LR 1140 2
Woodside Branch	Dean Forest Holy Trinity	Gloucestershire	87039	1840–1856	1842–1856	LR 1140 2
Worcester Branch	Worcester	Worcestershire	87039	1840–1868	1841–1982	LR 10286 2
Worcester District	Worcester District	Worcestershire	87039	1854–1910	1843–1878	LR 10288 2
Wotten-under-Edge Branch	Wotten-Under-Edge	Gloucestershire	87039	1842–1857	1850–1856	LR 1140 2
Yardley Wood Branch	Yardley Wood	Birmingham	87039	1847–1865	1864–1867	LR 1140 2

*Note: Some unit histories are located separate from the LR 1140 2 branch histories. Their call numbers are listed here.

Notes

- Unit Name is the branch or conference name listed in either the Family History Library catalog or the Church History Library catalog.
- The name listed in parentheses is the name of the hamlet or village as it is on maps today, if it is different.
- FHL Film Number refers to the microfilm number where the branch records can be located in the Family History Library.
- FHL Dates are the membership record's dates of coverage listed in the Family History Library catalog.
- *Manuscript History* Dates refers to the dates for the branch histories listed in the *Manuscript History*.
- CHL Catalog Number is the call number for the particular branch history found at the Church History Library.

The information about the Church units in the Three Counties, along with the descriptions of our research processes, may help interested parties who are seeking information about their ancestors from the area. Identifying place-names can help researchers locate which branches the early converts may have attended, possibly providing family historians some clues for other records to search, including Latter-day Saint membership records, the *British Mission Manuscript History*, and local tithe apportionment records to locate possible dwelling places.

Notes

1. "Wilford Woodruff's Baptismal Record, 1840," in *Wilford Woodruff's Journal*, 1:377–95.
2. This was a five-part series published by Jay Greaves Burrup: "150 Years Ago: A Look Back at Wilford Woodruff and the West Midland Mormons of 1840," *Herefordshire Family History Society Journal*. The dates and page numbers for the entire series are as follows: vol. 4, no. 6 (July 1990): 210–20; vol. 4, no. 11 (October 1991): 407–18; vol. 5, no. 2 (July 1992): 51–61; vol. 5, no. 3 (October 1992): 71–86; vol. 5, no. 7 (October 1993): 246–58.
3. Burrup stated, "Woodruff didn't return to the West Midlands until July 22. Thereafter, he noted that he didn't baptize many converts, preferring to let the local British Mormons who held the Priesthood perform the ordinance. Only occasionally did Woodruff list the converts' names in his diary." Jay Greaves Burrup, "150 Years Ago: A look back at Wilford Woodruff and the West Midland Mormons of 1840," *Herefordshire Family History Society Journal* 5, no. 3 (October 1992): 86.
4. *Wilford Woodruff's Journal*, 1:395.
5. An example is at the Fromes Hill Conference held at Stanley Hill on 21 September 1840 where several men's names are listed for priesthood ordinations, some of whom do not have baptism dates. *Wilford Woodruff's Journal*, 1:518.
6. By that time, most of the missionaries for whom we have records either had emigrated to Nauvoo or were preaching in areas other than Gloucestershire, Worcestershire, and Herefordshire. We did not follow their records after they left the area.

7. Thomas Steed, "The Life of Thomas Steed From His Own Diary 1826–1910," 5, 7, BX 8670.1 .St32, L. Tom Perry Special Collections, Harold B. Lee Library, Brigham Young University, Provo, UT. Also online at https://books.FamilySearch.org.
8. Examples of published materials would be the autobiographies found in Kate B. Carter, comp., *Heart Throbs of the West*, 12 vols. (Salt Lake City: Daughters of Utah Pioneers, 1939–51), or Kate B. Carter, comp., *Our Pioneer Heritage*, 20 vols. (Salt Lake City: Daughters of Utah Pioneers, 1958–77).
9. Examples of secondary records include life histories on FamilySearch.org or biographies published in Kate B. Carter's volumes.
10. *British Mission Manuscript History and Historical Reports, 1841–1971* (LR 1140 2, Church History Library, Salt Lake City). Volumes 4–11 contain the histories of branches in Britain.
11. Author communication dated 17 July 2014 from Jay G. Burrup, archivist, Church History Library, Salt Lake City.
12. Evva C. Benson & Cynthia Doxey, "The Ecclesiastical Census of 1851 and the Church of Jesus Christ of Latter-day Saints," *The Local Historian* 34, no. 2 (May 2004): 66–79.
13. Cynthia Doxey, "The Church in Britain and the 1851 Religious Census," *Mormon Historical Studies* 4, no. 1 (Spring 2003): 107–38.
14. "Gadfield Elm Chapel," http://lds.org.uk/gadfield-elm-chapel, (accessed 15 May 2015).
15. "United Brethren Preachers' Plan of the Frooms Hill Circuit, 1840," 248.6 U58p 1840, Church History Library, Salt Lake City. *Wilford Woodruff's Journal* states that on 14 June 1840, "The Preachers and members of the Bran Green and Gadfields Elm Branch of the Frooms Hill Curcuit of the United Brethren met at the Gadfield Elm Chapel . . . [and it was moved] that this meeting be hereafter Known by the name of the Bran Green & Gadfields Elm Conference of the Church of Jesus Christ of Latter Day Saints," in *Wilford Woodruff's Journal*, 1:458, 14 June 1840.
16. *Wilford Woodruff's Journal*, 2:61.
17. The Cheltenham Conference is listed for the first time in the general conference in Manchester on 15 May 1842, reporting a membership of 540 in 17 branches. *Millennial Star* 3, no. 2 (June 1842): 29. The Gadfield Elm Conference is not reported from that time on, because it was subsumed under the Cheltenham Conference.

18. The membership records of the two branches are listed in the Family History Library Catalog in three ways: Brans Green [Brangreen] Branch, Frogsmarsh Branch, and Brans Green or Frogsmarsh Branch, all on FHL film 86991, items 15–16. Another filming of Brangreen Branch is also on FHL film 86998, items 17–18.
19. James Palmer, "James Palmer Reminiscences, ca. 1884–98," 10, MS 1752, Church History Library, Salt Lake City.
20. *Wilford Woodruff's Journal*, 1:431, 4 April 1840.
21. The reason for using a "possible identification" category was because some individuals were found on the census living in the right area, but because no record existed on Family Tree or the other indexes, we could not be sure if they were the right people. For the purposes of later analyses, the "possible" category was included in the positively identified group because they were usually found on a census, even if they were not found on FamilySearch Family Tree.
22. *Wilford Woodruff's Journal*, 1:446, 10 May 1840.
23. "United Brethren Preachers' Plan."
24. *A Vision of Britain Through Time: Statistical Atlas, Social Structure*, http://www.visionofbritain.org.uk/atlas/.
25. Ronald W. Walker, "Cradling Mormonism: The Rise of the Gospel in Early Victorian Britain," *BYU Studies* 27, no. 1 (Winter 1987): 25–36. Philip A. M. Taylor, "Why Did British Mormons Emigrate?," *Utah Historical Quarterly* 22 (July 1954): 249–70.
26. Sometimes the census enumerator did not list any occupations for any family members. In other cases, we found that the individuals were elderly or young adults apparently living with their parents who may have had occupations recorded.
27. See the articles by Ronald W. Walker and Philip A. M. Taylor listed in note 25.
28. FamilySearch.org/learn/wiki provides a summary of the provenance of England's Tithe Records and how to search them.

Bibliography

1987 British Sesquicentennial Celebrations: Report of the British Isles Advisory Committee, March 1985, Office of the Europe Area Presidency.

Allen, James B., Ronald K. Esplin, and David J. Whittaker. *Men with a Mission, 1837–1841: The Quorum of the Twelve Apostles in the British Isles*. Salt Lake City: Deseret Book, 1992.

Barnes, James. "James Barnes Diary, 1840 August–1841 June." MS 1870. Church History Library, Salt Lake City.

Benson, Evva C., and Cynthia Doxey. "The Ecclesiastical Census of 1851 and the Church of Jesus Christ of Latter-day Saints." *The Local Historian* 34, no. 2 (May 2004): 66–79.

Bloxham, V. Ben. "Deed of Conveyance Between Thomas Shipton (as Grantor) of the One Part and John Benbow and Thomas Kington (as Grantees) of the Other Part Dated 4 March 1836." October 9 1984, 1–2. Transcript from a photographic copy of the copy in the Public Record Office, London.

———. Letter to James R. Moss, 21 March 1986.

Bloxham, V. Ben, James R. Moss, and Larry C. Porter. *Truth Will Prevail: The Rise of The Church of Jesus Christ of Latter-day Saints in the British Isles, 1837–1987*. Cambridge: Cambridge University Press, 1987.

British Mission Manuscript History and Historical Reports, 1841–1971. LR 1140 2. Church History Library, Salt Lake City.

British Pageant: Truth Will Prevail. http://britishpageant.org/character-bios/.

Burrup, Jay Greaves. "150 Years Ago: A Look Back at Wilford Woodruff and the West Midland Mormons of 1840." *Herefordshire Family History Society Journal* 4, no. 6 (July 1990): 210–20.

———. "150 Years Ago: A Look Back at Wilford Woodruff and the West Midland Mormons of 1840." *Herefordshire Family History Society Journal* 4, no. 11 (October 1991): 407–18.

———. "150 Years Ago: A Look Back at Wilford Woodruff and the West Midland Mormons of 1840." *Herefordshire Family History Society Journal* 5, no. 2 (July 1992): 51–61.

———. "150 Years Ago: A Look Back at Wilford Woodruff and the West Midland Mormons of 1840." *Herefordshire Family History Society Journal* 5, no. 3 (October 1992): 71–86.

———. "150 Years Ago: A Look Back at Wilford Woodruff and the West Midland Mormons of 1840." *Herefordshire Family History Society Journal* 5, no. 7 (October 1993): 246–58.

"Country Information: United Kingdom." *Church News,* 1 February 2010.

Carter, Kate B. comp. *Heart Throbs of the West.* 12 vols. Salt Lake City: Daughters of Utah Pioneers, 1939–51.

———. comp. *Our Pioneer Heritage.* 20 vols. Salt Lake City: Daughters of Utah Pioneers, 1958–77.

———. comp. *Treasures of Pioneer History.* 6 vols. Salt Lake City: Daughters of Utah Pioneers, 1952–57.

Carter, Sarah Davis. "She Came in 1853." in *Our Pioneer Heritage,* compiled by Kate B. Carter, 12: 226–30. Salt Lake City, Utah: Daughters of Utah Pioneers, 1969.

Clayton, William. "William Clayton Diary, 1840 January–1842 February." 29 October 1840. MS 2843. Church History Library, Salt Lake City.

Cook, David. Personal communication. Solihull, England, 2006.

Davis, William George. "William G. Davis Diaries, 1880–1882." MS 1689. Church History Library, Salt Lake City.

"Disgraceful Elopement." *The Times*, Friday, 4 April 1856.

Doxey, Cynthia. "The Church in Britain and the 1851 Religious Census." *Mormon Historical Studies* 4, no. 1 (Spring 2003): 107–38.

"England Bristol Mission Alumni Web Site," *EBMAWS,* http://www.mission.net/england/bristol/ensign/1998-03.html.

Eames, Samuel. "Samuel Eames Correspondence 1861." MS 9490. Church History Library, Salt Lake City.

Fales, Susan L. "Artisans, Millhands, and Labourers: The Mormons of Leeds and Their Nonconformist Neighbors." In *Mormons in Early Victorian Britain*, edited by Richard L. Jensen and Malcolm R. Thorp, 156–78. Salt Lake City: University of Utah Press, 1989.

Fielding, Joseph. "Diary of Joseph Fielding." BX 8670.1 .F46, L. Tom Perry Special Collections, Harold B. Lee Library, Brigham Young University, Provo, UT.

"Gadfield Elm at 175." *By Common Consent*, http://bycommonconsent.com/2015/06/13/gadfield-elm-at-175-4/.

"Gadfield Elm Chapel." *The Church of Jesus Christ of Latter-day Saints*, http://lds.org.uk/gadfield-elm-chapel.

The Gadfield Elm Trust. "The Gadfield Elm Trust." Aylton, Herefordshire: The Gadfield Elm Trust, 1996.

Gardner, Wayne. Interview by Carol Wilkinson, 31 May 2005, Gloucestershire, England. In author's possession.

Gailey, John. "History of John Gailey, undated." MS 11009. Church History Library, Salt Lake City.

———. "John Gailey, Reminiscence and Diary, ca. 1840–41." MS 1089. Church History Library, Salt Lake City.

Gibson, Simon. Interview by Carol Wilkinson, 13 September 2006, Monmouth, Wales. In author's possession.

Gilbert, Alan D. *Religion and Society in Industrial England: Church, Chapel and Social Change, 1740–1914*. New York: Longman, 1976.

Harrison, J. F. C., ed. *Society and Politics in England, 1780–1960: A Selection of Readings and Comments*. New York: Harper and Row, 1965.

Head, Ronan J. "Creating a Mormon Mecca in England: The Gadfield Elm Chapel." *Mormon Historical Studies* 7, no. 1–2 (2006): 93–94.

"The History of Gadfield Elm Chapel." *The Church of Jesus Christ of Latter-day Saints*, www.lds.org.uk/content/view/23/47/.

Holland, Jeffrey R. Address at dedication of Gadfield Elm chapel, 23 April 2000. Videotape in possession of author Carol Wilkinson. Transcribed by Carol Wilkinson.

Hunt, Wynnell M. *Cradley: A Village History*. Trowbridge, UK: W. M. Hunt & Cradley Village Hall Management Committee, 2004.

Journal of Discourses, 26 vols. London: Latter-day Saints Book Depot, 1854–86.

Kimball, Heber C. *Journal of Heber C. Kimball*. Nauvoo, IL: Robinson & Smith, 1840.

———. *On the Potter's Wheel: The Diaries of Heber C. Kimball*. Salt Lake City: Signature Books, 1987.

Kimball, Stanley B. *Heber C. Kimball Mormon Patriarch and Pioneer*. Urbana: University of Illinois Press, 1981.

The Latter-day Saints' Millennial Star. Liverpool, England. 1840–1970.

Lowder, Emily Hodgetts. "Emily Hodgetts Lowder—103 years." In *Our Pioneer Heritage*, compiled by Kate B. Carter, 7: 424–8. Salt Lake City: Daughters of the Utah Pioneers, 1964.

Ludlum, Sarah Ann Oakey. "Her Journey West." In *Treasures of Pioneer History*, compiled by Kate B. Carter, 5:257–58. Salt Lake City: Daughters of Utah Pioneers, 1956.

Mason, Jennifer, ed. "A Heritage of Love: An Account of the History of the Church of Jesus Christ of Latter-day Saints in the Cheltenham, England Stake, Written and Researched by Members of the Cheltenham Stake." M274.2 C516c 1987, Church History Library, Salt Lake City.

Maughan, Mary Ann Weston. "The Journal of Mary Ann Weston Maughan." In *Our Pioneer Heritage*, compiled by Kate B. Carter, 2:346–417. Salt Lake City: Daughters of Utah Pioneers, 1959.

McCleod, Hugh. *Religion and the Working Class in Nineteenth-Century Britain*. London: Macmillan, 1984.

Milburn, Geoffrey. *Primitive Methodism*. Peterborough: Epworth Press, 2002.

"Moorend Farm, Castle Frome, Herefordshire, To Sell By Auction." *Hereford Times*, 27 March 1841.

Moss, James and Lavelle Moss. *Historic Sites of The Church of Jesus Christ of Latter-day Saints in the British Isles*. Salt Lake City: Publishers Press, 1987.

"The Nauvoo Brass Band." *Contributor* 1, no. 6 (March 1880): 135–6.

Needham, John. "John Needham Autobiography and Journal, 1840 August–1842 December." Transcript. MS 4221. Church History Library, Salt Lake City.

---. "John Needham Autobiography and Journal, 1840 August–1842 December." MS 25895, Church History Library, Salt Lake City.

"Obituary: John Fido." *Deseret News*, 7 September 1881, 512.

Ockey, Edward. "Edward Ockey Reminiscence and Journal, ca. 1857–58." MS 11746. Church History Library, Salt Lake City.

Palmer, James. "James Palmer Reminiscences, ca. 1884–98." MS 1752. Church History Library, Salt Lake City.

Petty, John. *The History of the Primitive Methodist Connexion from Its Origin to the Conference of 1859*. London: Danks, 1860.

Phillips, Edward. "Biographical Sketches of Edward and Hannah Simmonds Phillips, 1889, 1926, 1949." MS 11215. Church History Library, Salt Lake City.

Pratt, Parley P. "Prospectus of the Latter-day Saints Millennial Star." M205.1 M646p 1840. Church History Library, Salt Lake City.

Primitive Methodist Magazine. Edited by Hugh Bourne. Bemersley Farm, Mow Cop, Cheshire, England.

"Proceedings at Dymock." *Hereford Times*, 14 November 1840.

Richards, Levi. "Levi Richards Papers, 1837–1867." MS 1284, box 1, folder 1. Church History Library, Salt Lake City.

Sansom, Charles. "Journal of Charles Sansom, 1826–1908 /prepared by great-granddaughter Doris Barber Smith; addendum research by grandson Howard and wife LaVon Sansom." M270.1 S229s. Church History Library, Salt Lake City.

Smith, Charles Nephi. "Diary and Reflections of Charles 'Nephi' Smith, son of Thomas and Mary Smith." https://familysearch.org/photos/documents/4972727?pid=KWJ8-Z8G.

Smith, Job Taylor. "Job Smith Autobiography, circa 1902." MS 4809. Church History Library, Salt Lake City.

---. "The United Brethren." *Improvement Era*, May 1910, 818–23.

Smith, Joseph. *History of the Church*. Edited by B. H. Roberts. 2nd ed. rev. 7 vols. Salt Lake City: Deseret Book, 1974.

---. *Joseph Smith Papers*, 3 series. Salt Lake City: Church Historian's Press, 2008. http://josephsmithpapers.org.

Sparks, Jane Ann Fowler. *Jane Ann's Memoirs*. Compiled by Marsha Passey. Montpelier, ID: M. Passey, 2004.

Spiers, John. "John Spiers Reminiscences and Journal, 1840–77." MS 1725. Church History Library, Salt Lake City.

Steed, Thomas. "The Life of Thomas Steed from His Own Diary, 1826–1910." BX 8670.1 .St32. L. Tom Perry Special Collections, Harold B. Lee Library, Brigham Young University, Provo, UT.

Taylor, Philip A. M. "Why Did British Mormons Emigrate?" *Utah Historical Quarterly* 22, no. 3 (July 1954): 249–70.

Thomas, Joan and Brian. *Garway Hill Through the Ages*. Almeley, Herefordshire: Logaston Press, 2007.

"Truth Will Prevail! UK Mormons Honour British Heritage in The British Pageant." *Mormon Newsroom*, http://www.mormonnewsroom.org.uk/article/truth-will-prevail-uk-mormons-honour-british-heritage-in-the-british-pageant.

"United Brethren Preachers' Plan of the Frooms Hill Circuit, 1840." 248.6 U58p 1840, Church History Library, Salt Lake City.

Van Wagoner, Richard S. *Sidney Rigdon: A Portrait of Religious Excess*. Salt Lake City: Signature Books, 1994.

Walker, Joseph. "English, U.S. Mormons Join Forces to Create 'Faith.'" *Deseret News*. 3 August 2011.

Walker, Ronald W. "Cradling Mormonism: The Rise of the Gospel in Early Victorian Britain." *BYU Studies* 27, no. 1 (Winter 1987): 25–36.

Wall, Francis George. "Francis George Wall—Pioneer of 1863." In *Our Pioneer Heritage*. Compiled by Kate B. Carter, 7:362–68. Salt Lake City: Daughters of Utah Pioneers, 1964.

Weight, Frederick. "A Brief History of the Life of Frederick Weight." MSS SC 3200, L. Tom Perry Special Collections, Harold B. Lee Library, Brigham Young University, Provo, UT.

Werner, Julia Stewart. *The Primitive Methodist Connexion: Its Background and Early History*. Madison: University of Wisconsin Press, 1984.

Whitney, Orson F. *Life of Heber C. Kimball*. Salt Lake City: Bookcraft, 1967.

Wilkinson, Carol. "The Restoration of the Gadfield Elm Chapel." In *Regional Studies in Latter-Day Saint Church History: The British Isles*, edited by Cynthia Doxey, Robert C. Freeman, Richard Neitzel Holzapfel, and Dennis A. Wright. Provo, UT: Religious Studies Center, 2007, 48–51.

Wilkinson, Carol. "Mormon Baptismal Site in Chatburn, England." *Mormon Historical Studies* 7, no. 1–2 (2006), 83–88.

Williams, William. "William Williams Reminiscence, 1850." MS 9132. Church History Library, Salt Lake City.

Woodruff, Wilford. "Elder Woodruff's Letter [Concluded]." *Times and Seasons*, 2 no. 9, 329.

———. *Leaves from My Journal.* Salt Lake City: Juvenile Instructor Office, 1881. Republished by LDS Archive Publishers, Grantsville, UT, 1997.

———. *Wilford Woodruff's Journal, 1833–1898, Typescript.* 9 vols. Edited by Scott G. Kenney. Midvale, UT: Signature Books, 1983–85.

Young, Brigham. *Manuscript History of Brigham Young, 1801–1844.* Compiled by Elden J. Watson. Salt Lake City: Smith Secretarial Service, 1968.

Online Sources for the Databases

Ancestry.com
FamilySearch.org
Freebmd.org.uk
History.lds.org/overlandtravels
Maps.familysearch.org
Mormonmigration.lib.byu.edu
A Vision of Britain Through Time, "Statistical Atlas, Social Structure," www.visionofbritain.org.uk/atlas/

About the Authors

CAROL WILKINSON is an associate professor of teacher education at Brigham Young University and taught for ten years as a religion transfer professor for the Department of Church History and Doctrine. She received her BEd degree from Durham University, England, and MS and EdD degrees from Brigham Young University. She has written several published works, including *The Restoration of Gadfield Elm Chapel*, *Mormon Baptismal Site in Chatburn, England*, *Temple Symbolism of the Body*, and *Run and Not Be Weary*. A native of England, she served in the England Bristol Mission, spending eleven months in the Three Counties of England.

CYNTHIA DOXEY GREEN is a former associate professor of Church history and doctrine at Brigham Young University. Her articles can be found in academic journals and books such as *Regional Studies in Church History* and *Strengthening Our Families: An In-Depth Look at the Proclamation on the Family*. Her research and teaching focused on family history and British emigration. Since her marriage to Richard A. Green and subsequent move to North Carolina, she continues doing family history research and speaking at local and national genealogy conferences and societies.

Index

A

age, of early converts, 116–17
agriculture, 24–25
Alliance, 168n5
apostasy, 16, 137–38, 153–54, 161–68
Apostles. See Quorum of the Twelve Apostles
Archbishop of Canterbury, 45
Arthur home, 73
autobiographical writings, 94

B

baptism(s)
    ages of converts at time of, 116–17
    in Bedford, 10
    finding number of, 95–97, 128n7
    first, conducted in England, 8–9
    at Hawcross, 94–96
    in Herefordshire, 44–45, 46, 49–52

baptism(s) (continued)
    of John Cheese, 86n22
    of Mary Ann Price, 79
    of Thomas Steed and family, 99
    Wilford Woodruff's record of, 65, 68, 86n13, 93–95, 128n4, 202
Barnes, James, 57, 68, 73, 77, 141
Bedford, 9–10
Benbow, Ann, 42
Benbow, Ellen, 180, 182
Benbow, Jane, 43, 105, 182, 184–86
Benbow, John
    contributes to Book of Mormon publication, 53, 196
    conversion of, 43–44, 105, 184–86
    emigration of, 138
    events focusing on family of, 182
    missionary efforts of, 46
    moves to Fromes Hill, 132n50
    occupation of, 133n55

Benbow, John (continued)
  pays emigration expenses for others, 141
  purchases Gadfield Elm, 193
  socioeconomic status of, 111–12
  tells William Williams of Mormon missionaries, 102
  Wilford Woodruff meets with, 42
Benbow, William, 42, 105, 184–86
birth years, 133–34n60
Bishop, Elizabeth, 155
blessings, of converts, 118–19
Bloxham, V. Ben, 219
Book of Mormon
  availability of, 47, 84
  and missionary work, 71–72
  publication of, 53, 64, 196
Boulter, Comfort, 142
Boulter, Thomas, 142
Bourne, Hugh, 27
Branch Database from the Record of Members, The Church of Jesus Christ of Latter-day Saints, 203–6, 214–15
branches
  boundaries of, 56n34, 124–26, 159–61, 220
  identification of, 220–21
  nineteenth-century in Three Counties, 78, 220–27
  organization of, 41, 54, 59, 65, 123
  records for, 108–9, 114–15, 116, 117, 128n6, 131n38, 142, 168n8

Bran Green and Gadfield Elm Conference. See also Cheltenham Conference
  branches assigned to, 124–25
  emigration from, 142
  membership of, 96, 129n14
  organization of, 54, 64–65, 68
  records of, 105–6, 132n44, 212, 214–15
  spellings of, 132n45
  in United Brethren Preachers' Plan, 59
  United Brethren's homes in, 32–33
Bran Green Branch, 108–9
British Mission Manuscript History and Historical Reports, 1841–1971, 203–6, 221–28
British Pageant, 182
Bromage, Elizabeth, 106, 126
Brooks, Ann, 212
Brooks, Mary, 118
Brooks, Susan, 42
Browett, Daniel, 57, 69, 119, 147
Brush, Frances, 115–16
Bundy, George, 147–48
Burrup, Jay Greaves, 202

C

Campbellites, 23
camp meetings, 27
Caroline, 130n17, 141, 168n5
Carter, Ellen Benbow, 180, 182
Carter, Sarah Davis, 146
Carter, William, 180
Castle Frome Church, 186

Castle Frome parish rector, 44–45, 186
Castree family, 161–62, 171n58
Castrey, Philip, 164
censuses, 206–7
Chatburn, 13–15
Cheese, John, 57, 68, 80–81, 86n22, 104, 133n55, 153
Cheese, Mary, 153
Cheltenham, 76
Cheltenham chapel, 174
Cheltenham Conference
  boundaries of, 125–26
  emigration statistics for, 139–40
  excommunication report for, 166, 167t
  flourishing of, 164
  Gadfield Elm Conference changed to, 76, 135n78
  membership and missionary success of, 76
  records for, 204, 229n17
Cheltenham Stake, 174
child labor, 25
christenings, 133–34n60
Church journals, 71–72
Church members, assist in missionary efforts, 60–61, 67–69
Church of England, 26–27
Church of Jesus Christ of Latter-day Saints, The
  beginnings in Lancashire, 5–16
  centennial in British Isles, 174
  connections between English and American Saints, 181–82
  difficult times in United States, 16–17

Church of Jesus Christ of Latter-day Saints, The (continued)
  early years in United States, 1–4
  growth in early 1840s, 123–27
  growth in England, 18–19
  growth in Three Counties area, 54, 57–60, 78–79
  records of, 92, 94, 96
Clayton, William, 15–16, 152–53
clergy, persecution instigated by, 44–45, 82, 186
Clifford, Elijah, 77
Clifford, Margaret, 77
Clowes, William, 27
"Cock Pit," 11
Cole, William, 106
Collett, Ann, 106, 142–43
Collett, Daniel, 106
Collett, Elizabeth Bromage, 106, 126
Collett, William, 106, 126
Colwall Branch, 158
conferences
  first, in Three Counties area, 54
  reports on, 123, 125
constable, sent to arrest Wilford Woodruff, 44–45, 185
converts. See also missionary work
  ages of, 116–17
  blessings and trials of, 118–22
  Church activity of, 209–10
  demographic background of, 107–9, 206–10
  emigration of, 96, 130n17, 138–54
  finding number of, 95–97

converts (continued)
  gender of, 115–16
  identifying, 92–95, 210–15
  occupations and social status of, 109–15, 133n55, 215–19
  preparation of, for gospel, 23–24
  research on, 91–92
  sources for names of, 201–6
  understanding, through conversion stories, 97–105
  who stayed in England, 154–68
Cordon, Alfred, 41
Cowdery, Oliver, 23
Crook, Margaret Lane, 157
Crook, William, 157
Cwm Circuit of Primitive Methodist Church, 30–31

D

Davis, Elizabeth Bishop, 155
Davis, John, 121
Davis, Jonathan, 161
Davis, William G., 156–57, 161
Davis, William, 155
Dilwyn, 83, 88–89n61, 95
dissenting religions, 26–31
Dow, Lorenzo, 27
Downham, 13–15
dreams, spiritual preparation through, 101–4
Dymock, 53, 64, 82, 83, 186–91

E

Eagles, Ann Sparks, 106–7
Eagles, Hannah Maria, 106
Eames, Samuel, 155
effigies, burning, 83

emigration
  and census information, 207
  destinations in, 152–54
  faithfulness of converts remaining in England, 154–55
  faith in, 198
  reasons for not emigrating, 156–58
  sources and records regarding, 96, 130n17, 138–43, 207–8
  trials of, 143–54
England
  Apostles depart for, 17–19
  missionaries' arrival in, 41–42, 52–53
  missionaries called to, 2–4
  religious conditions in, 26–38
  social, political, and economic conditions in, 24–26
evil spirits, missionaries afflicted by, 6–8
excommunication, 164–66

F

faithfulness
  and choice to emigrate, 138–39, 198
  of converts who stayed in England, 154–68
  Family Tree and determining, 209–10
  through trials, 149–52
Faith: The Musical, 182
family
  influence of, in maintaining branches, 126
  learning gospel through, 105–7
  and trials of emigration, 143–46

FamilySearch.org, 208–10, 214
Family Tree, 208–10
farming, 24–25
Far West, Missouri, 17
Fidoe, John, 154
Fidoe, Lydia Pullen, 154
Field, Mary, 146, 149–51
Field family, 149–51
Fielding, James, 5–6, 9
Fielding, Joseph, 4–5, 9–10, 13, 15–16
financial speculation, 2
fishing analogies, 50–51
Fowler, Jane Ann, 119–20, 143–44
Fowles, Adelaide, 148
Fox, Thomas, 95
Frogmarsh Branch, 105–6, 108–9, 132n44, 132n45, 142–43, 212, 214–15
Fromes Hill Conference
   branches assigned to, 125
   meeting place of, 134–35n77
   membership of, 96, 129n14
   organization of, 54, 64–65, 68
   records of, 228n5
   in United Brethren Preachers' Plan, 59
   United Brethren's homes in, 32–33

G

Gadfield Elm Chapel, 176–81, 193–94
Gadfield Elm Conference. See Bran Green and Gadfield Elm Conference; Cheltenham Conference
Gadfield Elm Trust, 179, 181
Gailey, John, 57, 68, 83–84, 100, 106
Gardner, Wayne, 176–77
Garner, Mary Field, 146, 149–51
Garrick, 4
Garway Conference, 73, 96, 221
gender, of early converts, 115–16
Gibson, Simon, 176–78
Gittens, Hannah, 106
Glover, Henry, 67, 74, 76
Goodson, John, 4, 9
Grant, Heber J., 174

H

Hallard, John, 211
Hallard, Mary, 211
Harford, John, 211
Harmony, 141, 168n5
Harris, Hannah Maria Eagles, 106
Harris, Robert, 138
Hawcross, 194–96
healing(s)
   of Francis George Wall, 118
   of Mary Pitt, 53, 186–91
Herefordshire Beacon, 53, 64, 196
Hill, Benjamin, 147
Hill, Francis, 210–11
Hill, Mary, 147
Hill Farm and Pond, 175, 184–86
Hinckley, Gordon B., 180–81
historic sites, 184–96
Hodgetts, Emily, 112, 144–46
Hodgetts, Maria, 145–46
Hodgetts, William Ben, 145–46
Holdt, Philip, 50, 128n1
Holland, Jeffrey R., 180–81
Holley family, 161–62, 171n58
Holmes, Elizabeth Cole, 105–6

Holmes, Francis, 106
Holmes, Hannah Gittens, 106
Holmes, Robert, 105–6
Holy Ghost
    bears witness of missionary message, 81
    Wilford Woodruff teaches by, 47, 80
Hooper, Hannah, 153
Hooper, Thomas, 153
Hyde, Orson, 3, 5–8, 11, 16

I

impressions, spiritual preparation through, 104–5
Index of Civil Registration of Births, Marriages, and Deaths in England, 208
Indian chief, 151
indigo blueing, 118
industrialization, 25

J

James, Hannah, 122
Jay, William, 74
Jenkins, Eliza Phelps, 104
Jenkins, T., 59, 69
Jenkins, William, 104
Jenson, Andrew, 203
Jones, Henry, 163–64
Jones, Samuel, 102–4
Journal Database, 202–3, 214–15
journals, 71–72, 84–85

K

Kay, William, 66, 67
Kimball, Heber C.
    called to England, 2–3

Kimball, Heber C. (continued)
    departs for England, 17–18
    experience with evil spirits, 6–8
    leaves England, 16
    meets Apostles at Far West, 17
    missionary efforts in Three Counties, 65
    strengthens Preston congregations, 11
    success of, 10–11, 13–15
Kimball, Vilate, 18
Kington, Thomas
    Church activity of, 68–69
    contributes to Book of Mormon publication, 53, 196
    conversion of, 46–47, 52
    emigration of, 138
    Job Smith baptized by, 195
    missionary efforts of, 47, 57, 66, 87n24, 87n27
    occupation of, 133n55
    ordination of, 86n24
    purchases Gatfield Elm, 193
    residence of, 186, 219
    socioeconomic status of, 112
    and truth seekers, 100, 101
    and United Brethren, 30–31
"Kitchen, the," 73
Knight, Elizabeth, 79, 88n59
Knight, Pamela, 104
Knowles, Joseph, 67

L

Lamanites, mission to, 23
Lancashire, Church beginnings in, 5–16
Ledbury, 65, 191

Leominster Branch, 85n8
Lilley, Richard, 133n55
Littlewood, Martin, 67
London Temple, 174
Lowder, Emily Hodgetts, 112, 144–46
Lucy, Jonathan, 158–59
Ludlum, Sarah Ann Oakey, 142–43

M

maps.familysearch.org, 214
Margretts, Susanna, 153–54
Margretts, William, 153–54
Margretts family, 164
Markham, David, 182
marriage, 157, 208–9
Marsh, Thomas B., 16
Mars Hill Conference, 165
Martin Handcart Company, 149
Matthews, Ann Fielding, 9–10
Matthews, Timothy, 9–10
Maughan, Mary Ann Weston, 104, 112, 121, 141, 144
Maxwell, Neal A., 176
meeting places, 79–80, 204–5
Methodism, 26–27
Millennial Star, 71, 84, 123, 138, 139–40, 164–66
ministers, persecution instigated by, 44–45, 82, 186
missionary journals, importance of, 84–85
missionary work. See also converts; Woodruff, Wilford
  American Missionaries in Three Counties area, 62–66
  anti-Church campaign's effect on, 173

missionary work (continued)
  Apostles depart for England, 17–19
  of Brigham Young and Willard Richards, 52–53
  British missionaries in Three Counties area, 67–69
  calling of missionaries to England, 2–4, 16–17
  and Church beginnings in Lancashire, 5–16
  content and message of, 80–81
  and continued growth of Church, 54
  of family members, 105–7
  methods for, 72–80, 88–89n61
  persecution in, 81–84
  preparation of converts, 23–24
  of Thomas Steed, 118–19
  training for, 70–72
  of United Brethren, 57–61
Moorend Farm, 186
Moravians, 30
Morgan, James, 66
Mormon Migration, 140–41, 207
Mormon Pioneer Overland Travel, 152, 207–8
Mormons in the Three Counties, The, 182
Moss, James, 175
Moss, Lavelle, 175

N

Nauvoo Brass Band, 148
Nauvoo Temple, 150–51
Needham, John, 67, 73, 79–80
Newman, John, 147
New Poor Law (1834), 25–26

New Toleration Act (1812), 27–28
Nonconformist religions, 26–31
North America, 140

O

Oakey, Ann Collett, 106, 142–43
Oakey, Rhoda, 143, 169n9
Oakey, Sarah Ann, 142–43
Oakey, Thomas, 106, 126, 142–43, 182
occupations, of early converts, 109–15, 133n55, 215–19
Ockey, Edward, 59, 111–12, 138, 186

P

Page, John E., 17
Palmer, James
   difficulties with Elizabeth Knight, 88n59
   emigration of, 138
   experiences persecution, 82, 84
   marriage of, 118
   missionary efforts and methods of, 68, 79
   records of, 210
Palmer, Mary Ann Price, 79, 88n59, 118
Patten, David W., 16
persecution, 81–84, 88n47, 119–22, 150–51, 161, 173
Peterson, Ziba, 23
Phillips, Edward, 138, 141, 147, 150
Phillips, Hannah Simmonds, 147
Philpotts, Mary, 166
Philpotts, Thomas, 122

pioneers, 207–8. See also emigration
pioneer trek, 181–82
Pitt, Mary, 53, 186–91
Pitt, William, 138, 148
place-names, 213–14, 228
polygamy, 173
poor relief, 25–26
Possons, M., 59
Pratt, Orson, 17, 18
Pratt, Parley P., 3, 18, 23
preachers, persecution instigated by, 44–45, 82, 186
Preston, Church beginnings in, 5–16
Price, Charles, 147
Price, Daniel, 79, 88n59
Price, Mary Ann, 79, 88n59, 118
Primitive Methodist Church, 27–31
Pritchard family, 156
public records
   convert identification in, 210–15
   description of, 206–10
Pullen, Lydia, 154
Pullin, J., 59
purse or scrip, traveling without, 77, 88–89n61

Q

Quorum of the Twelve Apostles
   departs for England, 17–19
   ordination of, 1–2
   reorganized and called to England, 16–17
   teaches missionaries, 70

R

Reform Bill (1832), 25
Richards, Jenetta, 10
Richards, John, 10–11
Richards, Levi, 62, 71–72, 73, 85n8
Richards, Willard
    arrives in England, 52–53
    called to England, 3
    as counselor to Joseph
      Fielding, 15–16
    gives Job Smith copy of Book
      of Mormon, 71
    goes to Bedford, 9
    meets on Herefordshire
      Beacon, 53, 64, 196
    meets with other missionaries,
      64
    missionary efforts in Three
      Counties, 62, 63–64
    ordained Apostle, 18
    in Sister Smith's dream, 102
Richardson, Thomas, 66, 67, 86n19
Rigdon, Sidney, 23–24
River Ribble, 8–9
Ruck, Elizabeth Collett, 106
Ruck, Robert, 126
Russell, Isaac, 4, 6–9

S

Sansom, Charles, 104–5
seekers, 97–101
sesquicentennial celebrations,
    174–76
Simmonds, Hannah, 147
Simmons, William, 194, 195
smallpox, 146
Smith, Adelaide Fowles, 148
Smith, Charles, 157–58
Smith, George A., 17–18, 62, 65,
    149
Smith, Job, 47–50, 71, 147–48, 154,
    195
Smith, Joseph, 1–3, 16–17, 71,
    148–49, 150
Smith, Sister, 101–2, 130n25,
    130n27
Smith, William, 154
Snailam, William, 67
Snyder, John, 4, 9
social status, 26, 109–15, 215–19
Sparks, Jane Ann Fowler, 119–20,
    143–44
speculation, 2
spelling, standardized, 211
Spiers, John
    baptizes Ann Weaver, 95
    cared for during illness, 61
    conversion of, 75
    emigration of, 138
    experiences persecution, 82,
      88n47, 119
    missionary efforts of, 57, 68–69
    missionary methods of, 73–74,
      76–77, 88–89n61
    and organization of
      Leominster Branch, 85n8
    receives preaching license in
      Leominster, 80, 89n64
    socioeconomic status of, 110
    taught by Brigham Young, 70
    as truth seeker, 100–101
"Spirit of God Like a Fire Is
    Burning, The," 101–2, 130n27
spiritual manifestation,
    experienced by Thomas Steed,
    99–100

spiritual preparation
    through dreams, 101–4
    through impressions, 104–5
Steed, Rebecca, 98
Steed, Sarah, 149
Steed, Thomas, 97–100, 118–19, 148–49, 163–64, 203
"Story of Strength, A," 176

T
Taylor, John, 3–4, 17, 41–42
tithe apportionment schedules, 220
trials. See also persecution
    apostasy caused by, 161
    of Church in America, 16
    of converts, 119–22
    in emigration, 143–46
    faithfulness through, 149–52
    in missionary work, 81–84
    pattern of, 1–2
Tringham, Elizabeth, 157–58
Tringham, Lindsey, 157–58
truth seekers, 97–101
Truth Will Prevail (book), 175
Truth Will Prevail (musical), 176, 182
Tunks, Isaac, 80
Tunks, Mary, 77
Turley, Theodore, 41
Twelve Apostles. See Quorum of the Twelve Apostles

U
unemployment, 110–11
United Brethren, 30–36
    and age of converts at baptism, 117

United Brethren, (continued)
    and branch boundaries, 126
    conversion of, 47–52, 54, 93, 102–5, 128n1
    give Gadfield Elm chapel to LDS Church, 193
    identifying homes of, 219–20
    missionary efforts of, 57–60, 74–75
    missionary work among, 45–47
    preaching style of, 80–81
    as seekers, 97
    socioeconomic status of, 107
    Wilford Woodruff's meeting with, 42–43
United Brethren Preachers' Plan, 47, 59–60, 85n3, 213, 219

V
Vision of Britain Through Time, A, 215–18
Vox, Mary, 95

W
Wall, Francis George, 118, 121–22, 146
Warren, Samuel, 74, 77
Weaver, Ann, 95
Weight, Frederick, 110–11
Wesley, John, 26–27, 28, 30
Weston, Mary Ann, 104, 112, 121, 141, 144
Wilding, D., 66
Williams, Mary Brooks, 118
Williams, William, 80–81, 102–4, 118, 122, 161
Willie handcart company, 143, 149, 169n9

Woodruff, Wilford
    arrives in England, 41–42
    attends conference meetings, 73
    baptismal record of, 65, 68, 86n13, 93–95, 128n4, 202
    and conversion of Thomas Steed, 98–99
    departs for England, 17
    effect of, on young converts, 104
    experiences persecution, 82
    meets Apostles at Far West, 17
    meets on Herefordshire Beacon, 53, 64, 196
    meets with other missionaries, 64
    meets with United Brethren, 42–43
    memorial commemorating missionary work of, 175
    missionary activities in Herefordshire, 43–47
    missionary efforts in Three Counties, 62–63, 65
    missionary work of, as example, 54
    people prepared for message of, 36
    performs baptisms at Hawcross, 194–95
    preaches at Castle Frome, 184–86
    preaches at Hill Farm, 184–86
    preaches in Ledbury, 191
    preaching route of, 213
    records of, 96, 210–11, 228n3
    in Sister Smith's dream, 101–2

Woodruff, Wilford (continued)
    success of, in Three Counties, 92–93
    teaches Benbow family, 105
    teaches by Spirit, 47, 80
    teaches United Brethren, 47–51
    and truth seekers, 100–101
    works with Brigham Young and Willard Richards, 52–53

Y

Young, Brigham
    arrives in England, 52–53
    attends conference meetings, 73
    denied as Heber C. Kimball's companion, 3
    departs for England, 17
    mantle of Joseph Smith falls on, 150
    meets Apostles at Far West, 17
    meets on Herefordshire Beacon, 53, 64, 196
    meets with other missionaries, 64
    missionary efforts in Three Counties, 62–63, 65
    and publication of Book of Mormon, 53, 64, 196
    in Sister Smith's dream, 102
    teaches missionaries, 70
Young, Mary Ann, 18

Z
Zion's Camp, 1